THE WILDFOWLER'S QUEST

Books by George Reiger

ZANE GREY: OUTDOORSMAN

PROFILES IN SALTWATER ANGLING

FISHING WITH MCCLANE

THE ZANE GREY COOKBOOK CO-AUTHOR

THE AUDUBON SOCIETY BOOK OF MARINE WILDLIFE

THE WINGS OF DAWN

THE UNDISCOVERED ZANE GREY FISHING STORIES

WANDERER ON MY NATIVE SHORE

THE SOUTHEAST COAST

FLOATERS AND STICK-UPS

THE BIRDER'S JOURNAL

THE WILDFOWLER'S QUEST

THE WILDFOWLER'S QUEST

George Reiger

Illustrated by

Joseph Fornelli

NICK LYONS BOOKS

LYONS & BURFORD, PUBLISHERS

For my mentors,
Ben Scott Custer and John Gottschalk,
and for my father,
and for every father who has taught
his sons that integrity and freedom
are what matter most in life, and that
wildfowling is an activity where both
can still be found.

Printed in the United States of America

10 9 8 7 6 5 4 3 2 1

Library of Congress Cataloging-in-Publication Data

Reiger, George, 1913–
    The wildfowler's quest / George Reiger
    ; illustrated by Joseph Fornelli.
        p.   cm.
    "Nick Lyons books."
    ISBN 1-55821-038-5
    1. Fowling. I. Title.
SK313.R45 1989
    799.2'4—dc20   89-8041
                                                        CIP

Contents

Part 4
Clubs, Conservation, and Whyfors

Introduction

I n my undergraduate days at Princeton, an art historian devoted to Asian cultures suggested that the essential difference between Chinese and Japanese art was the difference between profoundness and aesthetics. "The best Japanese art is exquisite work," he said, "but it doesn't wrench the soul the way a Shang bronze or a Sung landscape can."

Soul-wrenching is what distinguishes wildfowling from all other shooting sports. Dedicated wildfowlers hunt other game, of course, but we do so in much the same spirit of the lyrics that when we're not near the girl we love, we love the girl we're near.

Quail and pheasant are fun, but they don't demand the life-altering commitment that ducks and geese do. Grouse can change your life, but it's the dog work or the use of an heirloom gun that matters most, not the variety and majesty of the birds. As for shooting pen-raised mallards, it's pathetic sport—at best a reminder of younger dawns when great flocks of wildfowl whispered and muttered over the marshes like ghostly relics of the Pleistocene.

I bird whenever I'm outdoors on days when I can't be in a marsh with a gun. But birding is the naturalist's equivalent of Japanese art. It's a pleasing and highly aesthetic pastime, but it does not, cannot, wrench the soul the way wildfowling does.

True wildfowlers are naturalists. We don't enjoy large shooting parties, and we prefer pioneering in our travel to doing what everyone else has done. Whereas ordinary bird shooters are reluctant to visit a place new to them unless many others have already been there and put their seal of approval on it, wildfowlers seek out unbeaten tracks and travel alone or with a very few other time-tested companions.

When we speak of our native wildfowling tradition, we're actually speaking of several different traditions in one. First, there were Indians who dressed skins over reed or wooden forms and saved the best of these—what white men would later call "decoys"—from one season of abundance to the next, and imitated the sounds of ducks, geese, shorebirds, and turkey with that extraordinary instrument, the human voice.

In the upper Midwest there is a German-Scandinavian duck-hunting heritage that later emigrated across the continent and took root in the clubs of California. This tradition emphasizes gemütlichkeit and shooting, in about that order. It's good-natured sport, and even its excesses occur under a banner heralding, "Hail, hail, the gang's all here!"

A French tradition stems from the trapper-pioneers of the Mississippi watershed whose wellspring were the Arcadians who became Cajuns after settling in Louisiana. Conviviality has its place in this tradition, but subsistence hunting is at least as important as recreational shooting.

The Franco-American subculture gave us the artificial duck call, a device whose refinement is credited to a man named Glodo, generally spelled with two "o"s, but undoubtedly with an ending "eau" wherever this frontiersman's ancestors came from in France. Wooden duck calls only began to catch on in the East and Far West after World War II, and even then the most popular version in the Atlantic Flyway was the New York-manufactured Scotch call, designed to be shaken or played like an accordian by sportsmen lacking the competence or confidence to blow a mouth call. The duck call is symbolic of the Franco-American hunter—a sometimes stylish but always practical character, frequently linked to the extralegal slaughter of ducks but rarely to the waste of any of them.

Finally, there is a British/Dutch wildfowling tradition, itself divided between immigrants of the leisure class and those of the working class who built and manned the ships that brought the others and themselves to America. The Dutch are included in the Anglo-Saxon tradition, because they shared the same North Sea habitat in the Old World, and because fragments of a Dutch subculture are still to be found along the New York and New Jersey shores woven through with British ingredients from New England and the southern mid-Atlantic.

Because Americans speak English, and because our history books are mostly written by the Anglo-Saxon descendants of people who had been in deadly competition with the French and Dutch as well as with the native Americans whom we all displaced, we tend to overlook the important roles played by these others in the formation of this country and, hence, in its cultural complexity. We tend to forget, for example, that the word *decoy* is derived from the Dutch, and that the practice of flighting live-decoy geese out to attract wild birds has been practiced in Holland with white-fronts since the seventeenth century, even as it was practiced with Canada geese on Long Island and Cape Cod into this century. We also tend to forget that the two monumental American wildfowling books, *American Duck Shooting* (1901) by George Bird Grinnell and *A Book on Duck Shooting* (1939) by Van Campen Heilner, were written by heirs of the Anglo-Dutch tradition. (Midwesterners write waterfowling books, but they reflect the light-hearted nature of Midwestern sport; the Cajun tradition is oral, not literary, and there are no Franco-American books on wildfowling.)

The bond of Anglo-Dutch wildfowlers on this side of the Atlantic is the same one shared by Anglo-Dutch gunners on the other side: the tides. Gemütlichkeit was more likely to emerge as a Midwestern trait than an Atlantic coastal one, simply because duck hunting in a midwestern slough, or even on a shallow lake, doesn't carry the inherent risk that hunting in a constantly changing seascape does. Comradeship is an important ingredient of Atlantic coastal gunning, but carefree conviviality is not. It's far better to have a dull but dependable partner on a January hunt for sea ducks than an affable and heedless friend who forgets to secure the boat before he steps ashore. As Ernest Hemingway observed in another context, "Anyone who goes on the sea the year around in a small . . . boat does not seek danger. You may be absolutely sure that in a year you will have it without seeking, so you try always to avoid it all you can."

Although ducks and geese are my favorite quarry, I use the term *wildfowling* rather than the more familiar American word *waterfowling,* in order to encompass rail, snipe, woodcock, and even turkey, because these fowl are more truly *wild* than those incubator-hatched mallards whose execution over artificial ponds the average shooter calls "duck hunting."

This book begins in North America and moves abroad where much spectacular wildfowling is still to be had. Where appropriate, I've included a few names, addresses, and costs, less to promote anyone—since some of those listed will be dead or out of business by the time you read this book—than because a book of this kind constitutes a social as well as a natural history.

Most of these chapters were written over the past ten years when more changes have occurred in North American wildfowling regulations than in any decade since the 1930s. Rather than provide an introductory paragraph to each chapter to help establish its chronological context, most chapters stand as they were written: a reflection of a particular time, place and state of mind. Consequently, there may appear to be inconsistencies. For example, where some readers will see that I condone steel shot, others may feel that I condemn it. The fact is, as early as 1970 I argued that since lead would eventually come out of shotgun shells, just as it was coming out of paint and gasoline, duck and goose hunters should support the search for a suitable substitute rather than make a futile effort to save lead shot through rearguard legal action. We should accept the inevitable with conservation spirit and good grace, rather than be dragged kicking and screaming into compliance like the unreasonable hotheads the anti-hunters say we are.

When steel (iron) pellets were being field tested in the early 1970s, I urged that we not ban lead, but let market forces take it out of circulation. I proposed a tax on lead shot to benefit waterfowl and to raise the price of lead several dollars a box over steel shot. That would mean that the overwhelming majority of duck and goose hunters would buy and use the cheaper steel shot. With the majority of hunters having switched to steel, the lead poisoning problem would shrink to insignificant levels within a few seasons. Traditionalists who wanted to use black powder or old shotguns would not be forced to hang them on the wall or sell them as antiques.

This commonsensical proposal was steamrollered by extremists on both sides of what came to be perceived as a political issue. As too often happens in our society, we ended up with pages of complex regulations which no one likes and few respect. Furthermore, the national prohibition against lead shot in waterfowling has opened up a Pandora's Box of legal questions about its use in other forms of bird hunting. Yet because I grumble about steel's short-comings in my Florida chapter, that doesn't mean steel shot loads haven't been improved since then, nor that I've reversed myself about the desirability of getting lead out of most over-water shooting situations. Steel lacks the weight and, hence, the shocking power of lead. Steel patterns do not clobber birds as hard as lead. Nothing will change that fact. What can and must be changed are shooters' attitudes and techniques. Wildfowlers obliged to use steel must simply use restraint and pick their shots, especially when hunting hard-to-kill quarry like sea ducks and geese.

Nick Lyons and Peter Burford are rare and wonderful people, and even rarer and more wonderful publishers in having used for many years acid-free paper designed to last centuries. Since the literature of wildfowling dates back only about 150 years to "Frank Forester" (pen-name of Henry William Herbert) in this country and Lieutenant Colonel Peter Hawker in Britain, the acid-free paper beneath the type you're reading should provide future generations enough time and perspective to decide whether this book is a worthy addition to the genre.

That *The Wildfowler's Quest* has finally appeared after several disappointments and delays is due to the persistence of a large number of supportive people. Although there are too many to thank individually for a project that represents the best of forty seasons on four continents, I must single out the team of Nick Lyons and Peter Burford for their willingness to put their money where my mouth is.

I also want to thank artist Joseph Fornelli who, besides his love of wildfowling, is a fellow Vietnam veteran. Joe went over about the time I came back. Nonetheless, we shared what has now become more of a myth than history. If you were an American male of draft age during the Vietnam era, you either went or you didn't. It was sometimes harder to stay than to go, but Joe and I both volunteered.

Finally, I'd like to thank the editors of *Across the Board, American Hunter, Audubon, Field & Stream,* and *Wildfowling* in whose publications some portions of this book first appeared.

GEORGE REIGER
Heron Hill
Locustville, Virginia

North America

— 1 —

Mexico

Mexico is a microcosm of wildfowl-ing opportunity—a mini-continent of experience.

It's being poled out under the stars through a maze of mangroves to an improvised stand by a small lagoon that looks exactly like the dozen others your guide skirted or pushed across, except for the pintail, wigeon, *pato gato* (lesser scaup and ringnecks), and blue-winged teal—especially blue-winged teal—which lisp-whistle out of the dawn in a continuous stream until the ducks break off their attack about the same time the mosquitoes break off theirs.

It's standing waist-deep in skim-icy water in a forest of dead trees watching the sky for gadwall and wigeon and the channels for ringnecks and canvasbacks so bracketed by ghostly timber the birds have nowhere to flare but up for easy climbing shots or continue driving straight ahead so you miss the first shot because the bird is too close, and you miss the second shot because you can't turn fast enough in your chest waders to catch up with the target before it vanishes in the labyrinth of woody skeletons.

It's crawling across a salt-encrusted flat toward a flock of brant or pintail shimmering like a mirage in the heat waves rising from the baking sand and getting to your feet for the last dozen yards charge and nearly swooning with the effort, but killing a bird that glides dead and crash-lands a quarter-mile away where it resembles a kind of extraterrestrial wreckage in the desert light.

Mexico offers the most mysterious white-fronted goose hunting imaginable, where you and your companions stand next to drowned trees soon after first light and watch birds returning in flocks of thousands from feeding grounds dozens of miles away. You never actually see the birds until you step back to shoot, but motionless you watch their reflected movements in the mirror-calm water. When a goose circles low enough to be seen barely above the reflected branches of the tree next to which you're standing, you step back, kill it, and quickly step forward again before the survivors can pin-point the source of the terrifying sound. The flock swirls about anxiously, high and out of range. But they need water, and this is the place they roosted and ate grit the evening before, so gradually, nervously, they spiral down within range again, and the ritual is repeated.

Mexico can be an earthly paradise for the wildfowler; it can also be a brothel. Everything depends on your attitude. If you assume Mexico is the last near frontier for unrestricted shooting, and that anything can be had for a price, all your experiences there will be colored by contempt and corruption. If, however, you're able to avoid the gang-banging grounds—hunting camps where anything goes—you'll meet some wonderful people who'll guide you to some wonderful experiences.

The stress that arises between American sportsmen and Mexican outiftters stems from our differing attitudes toward precision, be it in time or machinery! Most Americans would tolerate the average Mexican's delusions of grandeur, his aggressively defensive *machismo,* and his country's unnecessary squalor, if this average Mexican would only try to meet us on time or maintain his machinery!

Mexico was conquered by medieval Spain, and a medieval distrust of efficiency and individuality still prevails. A Mexican honors who one is, not what one does. Work is neither good nor useful; it's something that has to be done—as reluctantly and as casually as possible. It's best to be born rich, or to win a lottery and become rich, so you don't have to work at all.

Mexicans are among the most fatalistic people on earth, and no "problema" is so great that it was not also inevitable and at least partially deserved.

Two of my Argentine hunting companions, Sandy and Stan Wilson, hunted ducks in the Yucatan with an American outfitter who calls himself "Pancho Villa." Pancho runs his operation out of Merida, which is a three-hour, one-way bus ride from the hunting grounds. Every morning, beginning not long after midnight, Villa runs minibus-loads of hunters to the coast where they spend about two hours in the mangroves before climbing back aboard the buses for the hot, dusty, and distressingly cramped three-hour ride back to the city.

One morning, the minibus in which Sandy and his dad were riding developed engine trouble. The driver flagged down one of his compatriots in another bus. After much arm waving and argument, the second driver backed his minibus up within a dozen feet of the disabled vehicle. The two drivers then tied a 200-foot length of hawser between the two machines. Both drivers jumped back aboard their respective buses, and the lead bus took off like a shot.

"He must have been doing thirty-five miles per hour when he hit the end of the rope," Sandy recalls. "Dad and I were sitting in the front seat. We just had time to shout a warning and to brace ourselves before we were jerked forward so hard some people in the back rolled all the way to the front! Guns and gear fell everywhere! 'Juan Fangio' backed up his bus, jumped out, and started yelling at our driver, who was pulling his hair and pointing to where the two bumpers had been yanked into cow-catcher shapes. The second driver suddenly pulled out a huge knife and began waving it at our driver. We figured we were about to see our man murdered. Instead, the second driver slashed the knot on our bus's bumper, ran back to his bus, jabbed his middle finger at our driver, and took off with the hawser snaking down the road behind him."

In nine visits to Mexico over the past forty years, I've experienced my own share of hazardous hilarity. In 1964, a friend and I were told to sound our 1940 rental car's horn before we reached any blind turns in the roads of Baja California Sur, and to listen for any horns coming from the other direction. People drove in the middle of those barely beaten tracks, and honking was our only hope for avoiding an accident.

When René asked what happened to drivers whose vehicles didn't have horns, he was told with a shrug, "They're killed." When he asked why people simply didn't approach curves at a slower speed, he was laughed at for being an "old woman."

One reason things don't always work in Mexico is because Mexicans are not team players or organization men. They excel in boxing and tennis, but not in soccer and basketball. They do well in baseball because it's the only team sport in which every player has a chance at bat and, hence, a chance at glory.

Mexicans equate gestures with success. Trying is as good as succeeding, especially if the effort ends dramatically. (Death is desirable for the best effect.) When their tendency to show off is combined with their fascination with blood, you end up with moments of inconclusive mayhem, ecstatic to locals but appalling to outsiders.

One morning in the Yucatan, my Texas shooting partner and I had thirty pintail, wigeon, and teal on the water by the time the sun was high enough for me to load a camera with color film. One of our two guides asked if he could shoot while I took my pictures. As it turned out, he was a decent shot and began working on his own fifteen-bird limit. But he was crippling twice as many birds as he was killing, because he didn't wait for the ducks to get within proper range. The two Mayans cackled with fiendish delight every time the one with the gun hit a duck and caused it to wince and limp back across the lagoon. Twice I took the gun away, once to demonstrate how to wait for the birds to circle close enough to kill, and finally to stop the pitiful carnage. It was clear the guide would just as soon *hurt* the birds as kill them. He and his buddy laughed uproariously when one pintail drake had both his legs broken so they dangled pathetically under the bird like landing gear that couldn't be raised. Although the duck was still in range, the guide used his last shell to shoot at another bird.

Corruption

Hunting south of the border reminds me of George Orwell's observation that "on the whole, human beings want to be good, but not too good, and not quite all the time." Bribes are paid at the beginning, middle, and end of some trips, almost reflexively. Federal wildfowling regulations are found in a fat little booklet updated and published annually, but this booklet is rarely seen, and even more rarely honored, at Mexican hunting camps. It wasn't until the end of my second trip across the border several seasons ago that I was able to track down one of the booklets and determine how many laws I'd broken in the meanwhile—beginning with a prohibition against afternoon shooting. (The closing hour has swung between noon and 3:00 P.M. in recent years, but since most of the Mexican camps I've visited condone, if not encourage, dusking, the rule is meaningless, regardless of the official hour cited.)

On one trip, had I known the law, I would have been able to bring back to the United States more birds than I did. Travel or possession limits of ducks and quail in most Mexican states (as elsewhere in North America) is twice one's daily limit. In Tamaulipas, however, the possession limit was then three times the daily limit. This exception—along with five bonus ducks in the daily bag—was made possible by the most influential American outfitter on Lake Guerrero. The cost of this exception was included in his "annual assessment" by local governmental officials, which his local manager told me ran to more than $100,000 a year. Instead of being able to bring out forty *patos* (ducks) and twenty *codorniz enmascarada* (bobwhite quail), a gunner visiting Tamaulipas at that time could bring out sixty and thirty birds respectively.

In order to bring out any number of birds, however, you must have a Mexican hunting license. Yet in order to pay local bribes, some outfitters charge their clients the $60 non-resident shooting fee, plus a $45 consular fee—and other *mordida* or "expedite fees"—without providing a license or even a receipt. Both the outfitter and the client know they're safe from harrassment once the hunter's "insurance fees" have been paid and so long as the hunter is under a "cooperator's" protection.

Having no license, however, can be sticky if you want to bring game back into the United States, since some sort of official paper is required to get the birds through customs. On my 1984 Yucatan trip, our shooting party was told that while all of us were "properly licensed," there were not enough license forms in Merida to provide each of us with proof of that fact. Not to worry, we were assured. By the time we left, we'd all have licenses to transport game back to the States.

Since I knew I was going to be hunting in Mexico again that season, I pleaded particularly hard for the license if only one form was available. When, to our collective surprise, a license *was* made available, the individual to whom it was issued wasn't even flying home with us. Therefore, we'd be carrying birds in for a man who was no longer in our party. Could it be done?

At the airport in Miami, an officious young turk in a customs uniform spotted blood stains on my styrofoam cooler and decided I'd made his day. While one of my companions watched my other luggage, I was hustled with the cooler to the office of the agricultural section where the young, and by now cocky, customs man told a weary, older official sitting behind a desk that I *alleged* there were birds in the cooler.

"What kind of birds?" asked the gray-haired veteran.

"Ducks," I replied.

"Where were you hunting?"

"The Yucatan."

"Was it good?"

"Excellent."

"What's your problem?" the senior officer asked his subordinate.

"There's blood on that ice chest!" the young man exclaimed.

"Ducks bleed," said the wise old gentleman who was looking more distinguished by the second. "And so will you if you don't get back on the job! We've got tons of drugs moving through this airport every month, and you bring me a duck hunter!"

Neither official asked to see my hunting license, and neither asked me to explain why George Reiger was carrying ducks shot by John Stowell. So conditioned was I by my week in Mexico, I nearly brought out my wallet to express my gratitude!

When I left Tamaulipas seven weeks later, my border-crossing was even more bizarre. My shooting partner and I both wanted to bring out birds. We nagged the camp operator until he finally came up with two licenses that had been left behind by two other hunters. One was a Texan whom my South Carolina companion thought he could pass for; the other was from Miami, and since anyone can be from Miami, I adopted the identity of the Miamian.

Just before leaving camp, my companion got cold feet and left his birds there. Our host was somewhat shady, and my buddy feared we might get a rugged screening at customs for that reason alone. I figured that if the Texas border officials wouldn't allow me to cross with my ducks, they were welcome to them. I was too curious to see what would happen to leave the birds behind.

When we landed in Brownsville, our pilot led us into a Customs shed where we talked briefly about the weather and the recent Super Bowl game with the local officials. Several pieces of paper were produced and signed and we were quickly on our way again. As soon as we re-boarded the plane, my companion tried to claim half my birds. He insisted I had a "moral obligation" to feed his "needy family."

"There's a tide in the affairs of men," I reminded him, "which taken at the flood, leads on to fortune, and we must take the current when it serves, or lose our ventures."

The pilot seemed impressed with my knowledge of Shakespeare, and we chatted while my companion sulked. It was then I learned we could have brought out an ice-house full of game! Although the pilot's boss doesn't pay bribes on the American side of the border, he brings other kinds of pressure to bear.

"There used to be a hard charger working here," recalled the pilot. "He didn't last four months. I have no idea where they sent him, but my boss suggested the Aleutians."

Much of Mexico operates under what I call the Melt-Water Theory of Economics. This is one way the Mexican is more Oriental than Occidental. A Chinese gentleman once told me that "money is like water, and contracts are like ice. I give you a block of ice, and you pass it on to somebody else who in turn passes it on. By the time that block of ice has passed through half-a-dozen pairs of hands, it's much smaller. But nobody has taken anything."

Since water is the essence of life, and since American water (the U.S. dollar) is especially "refreshing" in many dry areas of Mexico, you quickly learn that any personal whim will supercede law so long as your wants are well lubricated with loot.

The Refuge Hunt

One morning in the Yucatan, my gunning partner urged our two guides to move us to a more productive lagoon. Each hunter is assigned a guide, but hunters and guides are paired so that the shooters can be tucked behind mangrove screens in one boat while the guides use the other boat to retrieve ducks and to scout new territory. My partner and I had already killed eight ducks, and by any standard but Mexico's, we'd had a satisfying morning. The problem was we could hear our colleagues in the distance hammering birds for all their semi-automatics were worth. My partner was nearly delirious with envy!

The guides were as eager as we were to shoot more birds. They lose face if their shooters don't come in with at least as many birds as the next party, and it would have been disgraceful for them had we not killed limits of fifteen birds each when other parties were shooting twice or three times that many.

So the guides conferred briefly, shifted me into the second skiff, and push-poled us off on a twenty-minute expedition that included a portage over a dike separating two lagoons. We were poled through so many flooded tunnels in the mangroves, turned back around so many little islands, and taken across so many mini-lagoons that I lost all sense of direction. The sun became a meaningless ball of light shifting aimlessly around the horizon. Suddenly we were in a new lagoon where hundreds of pintail and blue-winged teal roared off the water, while dozens more sat fascinated before they, too, joined the other birds swarming like bees over the open water.

We didn't have out half our decoys when ducks began curling back. Although my partner and I were not in top form, every one of our misses was so quickly followed by a kill, my retrospective impression of the hunt is of constantly falling game. On several occasions, I played catch-up. I missed a duck with my first two shots, but nailed it just before the shotgun's muzzle slammed into an overhanging limb. I then listened intently for the splash on the other side of the islet where we were hidden. One drake teal buzzed the decoys and was shot at four times by the two of us before I caught up with the bird just as it disappeared behind the trees to my right. I thought I might have missed it but then saw the bird ricocheting through the understory. One of the guides struggled for ten minutes through a labyrinth of mangrove trunks, roots, and branches to retrieve the duck, which had lost its head and one wing during its violent fall.

The flighting and shooting were so intense, it took will power to stop. Even so, when we counted the birds we had three more than the twenty-two ducks we were legally entitled to plus the eight we'd killed earlier. We joked nervously and a little unhappily about our "Tamaulipas limits" as the guides poled us back toward the landing. They at least were in a less adulterated jovial mood, for regardless of how many ducks the other parties had shot that morning, our guides had found ample birds for us.

We were approaching the dike we had portaged across when a mysterious figure in a baseball cap suddenly darted out from behind some bushes and just as suddenly disappeared. I thought he was a member of the pickup crew who had come down to look for us. The abrupt silence and frozen attitudes of our push-polers, however, warned me that all was not well even before I heard one of the guides whisper, *"policia!"*

Instead of landing there, the guides began paralleling the dike, trying to look casual but obviously searching for another crossing. At one point, our two boats converged so that the guides could confer *sotto voce*. I asked my partner what was going on.

"My man said something about *departmento federale,"* he replied. "I think we're in a refuge."

Hoo-boy!

There were fifteen ducks in my jonboat, but three more than fifteen in my partner's. I was, therefore, not surprised when my partner's guide veered his boat away behind an island, and my buddy gave me the thumbs-up sign when they reappeared. He now had only fifteen ducks in his boat.

I don't recall much about the trip back, but I'm sure that not another word was spoken. I was angry and felt humiliated, but was not sure how much of my anger and humiliation was for having been caught in a refuge or for having been caught, period. It's wonderful how conscience-stricken even a rogue becomes when the long arm of the law is about to descend.

The club manager himself was at the landing to greet us. He was at his diplomatic best. With a look that gushed gallons of sympathy for our distress, he assured us that we'd not been in a refuge. "We don't allow hunting in the refuge," he explained with a straight face.

I pointed out that the guides had reacted guiltily at the first sight of the law enforcement agent, and if the guides didn't know the refuge borders, who did? Besides, the stranger in the baseball cap hadn't been hiding in the undergrowth because he liked to feed mosquitoes!

"You were hunting Victorio, no?" asked the manager. "Victorio is *not* in the refuge."

"We were *supposed* to be hunting Victorio, yes," I said. "But we moved and could have been hunting Timbuktu for all I know!"

"No problema," soothed the manager. "We will talk to the officials, and I am sure they'll agree you were not hunting in the refuge."

Back at the Rancho, my host gave me a "no problema" smile while standing with three Mexicans, including the man from the dike with the baseball cap and an army major wearing a Colt .45 in an unbuttoned holster. In a kind of intellectual displacement behavior, I became more concerned for the guides' welfare than for my own or my partner's. Our reputations would be blitzed, to be sure, but the Mexican guides stood to lose their licenses.

"How many ducks did you get?" the army officer said, smiling.

"There they are," my partner said, pointing to the birds being unloaded from the truck. "Two limits."

"Ah, so many *macho* pintail!" grinned the third man. "Not so many *patitos*."

"These gentlemen are excellent hunters," explained our host. "They save their shots for the big ducks."

"I see!" said the leering major.

"Shall we have a drink and talk about it?" suggested our host.

"*Bueno!*" agreed the Mexicans. Our host and the manager went onto the porch with the officials who began demolishing a bottle of Scotch, a bottle of brandy, and assorted bottles of tequila. I was too queasy to watch, so went back to my room and read.

When it was over, I was called to join the others under the palms for a picture-taking ceremony. The *federales* posed with us in various attitudes of triumph. One photo shows the army major down on one knee, pointing his .45 at a pintail drake. One of the other guests suggested the major take the bird home and have it mounted. Whether or not the major thought that a good idea, he forgot the bird when his party left ten minutes later.

After they'd gone, I apologized to my host for whatever the incident had cost him.

"This happens every opening week," he said. "The local authorities drop by so we can work out the rules for the rest of the season. This year we're supposed to keep tabs on the numbers and species of ducks we shoot. That's for their records. Off the record, they've agreed not to bother us again, but if we like, they'll harry the other clubs in the area."

A wag once observed that "the only nice thing about being imperfect is the joy it brings others." Mexico offers many opportunities for such joy.

Where-tos and How-tos

Mexico has some do-it-yourself hunting possibilities, but I recommend against wildfowling on your own unless you speak fluent Spanish and have an indulgent sense of humor. An old Mexican hand may sample the best the country offers, but few dentists and accountants on ten-day holidays will.

James Brannan of Gardena, California, is an old hand, and a letter he wrote me a couple of years ago so well captures the flavor of what true wildfowling in Mexico can be, he has graciously agreed to let me publish a couple of paragraphs from it:

"Duck hunting is very special to me. I love the whole experience, including the cooking and devouring. (It seems like *devour* is the right word, since I've never found—or even looked for—a delicate way to eat a duck.) Tomorrow I leave for two weeks of hunting in Mexico. I have a camp in the delta marsh of the Colorado River just north of where it joins the Sea of Cortez. It's an especially exciting place to be. Pristine, wild, and fortunately not too many hunters. Each season and each trip brings new adventure. Constantly changing water levels mean we must search out new areas and new access points, and experiment with new hunting methods several times each season. One time we'll be hunting from a canoe; the next, from a motor boat; and the next, on foot. One trip last season had this scenario:

"A two-hour flight from Los Angeles in my Cessna landing on a dirt agricultural strip, one hour by four-wheel-drive pickup, another hour in an outboard towing a canoe, one and a half hours paddling the canoe, then hiking with decoys packed on our backs for two miles through shallow water and mud flats—build a blind—set out the decoys and enjoy the last few hours of the afternoon flight. Then back to camp by the light of the moon and the navigational aid of Orion. A great day. All the senses working and the soul satisfied."

If you're not this independent and would just as soon have everything laid on for you, there are two types of hunting experiences in Mexico. The first is what I call the Club Experience, and it's well exemplified by Rancho San Carlos in the Yucatan. This resort accepts a maximum of sixteen people, but parties of ten or so are more common. If everybody doesn't know everybody else by the time you arrive in Merida, you'll soon be well acquainted after your outings in the mangroves.

The second kind of experience is what I call the Hotel Hunt. This is well exemplified by Hacienda Alta Vista where everything is so well organized, you don't quite feel you've ever left the United States. This is a less personal hunt, and you won't likely get to know anyone who is not already in your group. From the moment you arrive in Harlingen, Texas, to your flight back from Alta Vista's private runway, everything is managed by Alta Vista's very efficient, and, therefore, quite un-Mexican-like staff.

You're rarely aware of things breaking down or going wrong at Alta Vista, which, considering it's in Mexico, must be happening on an hourly basis. Only once during my stay, when an old patch gave way on the boat I was in, did I experience a *problema*. The guide continued on, hurriedly dropped off my partner and me, and then headed back with the boat half full of water. By the time he returned with a replacement hull, we'd killed eight or nine ducks. When I complimented the guide on his calmness under pressure, he explained there was nothing to get excited about since that was the third time the patch on that particular boat had given way that season!

Wherever I hunt, I enjoy sampling local flavors. This is more easily done at Rancho San Carlos than behind the chain-link and barbed-wire fence surrounding Hacienda Alta Vista. Because most of the best hunting was at the opposite end of Lake Guerrero from the camp, my partner and I took a couple of two-hour bus rides to reach the birds when the lake was too rough to cross by boat. Although not very comfortable, the bus rides provided us with our only views of local towns and terrain.

Despite declining waterfowl populations everywhere in North America, birds still concentrate in considerable numbers in both the Yucatan and Tamaulipas. The Yucatan features occasionally stupendous flights of pintail, wigeon, and blue-winged teal. Even more birds of greater variety can be found on Lake Guerrero. Recent reports, however, indicate the lake is being overshot. Whereas limits were once easy to come by, Guerrero visitors must now hunt longer and harder even to approach limits. Unless a front blows through to help your guides rally the birds off the lake, most shooters are fortunate to kill a dozen ducks, even during illegal, all-day hunts.

One advantage of Tamaulipas over the Yucatan is that if duck shooting is slow in the morning, you can always try quail shooting in the afternoon. Bobwhite are found along field edges where the survivors of your first flush fly to join a second covey, the second to a third, and so on until by the time you reach the end of the field, you may see "covey rises" of over one hundred birds.

There are quail on the Yucatan, but hardly so many. And there are no dogs at any of the duck camps there. The upland terrain is better suited for chachalaca, a gamebird rather like a hybrid grouse-roadrunner. I hunted chachalacas at Rancho San Carlos one afternoon, but without success. Like the local tarpon fishing, the largely improvised nature of such sport seems to create *problemas*.

On the Yucatan, you shoot decoying ducks from improvised blinds. There is no rallying of the waterfowl. At Lake Guerrero, the birds are supposed to decoy, but you're better off not using decoys, nor a permanent blind that pintail and wigeon will avoid after the first few weeks of the season. You'll kill a few early-morning teal and driven diving ducks from such permanent structures, but your best shooting occurs whenever you manage to wade downwind of one of the countless concentrations of coot whose constant uprooting of aquatic vegetation attracts dabbling ducks.

In the Yucatan, even in January, you can get by with a pair of low waterproof boots, a windbreaker for the pre-dawn trip out, and a short-sleeved shirt thereafter. Bring a *pint* of mosquito repellent, however, or try one of the new bug-repellent jackets. Avon's Skin So Soft is a surprisingly good repellent, and it's better smelling and probably less hazardous to your health than those liquids whose "active ingredient," DEET (Diethyl-meta-toluamide), will take the blueing off your shotgun!

By contrast, January hunting on Lake Guerrero means a snowmobile suit with insulated chest waders for long mornings in the frigid water. Mosquitoes are rarely a problem.

Mexican law prohibits you from carrying in more than fifty rounds of ammunition for each of the two shotguns you're allowed to bring. This was no handicap at Rancho San Carlos, which provides Remington shells (made in Mexico but under Remington specifications). However, this restriction may cause some despair at lodges elsewhere in the country. Although you pay roughly $13 a box for all local ammunition, the difference between Remington rounds and brands X and Y is considerable. Of ten easy shots at canvasbacks on Lake Guerrero, for example, I cold-cocked only five of the birds. Three were crippled by the lightly loaded number-6 shot and escaped when my resort-supplied semi-automatic jammed after the first round. Another canvasback flew by while I was still wrestling to clear a shell, and the last bird flew off after a fresh round went "poof" and its shot dribbled out the end of the barrel.

Since Mexican authorities now insist that you take in your own gun(s) and use a local guide—leading to still more bribery—and fill out something called a Model 91 Form on which you must list the value of your shotgun(s) so you can be charged for them if you try to leave Mexico without them, take in whatever you can of American shells, plus at least one double-barrel or pump-action shotgun. The pump is easier to fix than a semi-auto if it jams, and even if you lose one barrel of a two-barreled gun, you always have the other barrel to hunt with.

You pays your money and you takes your choice. You can expect at least one glitch a day on any trip to Mexico. You probably won't even be aware of glitches at a place like Alta Vista, thanks to its well-disciplined staff. On the other hand, so long as the glitches don't get out of control, I enjoy the color they provide. When I'm on vacation, glitched hunts are often more memorable than flawless ones. And I enjoy Mayan guides who whistle to their birds and say "Adios, patos!" whenever you miss.

2

Florida

$\mathbb{F}$ew sportsmen ever think of Florida as a wildfowler's mecca. Many go off with their families to Disney World and endure the overpriced fun rides without realizing they're less than an hour's drive from some of the best and most reasonably priced wildfowling left in North America. Florida has many of the attributes of Mexico and none of its liabilities. The weather and abundance of bird life are comparable, but there're no "hidden costs." Furthermore, having a vehicle in your own country means you're not as confined as you are in the isolated hunting camps of Mexico.

Dave Van Nest and Chris La Montagne of Space Coast Waterfowlers offer wonderful open-water layout shooting on the Banana River for diving ducks—mostly lesser scaup (bluebills), but with a few greater scaup (broadbills) seasoning the flocks. They also offer the fastest teal shooting (mostly blue-wings, but a few green-wings) anywhere in the United States. And if you want substantial variety in a single morning, the boys will take you from the willow-pothole backcountry of the St. Johns River to the periphery of Lake Winder where flocks of ringnecks, plus a few mottled ducks and fulvous whistling ducks, are waiting.

Even being there, it's hard to reconcile Florida's fabulous wildfowling with the fact that retirees still immigrate to the Sunshine State at a rate approaching a thousand people a day! Anywhere along the heavily developed coasts, you have trouble imagining there could be any ducks in Florida, much less secluded areas where the birds offer genuine sport.

What's most remarkable about my affection for Florida duck hunting is that it has withstood forty years of change. The memories of our youth become sweet in middle age and sweeter still with each passing year afterward. "Going home again" usually invites invidious comparisons from which the past emerges triumphant over the present. Yet my visit to south central Florida in January 1986 was even better than the wildfowling trips I used to make to Okeechobee with my father and older brother in the 1940s.

A good hunting expedition is made up of many special moments, with the most pleasurable ones being unexpected. For example, my companions and I never anticipated shooting snipe when we went to Florida to hunt ducks. But after each morning of ducks, we shot in the afternoons on, perhaps, the best snipe grounds in the nation. I'd brought seventeen rounds of number-8 shot for close teal, but quickly went through those shells with snipe. With four birds still to go for an eight-bird limit, I was reduced to express 6s bummed from my companions.

The snipe held close that first afternoon in thirty-plus mph winds. When they flushed, they climbed high before abruptly turning back. The birds then accelerated from thirty to seventy miles per hour in their own small lengths. A pellet of number-6 shot may bring down a snipe more effectively than a pellet of number-8, but more pellets are needed for a pattern sufficient to hit one of the small, darting, swept-back-winged targets. An ounce of number-8 shot has approximately 410 pellets, while an ounce of number-6 shot consists of only 225 pellets. I consoled myself for my many number-6 misses with this ballistic trivia.

Flooded Willows

Our first morning in Space Coast country was windy and spitting rain. My companions and I met at Dave's and Chris' headquarters for coffee and doughnuts but were soon aboard jonboats heading south up the St. Johns River through lakes Poinsett and Winder. Without any clear idea of where I was going or what to expect, I kept my head down, keeping my glasses dry and listening to the whine of the outboard and the hiss and applause of water racing under the hull.

After forty-five minutes of running in the dark, and just before dawn, Dave waded ahead of our party of four along a flooded trail leading through a cypress stand to a pothole surrounded by bushy willows. Dick Graham didn't have chest waders, so Dave selected a shootable opening for him that wouldn't put Dick in over his hip boots. Then when Dave set out the decoys, he left most in front of Dick. But decoys seemed to make little impression on the birds, and Dick ended up with fewer op-portunities than those of us able to wade out and seize the day. Dick's brother, Bob, Mel Baughman, and I quickly killed limits of five teal each.

The initial shooting distance was about thirty feet. The blue-wings (and one green-winged hen) swept in low over the willows and were gone quicker than you just read about it. Forewarned about the circumstances and favored with insert chokes for my Browning over-and-under, I cold-cocked my first three teal with three shots from a skeet-choked barrel. Made over-confident by this success, I was twice behind another bird tipped by both Dick and Bob. Mel humbled us by killing the duck with his .20 gauge side-by-side at extreme range.

The shooting was spectacular, but the variety of birdlife in the dawning swamp was more so. Besides teal zipping over the willows, stately flights of white and glossy ibis, occasional wood storks, anhingas, and even sandhill cranes lent their eerie profiles and calls to the pan-orama. Coots clucked, whistled, beeped, and croaked just out of sight in the willows, while wood ducks weeped, and mottled ducks quacked. We would have been happy to finish our limits with a shot at either one of these latter high-point birds, but the woodies flew early, and the mottled ducks were decidedly decoy-shy.

Since a cold wind was blowing, we were surprised to see several highly active alligators, including one basking whopper over twelve feet long. Dave told us he was thinking about taking us teal hunting two days later in an area where, if we didn't retrieve our fallen ducks immediately, we stood a good chance of losing them to alligators or turtles. He said the renaissance of the alligator was the reason the St. Johns' water-snake population, especially poisonous cottonmouths, had fallen so dramatically in the past few years, and also the reason no dog-owning wildfowler would use his retriever in some sections of the river.

Mel digested this good news/bad news and decided he'd still rather see more water snakes than risk losing a dog, or his leg, to an alligator. Nervousness about alligators is as old as wildfowling in Florida. In 1875, F. Trench Townshend noted that "the pools left by the overflow of the lake we found swarming with alligators; in one not fifty yards in diameter I counted thirty-five of these hideous reptiles, ranging from eight to twenty feet in length. It made us at first rather nervous, when wading after duck through water and mud up to our waists, to know that the next step might be on the back of an alligator lying buried in the mud, with the probable result of losing one or both legs, but impunity from such accidents quickly made us bolder."

Unexpected offerings, such as human legs plunging past their heads, are undoubtedly more frightening than appetizing to alligators. The only time I've ever witnessed a wild alligator taking prey, the saurian stalked a swimming coot for five cautious minutes before submerging and pulling the bird under. Unless prey is moving, I don't think an alligator shows much interest in it. For that reason, a crippled duck may intrigue an alligator, but a dead bird floating in a pothole is more likely to be pulled under by a turtle. A small man is too large for even a large alligator to swallow, so despite the saurian's capacity for twisting off arms and legs by furiously churning, those twenty-footers Mr. Townshend saw would probably have been more afraid of him than he was of them.

At least I kept telling myself that while charging after my own fallen birds.

Snipe Again

We took a midday break to pluck ducks at Space Coast headquarters. Plucking and gutting are not something you can put off for long in the warming, humid weather of central Florida. With everyone participating in the dis-assembly line, we soon had our birds ready for the freezer. At that point, Dave allowed as how he knew where a few more snipe might be found. What he showed us—after a false start that had the others convinced they were on another kind of "snipe hunt"—was the most fabulous shorebird shooting of my life.

Hundreds of snipe were scattered over a forty-acre pasture not far from the highway, and birds got up with every step we took. Our initial search for the birds had been fruitless, because we'd looked on terrain where there was too much water. Snipe prefer boggy, well-manured pastures where recent rains draw succulent worms and other invertebrates to the soil's surface without drowning them. I've shot snipe in half a dozen states, including my own marsh in Virginia, but in all those places, the birds were in transit and an unexpected bonus on hunts for other lowland fare. Snipe in Florida, however, are on their wintering grounds, and they clearly make the most of that state's poorly drained interiors grazed and fertilized by herds of cattle.

Shooting the birds was only part of the challenge. Keeping your eye on the precise spot where each snipe fell and walking directly there without being distracted by the alarm calls of other flushing birds, or by the movements of other shooters, was nearly as difficult as hitting the snipe in the first place. Having a dog might have helped, but I suspect the abundance of scent would have driven the animal crazy.

Shooting where birds are getting up with each step, and cattle are lumbering by on every side, is nerve-wracking exercise. A low-flushing target cannot be safely tracked even when you're reasonably sure your companions are behind you. At the same time, if you're too much in front, you'll inhibit their shooting or run the risk of getting shot yourself. I tried to calculate where most of the flushing snipe were going and hurried to intercept them. I took a position well out of range of my friends and under the birds' flight line and consequently had the closest thing to driven snipe possible on this side of the Atlantic. I killed most of my limit with high incoming shots.

Despite this methodical approach to the sport, I fired over thirty shells to kill eight snipe. I was consoled by the fact that with my last borrowed shell, I killed my last, limit-filling bird. I'd borrowed seven shells from Dick Graham and had almost casually killed my seventh snipe with the first of them. However, with only one bird to go, I tensed up, and by carefully tracking the next five targets, I missed every one of them. I was aiming the shotgun, not instinctively swinging it. With one shell left and none others to be begged, I began lecturing myself. I knew that the more tense I became, the more certain I'd miss. "Relax," I advised myself. "Treat this shot as though you have a dozen shells to spare." Almost casually then, I swung past the next snipe, squeezed the trigger, and watched it fall.

The little victories are remembered longest.

Yesteryears

Our second morning was devoted to layout shooting for scaup on the Banana River. For Dick and Bob, this was an opportunity no longer possible in their home state of Maryland where the political clout of landowners with shore blinds has resulted in the outlawing of most forms of boat shooting—especially from short, low hulls anchored in the middle of a river or bay.

My state of Virginia still allows layout shooting, as did New York where my brothers and I first tasted greater scaup hunting from a fourteen-foot plywood boat with brushed-up panel sides. Some mornings, wavy lines of broadbill stretched completely across the sky over Fire Island Inlet, and when tiny fractions of those lines broke off and hurtled down toward our decoys, the speed of those birds was so great that, when hit, they skipped and cartwheeled twenty or more yards across the surface before skidding to a halt. Sometimes, instantaneously, and always heartbreakingly, those same birds dived and rarely reappeared. I silently pledged not to let that happen on the Banana River.

Unbeknownst to most Floridians, the Banana River has a long and luminous hunting history. Beginning in the 1870s and peaking just after the turn of the century, Florida became well known to wealthy northern shooters who killed tens of thousands of birds each winter on the Indian River estuary between Palm Beach and Cocoa where scaup rafted literally by the millions.

By 1898, however, the editors of the United States Cartridge Company's *Where to Hunt American Game* warned that although "much game is still to be found there . . . these rivers are so much sailed over by houseboats containing sportsmen that the draught on the game is felt." Still, the editors suggested that "on the east coast of Florida, adjacent to the Banana and Indian rivers, is a great place for wild fowl, Merritt's island in that neighborhood and the peninsula opposite being especially good duck-shooting grounds."

Yet by 1947, when Lou S. Caine contributed the Florida chapter to Eugene V. Connett's *Duck Shooting along the Atlantic Tidewater*, the heyday of the Banana River was history: "Years ago the famous Canaveral Club, located on the headwaters of the Banana River, was in its prime. Founded about the time the East Coast Railroad went only as far as Titusville, it consisted of a spacious clubhouse at the head of a lagoon only a stone's throw from the ocean. Today, the club is a forlorn wreck of its former glory.

"There are now no worthwhile duck clubs in Florida," Caine concluded. "In fact, duck hunting, as far as the natives of the state are concerned, plays a very definite second fiddle to deer, turkey, and quail, and it is northern sportsmen who really appreciate it."

When Titusville was the end of the line, many among the fashionable wintering crowd who'd come south on Flagler's railway came expressly for the renowned duck shooting. Gradually, however, the railroad pushed on and the ducks declined. Visiting sportsmen took up marine angling and turned to quail and turkey—game they saw little of up north. Tourist wildfowlers shot canvasbacks in the mid-Atlantic or mallards along the Mississippi; there was no point in going all the way to Florida to shoot the smaller and less fashionable scaup and teal.

Gradually, from the 1910s to the 1940s, Florida was forgotten as a wildfowling mecca. Even local hunters came to think that duck hunting represented a waste of the state's sunny skies and salubrious weather. In winters following World War II, the King brothers, who owned Stuart's Pelican Hotel, used to tease my father for trying to find local people to take him and his sons on long round-trip drives to Lake Okeechobee merely to hunt ringnecked ducks—even if the lake did have the most spectacular concentrations of these birds the world will ever see.

Each expedition was like a voyage in a time machine to pre-Columbian Florida. I clearly recall the urgent whisper of wings in the darkness as we put out our Mason factory decoys, and the first light of dawn when ringnecks, occasional bluebills, and sometimes mallards and teal crisscrossed the heavens at every altitude. Just the sound of the wildfowl was a narcotic to my soul.

The only drawback to Florida duck hunting then was the scarcity of other shooters. On calm days, there was no reason for the birds to move much after dawn. Although an occasional bass fisherman helped, we had to rely on gusty weather to stir the ducks off the open water. Since we went duck hunting on days too rough to fish offshore, there was generally sufficient wind to move the birds. But not always. It was sometimes blowing a gale at the St. Lucie Inlet but flat as a fritter on Okeechobee. On calm days, we'd have to content ourselves with a coot shoot and watch clouds of nervous ducks swirl up and settle down on the lake every time we fired at a coot. Occasionally a fragment of those clouds would come our way and make the day.

In the 1940s, the daily limit was never more than eight ducks. Yet from 1973 to 1985, point-system values for teal, pintail, and wigeon, and bonus seasons for scaup, provided limits of ten ducks a day. With birds better concentrated and with easier access to them than in the 1940s, far more Florida shooters killed far more ducks per outing in the 1970s and early 1980s than in the "good old days" of my youth.

The Banana Estuary

Dave Van Nest told us we'd see between 60,000 and 75,000 scaup during the morning flight on the Banana River. Approximately one percent of those would pass directly over our decoys. He intended to rotate several parties, two by two, in one layout boat, starting with two hunters from Minnesota. Dick and Mel would follow them, and if Bob and I still hadn't shot our limits from one of the mangrove islands in the estuary, we'd try the layout boat last. What none of us reckoned with was the ferocity of the weather.

As soon as we opened our motel door, I was happy that Bob and I would be shooting standing up, rather than lying down in a low-profile boat. Wind and rain were gusting to more than 35 knots, and when we stepped outside, water quickly penetrated every pore of our "waterproof" clothing.

After meeting our guide, Ron Taylor, launching his boat, running to our hunting site, and putting out the decoys, we still had close to an hour before legal shooting time. So we unfolded three aluminum lawn chairs, sat butt-deep in our chest waders in the bay, and discussed the meaning of life while lightning crashed on the horizon around us.

Like other Florida guides, Ron doesn't carry a shotgun. This was a state law at the time (since changed), and one of the subtle pluses of hunting in Florida. You never suffered the indignity of a guide who not only *called* the shots but *took* half of them as well! Ron pointed out that

Florida guides have always prided themselves on their ability to locate ducks for their clients: "We're the ones who actually *hunt* the birds," he said. "Shooting the ducks is the client's responsibility. If he doesn't shoot well, that's a pity, but it doesn't reflect on our ability (or inability) to put him into the midst of them."

On the other hand, Ron feels strongly that a back-up gun for the guide is indispensable when using steel shot for diving ducks. "We'll eventually have to use steel shot for all waterfowling," Ron predicted, "but that inevitability shouldn't blind us to the fact that steel lacks the shocking power of lead. Bay and sea ducks die hard, and I'd like both of you to double-shoot every bird you hit. Even then you'll lose some."

This prediction came true with the very first duck. As the light came up, we put away the lawn chairs and were taking our positions near the mangroves when a common scoter hen worked her way upwind to the decoys. I waited until she was right over the plastic birds and not more than twenty-five yards out before firing. She splashed into the water and disappeared. Bob and I quickly waded to where she went down, but she resurfaced more than forty yards from us. We each fired, but our shots hit the back of a wave just as the swimming duck dived in the trough on the other side. If she came back up, we never saw her.

Steel shot is the best argument in favor of three-shot pump-guns and semi-autos over double barrels. Even then, regardless of how many rounds your gun can legitimately hold, you'll lose a depressing percentage of the diving ducks you knock down.

Some readers may doubt my claim of sub-Arctic sea ducks in Florida. Others may wonder why I'd "waste" shot on such an allegedly bad-tasting duck when better-eating scaup were on the agenda—especially after I admit that both scaup and scoters at the time counted as twenty-point birds.

First, sea ducks were abundant in Florida during the 1985–86 season. One of Space Coast Waterfowlers' clients even killed a common eider hen. Not long after our hunt, the extreme cold set the stage for the *Challenger* space shuttle disaster.

But the principal reason I tried to bag the scoter is that I've always preferred the extraordinary to the ordinary. Although I've shot hundreds of scoters from Maine to Alaska, the idea of sea duck shooting in Florida tickled my unconventional fancy.

Next, I'm one of those rare individuals who has actually tasted scoter and am consequently unwilling to parrot all the erroneous clichés about how inedible they are. As with any food, quality lies in the preparation and cooking. You have to take more pains with scoter breasts than with Canada goose breasts, for example, but the extra care is worth the effort.

Finally, and most obviously, a scoter in the hand is worth a yet unseen pair of scaup on the wing. Although Bob and I had heard much about the fabulous Banana River scaup flights, we hadn't yet seen a scaup and were prudent enough to take our shots as they offered.

During that dawning hour in the tempest, two dozen scoters (all of them the black or common species) flew within gun range, and we saw possibly three dozen others out of range. Bob and I each collected a scoter as our first bird of the day, but immediately lost interest in sea ducks when the first waves of scaup came flighting over from the Indian River.

For forty minutes, they came in undulating phalanxes—10,000 of them at least. Ron said that in an ordinary winter 30,000 to 40,000 scaup winter locally, but that that frigid season there were nearly twice the usual number. In the rain and gloom, we saw fewer than one-sixth of the birds that actually moved that morning.

"There's just as much food for the ducks in the Indian River as the Banana," Ron observed. "Yet the scaup have always preferred feeding in this lagoon and roosting on the other. If the wind and rain weren't forcing so many birds south and west of us, you'd see something to tell your grandchildren about."

What we saw was still worthy of a grandfather's reminiscence. Birds swept over in continual ranks. When it was soon apparent that enough pairs and singles would swing down to the decoys—indeed, Bob and I quickly collected three each that way—I decided to finish my limit with a pass shot—a bird taken at full speed rather than one with flaps down over the decoys. I spent twenty silly minutes moving from one position—where a flock had just gone over—to another, where they'd just done the same. I was always too late or too soon. I finally waded back to Ron and Bob standing near the decoys—just in time to intercept a flight passing thirty-five yards up.

I was behind the scaup with the first barrel, but caught it with the second. It turned out to be a drake broadbill that, in addition to having both wings broken, must have taken at least one pellet through the neck or chin into the brain, for he was the only cold-cocked bird of our outing. The drake still sculled feebly in a circle with his head under after hitting the water, but he wasn't going anywhere, and he was as close to a clean kill as you may expect with steel shot on diving ducks. Furthermore, like all steel-shot birds, the scaup bled so profusely, he turned the water gray around him.

Bob completed his limit with one of a pair of Florida ducks that came suddenly out of the driving rain. In contrast to our frustration with steel's capacity to kill diving ducks, Bob was able to knock down and eventually collect his dabbler with shots that were all taken at extreme range.

While retrieving the bird on the comber-crested bay, Ron half-filled his boat with water. He returned to the mangrove island where we helped him unload all the gear before he would take the boat off again to run in high-speed circles with the plug out to get rid of enough water so we could reload the boat for the pounding and anxious run back up Newfound Harbor.

The Drowned Lands

When further delays in the *Challenger* launch prevented us from hunting pintail and wigeon on the adjoining Merritt Island National Wildlife Refuge, our group returned to the St. Johns River for our last duck hunt. We decided to shoot as many as fourteen teal in the scrub willows before going out to Lake Winder to round out our limits with ringnecks.

Writer Charles E. Whitehead described a day of duck shooting in the 1850s with several friends on a Florida river that may have been the St. Johns. The first part of the hunt was spent poking around in what Whitehead called the "drowned lands," shooting mottled ducks (which he called "black ducks") and wood ducks. Then his group decided, as ours did 130 years later, to move onto open water and finish with a flourish on rafting birds. Ours were ringnecks, but Whitehead's were teal, "blue-wings, all of them, not a green-wing among them."

As his party made its way downstream, Whitehead described the timeless beauty of Florida's interior wetlands:

"The level waste of sedge extended beyond the vision, waving in the wind. The constant opening and closing of watery passages, the little reed-locked lakes, the tortuous course we were obliged to follow, the sameness of the grouping of the reeds and little islets, repeated over and over again till the mind was all afloat as to locality and distance; the weird trees with their dead and naked arms, and the occasional mass of broken reeds and matted driftwood that in the summer had formed the alligator's lair, all contributed to impress the mind with a feeling of strangeness and solitude. The wild birds, too, were unwontedly familiar in their demeanour. Marsh hens [coots and gallinules] ran over the drifts before the boat, and gulls came screaming around us."

When Whitehead's party came to the edge of the open water, "a glance ahead showed the farther end of the pond literally covered with ducks." The shooters, including a young woman, each got into a different boat rowed or pushed by a black man. The party split up with some of the hunters flushing and others waiting for the birds to fly over:

"Away down the marsh came the frequent boom! boom! of my comrades' guns, but it did not seem to interfere with the comfort of the ducks, who still fed on, though keeping out of shot from where I sat. Soon the report of the guns coming nearer caused the ducks to crowd together with all their heads up. There was a long pause, and then a negro's voice sounded close by: 'Mars Jackson, mark!' followed by the clear ringing of a double shot, and at the sound up went my flock of ducks. Three or four arose first, and then the whole mass cleared the water; and the beating of their wings on the surface was like a long-continued roll of thunder. I had no conception, before they rose, of their multitude. It seemed as if they could be counted by tens of thousands. When they had attained a sufficient height to overlook the meadow, they wheeled like the line of an army, and apparently catching sight of the other boats, came with the bright linings of their wings turned to the sunlight, and their countless pinions, hurtling through the air directly over the place where we were concealed. I had given Scipio, as a reward of merit, the musket I had brought with me, directing him to take his own time, and fire as he chose. He, however, could not wait for the best shot, but fired as one wing of the army wheeled over us. The aim was not a bad one, for a dozen ducks fell at the shot, and several more at intervals came slanting down from the flock. The effect of this unexpected attack drove the wing of the flock into the main body, clustering them together in a compact mass, when I fired both barrels. My stronger shooting gun bored a hole through the black mass, and twenty-seven ducks fell on the open water, and two or three went down aslant into the reeds. Three and a half dozen ducks was the contribution that one flock made to our booty. I still looked longingly after them as they went floating around the horizon, like banks of minute flies that wave at midsummer from prominent points on the shores of great lakes, undulating with the wind.

But they passed away in the dim horizon, probably being unwilling to make another trial of the Drowned Lands."

Flock shooting offers little pleasure to modern sportsmen, but the sight of waterfowl concentrations always does. As our party came to the edge of Lake Winder, we flushed several thousand teal. They clustered and swarmed across the horizon more like bees than birds and were soon out of sight over the reeds. They left behind several rafts of ringnecked ducks that boiled up and swirled to the far side of the lake before returning to another resting spot on the open water.

Another one of Space Coast's clients was already on the lake, waist-deep in the middle of a vast submerged grass bed. He was being tended by still another client from Oregon who'd gone to the expense of acquiring his own airboat. The two men's plan had been to flush the birds off the open water, improvise an open-water blind from cut brush, put out a couple dozen decoys, and shoot the ducks as they returned. So far, only the first three parts of the plan had worked.

Chris was our guide that morning, and as the two airboat-bound clients described their predicament, I watched his eyes exploring the horizon. In a few moments he'd decided where each of his parties would find the fastest shooting. He told the airboaters to pick up and follow us. After checking on still another of Space Coast's parties, Chris took us into a small, flooded bay from which we flushed several dozen ringnecks and a dozen teal. He put insufficiently wadered Dick and brother Bob at the upper end of the bay, and Mel and me in deeper water nearer the entrance. Mel and I were told to let the birds flying into the bay go past us and then salute any survivors coming out. If the ducks looked as though they weren't going into the bay, we could take those in range. "Your collective points come to no more than six ringnecks," Chris warned, "so one or two flights should do it." He then led the airboaters to another bay farther around the Lake.

Organized optimism seems to amuse the red gods. Several ringnecks crossed the mouth of the bay without giving either one of our sub-parties a chance at them. Then a hen ringneck came from the only direction for which we weren't prepared, but I managed to kill her at extreme range.

Mel and I then let a couple of singles go by with the hope they'd continue up the bay, but they didn't. So the next one that churned overhead, a handsome drake, I folded. Since I was done, I asked Mel to switch sides with me, but he figured he'd eventually get shots from where he stood twenty feet to my right. Two other ringnecks went by, in range of my three-inch 12-gauge shells, but not, Mel felt, for his two 3/4-inch, 20-gauge shells.

At last, a mixed flight of teal and ringnecks went far enough up the bay for Dick and Bob to knock down three. Two were ringnecks, and the third was a drake blue-wing in the best breeding plumage we'd seen on the trip. Dick decided to have it mounted, and although two of our party were still shy of their limits, we decided to end the hunt on the happy note of the prime blue-winged drake.

All of our party shot well that January, and this pleased the guides as much as it did us. We were, in turn, pleased with the guides. Having enthusiastic and honest youngsters organize your trip and lead the way adds immeasurably to any hunting expedition. I was, furthermore, impressed by the way Dave and Chris handled clients who skybusted. Every time a shooter knocked down a distant bird that became a swimming cripple, Dave or Chris would take the man, *along with all his friends,* out to look for the downed duck. More often than not, they didn't find it. Yet the half-hour or more spent looking for it, while other birds continued to fly by and even land in the deserted decoys, soon persuaded all the hunters to pass up any doubtful shots.

I was also impressed by how Dave and Chris handled potentially risky situations. On the run back across Lake Poinsett with winds gusting to forty mph, Chris organized a convoy of small craft with his large semi-V hull in the lead; the smaller, flat-bottomed jonboats in the middle, and our large work-launch bringing up the rear. Each boat had one hunter ready with an anchor in case of engine failure. In our boat, a second hunter (me) was assigned drain-plug duty. As soon as we reached planing speed, I pulled the plug to let the sheets of incoming spray drain out the stern. I was so busy keeping weeds and other debris out of the hole, I was unaware we were across the lake until Chris told me to put back the plug. Dave, meanwhile, had taken the airboaters around on a sheltered trail too shallow for outboards.

We shot snipe again that afternoon. I managed to improve my ratio by killing eight birds with nineteen rounds. I took mostly high, overhead snipe and my last shot stopped a bird in mid-flight and helicoptered it down so slowly, I was able to walk over and catch it in my hand before it hit the ground.

Lake Okeechobee

Some mornings in the dark at the lakeside towns of Moore Haven, Lakeport, Clewiston, and Okeechobee, the snarl and roar of outboards and airboats is so deafening you wonder whether you'll see more ducks than hunters when the sun comes up. Yet somehow, Lake Okeechobee's 450,000 acres manage to absorb the mobs of men and machinery. Even more amazing, a significant percentage of hunters come off the lake and out of the fringing marshes, day after day, with limits of ringnecked ducks.

The ringneck is exceptional among American waterfowl for having expanded its traditional breeding range over the past half-century. Once uncommon in upper portions of the Atlantic Flyway, an estimated 6,000 now breed in Maine. An additional 10,000 breed from New York's Adirondack Park to Prince Edward Island, Canada. Although the Mississippi Flyway still has more ringnecks than the Atlantic Flyway, and although Louisiana still hosts more wintering ringnecks than any other state, Florida is a close second. Furthermore, while Louisiana's 70,000-plus ringnecks are distributed throughout the state, Florida's 60,000-plus ringnecks are mostly found on or around Lake Okeechobee.

Unfortunately, the eastern expansion of the ringneck has stopped and may be in remission. This is distressing to wildfowlers, because ringnecks are so much more reliable as breeders than the traditional trophy diving ducks: canvasbacks and redheads. The brood-rearing success of ringnecks is greater than any other duck species, providing an average 1.7 immature to adult ratio during the fall flight.

In addition, ringnecks are by far the tastiest of all diving ducks. Wintering canvasbacks and redheads now consume large quantities of shellfish to survive, but wintering ringnecks feed primarily on seeds, tubers, and the leafy parts of aquatic vegetation. Even ringnecks that winter on estuaries feed mostly on plants. Snails and other invertebrates never make up more than about 11 percent of their diets.

In the late 1940s and early 1950s, my father, brothers, and I shot a goodly number of big ringneck drakes that weighed close to two pounds. Today one rarely shoots a drake weighing more than a pound and a half. This may be because ringnecks find fewer areas today where they can feed undisturbed and develop fat reserves for the migration north. This may also be because fewer birds today live more than a few years; hence, few reach the species' maximum size.

Even though divers are more tolerant of shooting pressure than other ducks or geese, biologist Clarence Cottam observed in the 1930s that scaup become night feeders rather than continue suffering attrition from heavy gunning. The same is true of ringnecks. Some flocks even abandon heavily shot wintering grounds. The flocks fracture into small groups and pairs that disperse to small ponds and potholes earlier than such springlike behavior is scheduled. Such a vanishing act occurred on Okeechobee in January 1986 and left hundreds of hunters staring into largely empty skies during the last two weeks of the regular season.

Okeechobee may disappoint hunters seeking variety, since 90 percent of the ducks found there are ringnecks. Still, the lake appeals to many because its fishing camps and marinas provide rental boats and motors, making it one of the few areas in the country where nonresident wildfowlers can readily organize their own hunts. Maps and information can be obtained from the Glades County Chamber of Commerce, Box 490, Moore Haven, FL 33471. If you prefer hiring a guide, at least for your first experience on the lake, write Calusa Lodge, Route 2, Highway 78, Moore Haven, FL 33471; Ernie Glover, Route 2, Box 222, Lakeport, FL 33471; or Scott Driver, 4526 Southeast 21st Court, Okeechobee, FL 33472. Their services cost roughly $75 per hunter per day. Each guide takes out two hunters per boat, so plan your trip with a partner or in multiples of two.

This is also true of Space Coast Waterfowlers, 5150 S.R. 520, Cocoa, FL 32926. Dave and Chris charge $100 per hunter per day, but their extra service and the greater variety of shooting are worth the extra money. Dave and Chris fly over their hunting grounds before the season and then every week during the season to make sure they know where the greatest concentrations of ducks are. They're also the only guides hunting birds adjacent to the half-million-acre Mormon ranch that protects a significant portion of the St. Johns watershed. They'll show you parts of Florida that not even the Seminoles know about. Okeechobee offers satisfying shooting, but the camaraderie and contentment you'll find on the St. Johns and Banana rivers convert these outings into world-class experiences.

—3—

North Carolina

Core Sound

In the fog, the ducks appeared like ghosts, brief and insubstantial, and were gone again, vanished, before my companion and I realized we might kill one. We chewed our missed opportunity until it was limp with denial:

"Why didn't you shoot?"

"I couldn't tell what kind they were."

"What difference does that make? They were scaup or redheads and both are legal."

"But it was your turn to shoot."

"That holds only for singles and there were a dozen of them."

"But the birds were on your side of the blind. You had a better chance than I did."

"They seemed a little long."

"They were perfect and you know it!"

"Okay, so we weren't ready."

Being ready is less a matter of timing and position than a state of mind. My companion and I had each killed a duck soon after climbing into our blind a mile or more out in Core Sound behind a yet unseen horizon of desolate barrier banks. We were still gloating over our success and comparing the subdued beauty of the hen broadbill with the more elegant flair of the redhead drake when a ghostly flock of diving ducks sped by us in the mist.

Had the birds come an hour later, when our self-satisfaction had waned and we were again primed for action, I'm confident we would have killed two or three of them. But wildfowling is like that: periodic picture-book kills suspended from a long chain of missed opportunities.

When you're on the downside of forty-five, any winter day on a bay reminds you of younger outings. Your body may be locked into relentless time, but your mind is always free to wander like a child through a pleasantly cluttered attic. Under thirty and you're still making memories; past forty-five and you're as often dusting off moments from the life of the lad you were as putting fresh impressions in the trunk upstairs.

So it was that my sampling of North Carolina wildfowling was both new and familiar. I'd never before hunted ducks from a fifteen-foot-high stake blind. Yet the superior view of incoming birds reminded me of a younger dawn when I killed my first wood duck from the top of a quarry wall.

My banded redhead drake was like another banded drake diver taken on Long Island's South Oyster Bay. That bird, a broadbill, was killed from a flock that swept low over the decoys just off Meadowbrook State Parkway. He turned out to be at least eight years old.

The Core Sound bird also reminded me of my first redhead drake, killed while hunting near Annapolis between military tours in Vietnam. That drake was one of a pair I doubled and longed to have mounted, but without money for such luxuries, and with a promise to a girlfriend to supply her with a wild duck dinner, I reluctantly plucked—but then heartily ate—the prize. The next year the redhead season in the Atlantic Flyway was closed, and it was more than a decade before I could collect a replacement mount.

With its clay-red head, jet-black breast, gray vermiculated back, bright yellow eyes, and white-banded, black-tipped, and slate-blue bill, the drake redhead is the most handsome of the bay ducks. No wonder the species is regarded as a trophy and attracts hunters from all over the eastern United States to Core Sound to try their luck and skill in taking one.

But the knowledge of a good blind builder is even more important than that of the shooter. Of four parties of two gunners each serviced from one twenty-four-foot tender, outdoor writing colleague Art Carter and I were the only ones to see any redheads. The others killed pintails, black ducks, buffleheads, red-breasted mergansers, and a common scoter—none of which Art and I saw. Yet our four blinds lay on a line less than three miles long.

Although the other hunters would have enjoyed seeing redheads, they were satisfied with their variety of game and ample shooting. But Art and I had come specifically for redheads, and our guide knew that as well as he knew the territory of his blinds well enough to provide us with exactly the species we wanted.

Each hunter is expected to wear chest waders and do his own retrieving, so Art and I had an opportunity to walk for hundreds of yards around our blind on the hard sandy bottom. I had been concerned about rumors of baiting and was, therefore, relieved to find that the only duck food in the crystal-clear water were two beds of naturally rooted eelgrass.

Hunting with Carter means that you frequently share in his phenomenal luck. He reminds me of a story about Napoleon Bonaparte. One of Bonaparte's generals wanted his aide de camp promoted. Bonaparte listened to a litany of the young man's credentials: his lineage, his wife's lineage, his academic record, his past campaigns, and so forth. Impatiently Bonaparte interrupted, "Yes, yes! But is the young man *lucky?*"

I never met Carter's wife, and I know nothing about his academic record. But he'd certainly improve the odds of any group, team, or army of which he was part. Most outdoor writers consider themselves lucky when the weather allows them to get a story of any kind. Carter, by contrast, expects his trips to be crowned by ideal weather and personal trophies. He took the largest salmon of Iceland's 1983 angling season and a world-record pike in Sweden. Later during the North Carolina tour, Art combined skill with his exceptional luck to shoot a double of snow geese near Bodie Island—after he'd photographed the birds hovering over the decoys from a position far out of shotgun range.

When host Joel Arrington stood to shoot, his gun misfired. The guide missed, period. The startled geese fell back on the wind over Carter who put down his camera and picked up his gun. Those birds didn't have to go Art's way. They could have flared to either side of the blind or climbed against the wind. But they drifted conveniently over Carter's head as everything else in his life seems to do.

The snow geese incident might seem to be only ordinarily good luck. But what happened at Core Sound wasn't. It was the most extraordinary luck imaginable. The red gods don't smile on this boy; they dote on him!

After I'd petted and put my redhead on the seat between us and philosophized about the special qualities of this particular species, Art allowed as how he'd never shot either a redhead or a banded bird.

"I'd give my eyeteeth to get a duck like yours," he said.

Such heart-worn-on-the-sleeve yearnings embarrass and even frighten me. In my experience, the red gods delight in crucifying hope whenever anyone speaks optimistically or makes the slightest appeal to their charity. Even when signs are propitious, I'm especially careful to keep my thoughts to myself, knowing how capricious the gods can be. I would have calculated the odds of either one of us killing another banded redhead drake about equivalent to our shooting a stray European wigeon. The gods had already sent us one. I couldn't conceive they'd send us another. And once Art spoke aloud his plaintive appeal, I feared we might not see another bird of any kind!

Well, we did. And I'm not just talking about the ring-billed gulls, gannets, pelicans, cormorants, and even a few vagrant kittiwakes that sailed by our blind. Nor about the palm warbler that landed at eye level on the blind wall. Nor even about the second redhead, a hen, which I killed.

I'm talking about the astonishing fact that less than five hours after Art shamelessly begged the red gods for a banded redhead drake, he sat stroking the feathers of one carrying an even older, sand-polished aluminum ring than the one my bird sported.

Don't ask me how he does it. It was his turn to shoot, and the gods delivered the bird to him idling over the decoys—and they didn't even ask for his eyeteeth!

Pamlico Sound and Mattamuskeet

Smart wildfowlers take their recreation at least four days at a time. They know that half those days will probably be spent staring at a vacant horizon, or huddled in an open blind in a storm so intense that even if ducks appear, the hunters will be too bundled up and numb with cold to do much about it. The third day may provide perfect weather, but poor flighting. However, the fourth day is invariably the one that dreams are made of.

Although Art and I had good hunting elsewhere in North Carolina, the peak of our visit came at Lake Mattamuskeet. This was the day after a day on Pamlico Sound where neither one of us fired a shot. We watched clouds of canvasbacks swirling up and resettling half a mile away—inside the national wildlife refuge.

Although I was eager to write an update on canvasback, I was not eager to spend another day in a cramped fifteen-foot boat-blind with two other equally frustrated people. We'd sat with no place to lie down from dawn to twilight in weather so calm it had taken over a hundred yards for the few ruddy ducks and buffleheads in our vicinity to get airborne. By the time the wind picked up, it was too late in the afternoon to give us more than a good soaking while running back to the landing in the dark.

Although we were scheduled for a return to Pamlico the next morning, Joel pleaded our case with outfitter Bob Hester. I don't know what Joel promised him, but Hester assigned the three of us to a blind on the north side of Lake Mattamuskeet overlooking freshwater ponds that had been planted the previous summer with milo and millet.

The cold front that hit us at sunset on Pamlico Sound generated fierce winds during the night, and the temperature plummeted to Arctic standards. We found ice coating the decoys left out by a previous party, and the radio predicted snow flurries by noon.

The wisdom of wearing chest waders for all wildfowling in North Carolina rose as suddenly as the water did when I stepped into a soft hole while wading the last few yards to our assigned blind. My chest waders also helped retain heat contained by my insulated underwear, two pairs of socks, a goose-down jacket, a woolen face mask, down mittens, a down cap with ear flaps, and a flannel-lined, waterproof parka. I looked like a camouflaged Yeti, but I was warm, and I could still swing my arms well enough to shoot.

After watching a couple of flights of pintail work to the edge of range before falling off on the wind, I asked guide John Mullet what he would do. He oracularly suggested that "All you don't shoot at, you don't get," so I saluted the next drake that hove into extreme range and was pleasantly surprised to see the bird fall dead even as Arrington muttered, "Too far."

For Joel, the bird *was* too far. In the huge blind, which four of us occupied with room to spare, Joel—standing at the other end of the front wall—was fifteen feet farther from the bird than I was. Furthermore, he was shooting an open-choked, 2 3/4-inch chambered gun with only an ounce and a quarter of number-6 shot. I was using a full and modified over-and-under with a selector switch, enabling me to give the full choke barrel priority with a bird at extreme range. In addition, my three-inch shells were Federal Premiums packed with 1 5/8 ounces of copper-plated number-4 shot. That's one of my lucky loads, and as every hunter knows, feeling lucky makes you confident, and feeling confident makes you a better shot. I could have used 1 7/8 or even two ounces of shot, but over the years, I've found that 1 5/8 yields more consistent killing patterns with my gun than heavier loads. Once again, if you have confidence in something, that's more than half its effective use. Number-6 shot is my preferred load over decoys, but number-4 is a heavier, bone-breaking pellet. Since it was unlikely we'd lose many cripples in the dike-enclosed pond, I opted for the long-range, *knock-down* potential of 4s over the shorter range, *killing* power of 6s. As it turned out, I still killed cleanly most every bird I hit.

After demonstrating that the birds were not too far—at least for three-inch shells fired from the near corner of the blind—I was expelled from that corner. Arrington and Carter improvised a rotation rule that soon had me at the far end with the two of them jockeying for position in the near corner. Joel ended up in the middle, but was promptly rewarded for being a proper host when a dozen green-wing teal suddenly appeared inside the decoys. He was the only one quick enough to stop one of the birds, although Art and I gave all the credit to his improved cylinder choke.

We saw over 2,000 pintail and other ducks that freezing morning at Mattamuskeet, plus dozens of Canada geese and hundreds of tundra swans. Only a small percentage of all those birds came within range, but enough did to provide us with a shot every ten minutes or so. When we quit shooting, we had ten pintail, a teal, a wigeon, and a mallard. All the ducks, but two pintail, were drakes. Counting a pintail and a mallard we knocked down but lost, we shot five ducks each, plus a Canada goose that Art took back to South Carolina for his Christmas dinner.

The highlight of the day was not our shooting, but the birds flighting from the unseen lake—sweeping over and out of sight again into snow-dusted skies. The ducks flew to find food, but their need was not so desperate as to cost them their caution and us our sport. No sportsman enjoys taking advantage of ducks down on their calories. They're too easy to kill and too thin and poorly flavored to eat. Well-fed birds riding the first winds of winter, however, are a delight to the eye, to the gun, and to the palate.

Hester on Hester

A good way for a curious wildfowler to start in North Carolina is to write Bob Hester at Route 1, Fairfield, NC 27826. Hester provides access to some of the best duck shooting left in the Atlantic Flyway. Costs for Hester's guides range from $110 per hunter per day to $75 per hunter per day if there are four people in the party.

I stayed at a local inn where the rooms were cheap—$17.50 for a single; $22.50 for a double—but marginal. I was too tired to care about the dirty sheets, poor plumbing, and erratic heat—but should have eaten elsewhere. Fortunately, there are elsewheres.

John Mullet told us that Hester instructs all his guides to "call just enough so the birds don't hear you." When we got back to Hester's headquarters, I asked him to elaborate. Bob said that clients expect to hear the guides honk like geese and quack like ducks. So Bob makes sure that all his guides are equipped with first-rate calls with lanyards and whatever bird bands they've collected over the years and crimped on for special effect.

"But the truth is," said Bob, "most hunters, and this includes the guides, don't know the first thing about waterfowl calling. Take Canada geese, for example. The *'awronk'* most hunters blow means little to a goose. It has as much to do with his looking for a place to eat as a smoke alarm does to a dinner bell! If more hunters spent time in a refuge listening to the sounds the birds actually make while feeding, hunters would be embarrassed to repeat their silly *'awronk, awronk, awronk.'*

"A gander sometimes makes a drawn-out *'awrooonkk'* while landing. And geese joining other geese make a breathless—at least it makes you breathless to duplicate it with a call—*'ronk-ronk-ronk-ronk!'* Yet the only sound you'll hear all the time from feeding geese is a kind of murmur. You'll never hear competitors in a goose-calling contest make that murmur because they know the judges will downgrade them for it. Most judges, like most hunters, have heard more artificial goose calls than geese. They don't know the way geese really communicate. Since most of my clients have never heard a flock of geese talking on the ground, I tell my guides to give the clients what they expect to hear—namely, the sounds geese make when they're alarmed or just flying around—but not so loud the birds may be alarmed by the noise."

Art Carter took umbrage at Hester's theory, but was willing to concede geese if Bob would allow that ducks were different.

"Not at all," said Bob. "Ducks mutter and chatter when they're feeding and secure, and that's the only sound that incoming birds want to hear. The problem is that duck chatter is difficult to send any distance on a windy day. A single quack is all I recommend then. I know Midwesterners feel you need a high-ball call just to get a passing duck's attention, but if you've put yourself and your decoys where the birds want to be, you don't need to call at all.

"Some days you don't even need decoys. We find that ducks and geese become so decoy-shy toward the end of the season, you're better off sitting downwind of the decoys, or even occupying a well-sited blind without decoys, than using the same stool in the same place day after day."

Bob is an original thinker in other respects. He has a plan, which a contemptuous federal biologist characterizes as "hare-brained," to establish a resident Mattamuskeet flock of blue geese. Bob hopes to provide an alternative trophy for goose hunters disappointed by the continuing decline of wintering Canada geese in North Carolina. Since a blue goose is an unusual sight in the Atlantic Flyway, and since the Mattamuskeet area has historically hosted 1,500 lesser snow geese, of which about half are of the blue color phase, Hester is certain that if he can only increase the local blue goose population, he'll have hunters coming from all over the eastern United States to collect one of these scarce birds.

Fish and Wildlife Service critics claim the notion is impossible: "Snow geese, far more than Canadas, need to make migratory flights to trigger their nest-building and egg-laying instincts," one told me. "These birds will try to walk to Canada if they're pinioned and can't fly. Unless you can trick them into thinking they've made the journey, captive snows rarely breed. Hester says he'll have a huntable population of blue geese by 1990; he'll be lucky to have a hundred breeding pairs by that date—which was his goal for 1984!"

Hester's other extra-curricular activity on behalf of wildfowling has already met with success. In the mid-1970s, Bob began appealing to state and federal agencies for a tundra (alias, whistling) swan season in North Carolina. William J. L. Sladen of the Wildfowl Trust of North America resisted the proposal, warning that the sudden swelling of swan numbers in North Carolina from 1972 on has had less to do with improved production on the birds' western Arctic breeding grounds than with a shift in the core of the eastern wintering population from Maryland to North Carolina. There were not that many more swans overall, Dr. Sladen insists—only more swans in North Carolina.

Swans have declined in Maryland due to the decline of rooted aquatic vegetation in the tributaries and bays of the Chesapeake, he explains. They've increased in eastern North Carolina due to the creation of vast corporate farms where tens of thousands of winter wheat acres are available for feeding, and two large sanctuary lakes are used for roosting. Dr. Sladen stresses that the tundra swan is a late-maturing species with a continental population of less than a quarter-million birds. State and federal wildlife agencies should have carefully determined just how much shooting pressure swans can sustain before acceding to a handful of guides and farmers from eastern North Carolina who wanted to see the birds hunted.

Other, mostly state, biologists felt there was no reason the tundra swans could not be shot since, even as early as 1972, more than 60,000 wild swans were using North Carolina as their winter home. A decade ago, however, biologists warned Hester that politics, not science, was the issue. Bob didn't at first understand what politics had to do with it. So long as state biologists were telling him there were more than enough swans for hunting, why not open a season? Swans have been shot in

North Carolina since colonial times, and Bob personally knew dozens of people who wanted to hunt them.

Hester eventually found an ally and mentor in physician Thomas Stokes, who pin-pointed the fundamental problem with Bob's campaign. Stokes observed that the average politician doesn't know a swan from a snow goose. Nor does he feel a compelling need to know the difference. The only way a politician can be persuaded to know anything is for a significant number of his constituents to tell him it's important.

Stokes became the chairman of a Swan Now Committee. With donations from fifteen sportsmen to kick things off, he began a letter-writing campaign to every politician with the least possible interest in the matter. Bob Hester helped organize support in eastern North Carolina, and legislative offices were soon deluged with letters demanding a swan season. State legislators and congressmen passed the pressure on to the U.S. Fish and Wildlife Service, which gave its approval in 1984 for the first swan season east of the Mississippi since 1918.

The Ultimate Wildfowl Trophy?

We were worried. We had been alternately sitting and standing in a ditch between two fields of winter wheat for nearly two hours and hadn't yet seen a flight of anything. Wildfowling usually involves some waiting, but because our binoculared vision included the air space over several square miles of flat eastern Carolina acres, and because swans were reputedly abundant in the vicinity, the empty sky was disconcerting.

Even Dick Braeme, a wildfowl biologist and our volunteer guide for the hunt, was concerned. "Don't worry," he said to reassure himself as well as the rest of us, "the birds were here yesterday; they'll be here today."

Scouting is the key to all successful wildfowling. With so many fields in the area for the swans to visit from their two refuge lakes, Phelps and Pungo, Dick had spent two full days finding fresh swan droppings and then the farm owner to get permission to hunt. Even so, we had a delay. The farm manager came charging out in his truck to run us off "his" field, because he'd not been notified by the owner that anyone would be hunting there. Ultimately, however, his visit gave us heart. When he found we were after "sky carp," as he called the swans, he wished us luck and assured us that, although swans didn't move around as early as ducks or geese, if we stayed put, we'd soon have more than enough birds for a trophy each.

In our party of five, Dick Braeme and Joel Arrington had killed swans during the first North Carolina season. Journalist Jim Phillips, conservation administrator Mike Corcoran, and I were the rookies. When we asked the veterans what they thought about swan hunting, Dick and Joel were evasive, only mentioning the unexpectedly light shot needed to kill the big birds.

"Number six is more than adequate so long as your target is under thirty yards and you shoot the bird in the face and eyes," said Joel. Dick added that if you waited until they were "tits and tummy to the wind," you could probably kill a bird with a well-thrown rock.

I'd brought my over-and-under with a favorite load of number-4 shot in the improved-cylinder barrel chamber and a heavier load of copper-plated BBs in the modified-choke barrel chamber. As it turned out, I fired only the improved cylinder barrel—once to kill my swan and later to help Mike's bird stay down. The first shot was at twenty-five yards; the second at forty. Of the five birds we shot, only Mike's required a second round. Joel cold-cocked his bird with 1 1/4 ounces of number-6 shot. So much for the myth of an invincible bird requiring buckshot, if not a heat-seeking missile, to kill.

I asked Dick whether the permit system used by the state to license swan hunters facilitated poaching.

"No doubt about it," he replied. "Landowners are probably not killing any more swans than they used to—although some farmers go out of their way to try to run the birds down in their pickup trucks. The new problem is that with hunting permits in circulation, some hunters keep killing swans, one at a time, carrying them off the field, and using their permits only when they have to. When they're caught, or on the verge of being caught, they tag the swan they have in hand and stop for the season.

"While I don't condone such behavior," Dick continued, "as a wildlife biologist concerned with the species and not individual birds, the combined legal and illegal kill of swans each year in North Carolina is still under 10,000—a number sufficient to guarantee a healthy local wintering population well into the future."

Like all wildlife controversies, the one over swan hunting has less to do with facts than feelings. Some biologists worry that hunting mortality may warp the trend of natural selection; others point out that such is true with any game species. Some Carolina farmers treat wintering swans like the enemy; others regard the great white birds as angels. Some hunters value the swan permit as a way to shoot a "long-necked goose" for Christmas dinner; others as a way to acquire a trophy mount. A handful even acquire permits but never intend to use them.

All hunting involves cultural values. Americans belittle southern Europeans for killing songbirds. Yet the mourning dove is classified as a "songbird" in many of our northern states. Furthermore, European thrushes are larger and provide more meat than the "game" sora rail.

Many people, including some hunters, believe that swan hunting is unethical. They can't explain why they feel this way, only that it's somehow wrong to shoot one of the snow-white birds. Yet so long as hunters quickly dispatch any cripples, and so long as every killed creature is used, shooting a swan is ethically no different from shooting a deer, to which we as fellow mammals are evolutionarily much closer.

So if neither science nor ethics lies at the core of the swan hunting debate, what does?

Aesthetics. Many people like to see a swan. They feel their lives are enlarged by the proximity of the monumental birds. If hunting pressure causes North Carolina's wintering swans to become, as visitor Nathaniel H. Bishop found them well more than a century ago, "exceedingly wary" and unable to be approached "within rifle range," where does this leave someone whose principal pleasure is in watching them? Has the state's Wildlife Resources Commission considered those who want to observe and photograph swans as well as those who want to hunt them?

Man has always exploited swans. Even the mute swan of England, protected since medieval times, was formerly managed by the Crown and the various manufacturing guilds for its meat and feathers. Only young swans, or cygnets, were eaten, and in 1274, they were worth three shillings (thirty-six pence) each. That same year, wild geese sold for only five pence, and pheasants for four. Up until the discovery of the New World and the subsequent introduction of the turkey to Europe, swans were a traditional holiday meal for British nobility.

Many nineteenth-century American sportsmen knew as much about the succulent flavor of young swans as thirteenth-century English aristocrats. A select number of twentieth-century hunters have rediscovered that exquisite taste. I set a young or "gray" tundra swan before six discriminating game gourmets. Four of us voted swan superior to Canada goose; the other two voted it as good as goose.

"A gray swan is the best eating bird that flies," declared a Carolina waterman. "The best way to deal with an old bird though is to put it in an oven at 350 degrees and check it every day 'til it's done."

Swan's down is better insulation than goose down. The Hudson Bay Company sold 108,000 swan skins between 1820 and 1880. These were turned into clothing and powder puffs. Russians shot Bewick's swans for the market until the 1940s, and the birds' tough skin and warm soft pelts were turned into everything from caps to wallets. In ancient times, swan windpipes were dried and fashioned into flutes, and in Iceland the feet were made into purses. In the centuries before the United States and Japan redesigned the wealth of nations, swans were merely another commodity like turnips, timber, and human labor. Now as even our most affluent and sophisticated societies strain under the weight of ever-increasing humanity, a return to less refined perspectives may be inevitable. All creatures, including humans, will once again have their price.

The swans finally appeared at 9:15 A.M. Family groups rose off distant Phelps Lake and were clearly visible for up to four full minutes before swinging over our decoys. If they had been black rather than white birds, we could have watched them against the pale sky for more than twice that long while they worked our way. Their steady approach and their constant calling were soul-stirring stuff. Dick yelped back at them, and I even gave a bark or two without flaring the birds.

We pressed against the ditch bank while the swans ponderously approached our spread of snow goose shells. Unfortunately, the incoming birds were back-lit by the rising sun so it was impossible to distinguish the gray young of the year from their white parents. Two of our group wanted white birds to mount; the others wanted gray birds to eat. I killed an adult by mistake; Phillips did the same with a gray bird, so we swapped. By 1:30 P.M. we'd lunched, showered, checked out of our motel room, and started our journeys home.

Jim and I shared his vehicle for the trip north. We'd been exultant in the field. Yet the more distance we put between ourselves and the shores of Albemarle Sound, the more we questioned whether what we'd done was a "trophy experience."

"A swan's not a real trophy," Jim concluded. "We didn't work hard enough for those birds. Less than twenty-four hours after walking out my front door, I'd killed what many hunters would regard as the ultimate wildfowl trophy. Dick Braeme did the scouting, so he may have earned his bird, but we didn't."

A trophy hunt has two indispensable ingredients. First, the quarry must be scarce or a species that only a relatively few people will ever have the chance to shoot. Second, the quarry must be challenging to hunt. An easily acquired prize is no prize at all.

Tundra swan shooting satisfies the first requirement. Swans are large (averaging fifteen pounds) and beautiful birds, and North Carolina (and in 1988, Virginia) are still the only states east of the Mississippi that allow their legal pursuit. However, as the principal wintering ground for the species—over 100,000 are now found in the four counties separating Albemarle and Pamlico sounds—eastern North Carolina is the only place on the continent where a hunter seeking a swan trophy has an almost certain chance of acquiring one. Ironically, it's that certainty which subtracts from the trophy experience of hunting them.

Although tundra swans have been hunted in Utah's Great Salt Lake valley since 1962, and more recently in several other western states, the birds are not as concentrated, or as abundant, in the West as they are in North Carolina. Furthermore, because they've been hunted in Utah for a quarter century, they're wary and difficult to decoy. Thus, western wintering tundra swans are rated as superior trophies to those shot in the East. Birds in the Carolina wintering population are still too tame and trusting to represent anything more than ponderous targets twenty and thirty yards away.

Half a century ago, when Van Campen Heilner shot a swan on the Baltic coast, waterfowl generally, and swans in particular, had passed only a few milestones in their recovery after the heavy-handed commercial shooting that had thinned their ranks before the turn of the century. As Heilner's friend, Dr. Herbert Blume, member of the Danzig Senate, pointed out, what saved the sport of wildfowling were "the nobility in Europe and the duck clubs in America."

Heilner discovered that the Poles and Germans shot geese and swans with rifles and scorned the American use of shotguns. "Would you shoot a stag with a shotgun?" they asked. Heilner could make no reply to satisfy them.

After he killed a scarce European whooper swan, a bird of the same species (but different race) as North America's trumpeter, and did it with a shotgun while pass-shooting old squaw ducks, he wrote, "I felt sick. I always wanted to shoot a swan and now I think I shall never want to shoot another."

Yet Heilner did not regret the killing so much as he regreted the ambiguity of shooting a still-threatened species and, perhaps, the fact that he didn't kill it cleanly. The bird lay on the water, "dying in circles, its beautiful snow white plumage all stained crimson."

All of us regret the shots we bumble and the birds we cripple. What wildfowlers never regret is the hunting of an abundant species and cleanly killing the birds so they land with resounding thumps or mighty splashes—"the water spouting into the air like a geyser," as Heilner described his swan's fall.

In my own case, I regret only that by the time I'd made up my mind to take the lead swan among the first four incoming birds, he was so close to the ground that when I popped up to shoot, I had to fire *at* the bird, rather than *below* him, or risk blowing off the heads of two of Dick Braeme's decoys. As a result, the swan was not centered by the pattern. Although unable to move, the bird had to be given the coup de grâce by smacking his head several times against the frozen ground— hardly a fitting conclusion to a trophy experience.

Were I able to replay the day, I'd let that first group go and select another bird out of a long line of swans that sailed thirty yards over less than an hour later. Such a bird would have been cleanly killed. Further- more, had it fallen and crushed one of Dick's decoys, that would have given us something to talk about for years afterward. By contrast, paying for decoys damaged by gunfire is an embarrassment no one even wants to think about.

Swans will always be a controversial species. Perhaps it goes against the grain of American sensibilities to think of such birds being hunted. Perhaps, we're just unwilling to discuss the economics of anything as beautiful as the great white birds flighting off Phelps and Pungo lakes and undulating over the frozen fields of corn stubble and winter wheat. Yet unless we do establish financial reference points for swans, every one of us—be he a bird watcher, hunter, or even someone who dismisses swans as "sky carp"—will have no voice in determining the fate of these birds.

Sir Peter Scott wryly observes in his book on swans that "man made conservation necessary." He ends this book with a plea for "universal, rational birth control," for without it "all conservation efforts will be in vain." Until then, we must learn to make room for every equation in the mathematics of conservation. Sir Peter noted that all migratory wild birds "can and ought to be exploited as a profitable amenity. Watching and studying wildlife is an increasingly popular leisure activity; shooting is also a legitimate pastime, when subject to careful control, though only one shooter can kill a bird whereas many people can enjoy its flight. Wildlife and wild places can be as much of a tourist attraction as stately homes and seaside piers, and will bring prosperity to the district in which they lie."

By making room for all forms of wildlife appreciation, we can have our swans and eat them, too. Photographers will be able to take pictures of the birds in wildlife sanctuaries, while wildfowlers may find the same birds a few miles away a satisfying hunt.

The balance won't be easy to maintain. Wildlife preservationists have a powerful ally in the image of the swan as an enchanted princess dancing to the music of Tchaikovsky. Using political rather than scientific consensus to establish swan seasons—as Bob Hester did in North Carolina—is a double-edged sword that can be turned against wildfowlers. It behooves all of us who admire and enjoy wildlife to encourage biologists and ecologists, not legislators and business executives, to cast the deciding vote in resource allotments.

4

Ohio

Declining Ducks

Everyone agreed it was an inauspicious start. Cyrus Nielsen, who has been guiding and trapping on the marsh for more than sixty years, called the 1984 opener, "the worst ever." By noon, when my hosts (Oakley Andrews, Dugie Pearson, and Keith Russell) and I left Cy's huge multi-directional blind ("lucky #16," or the "Hilton"), we'd killed only seven ducks.

The wind was southwesterly and warm, but its 20-knot gusts should have stirred clouds of birds off white-capped Sandusky Bay—had there been clouds to stir. Instead, only a few pairs, trios, and quartets of mallards, gadwall, and wigeon circled us at extreme range after several teal and wood duck had made their characteristic Kamikaze dawn assaults.

My hosts were waiting for me to take the first shot, but because I didn't know that, and because I was unfamiliar with the setting and, therefore, from which direction the birds would likely appear, several woodies and teal came and went without being saluted. A drake blue-winged teal finally pitched and listened to our Alphonse-and-Gaston routine before buzzing off, unexpectedly, downwind. By the time I rallied to the shot, I had to take two to down the little "breakfast bird."

When larger ducks began to appear at sunrise, they warily worked over the blind as though it was the last day of the season, not the first. Even before we examined the drake mallards and gadwall we killed at extreme steel-shot range, and before we compared notes with other hunters back at the landing, we suspected the truth: most of what we were seeing were adult birds, wise to the ways of wildfowlers.

For five years, the U.S. Fish and Wildlife Service, urged on by Ducks Unlimited (DU) and other sportsman's groups, had maintained the same-length seasons and limits for most species of waterfowl in the face of dramatic population declines. The theory was that by gathering harvest data over five years in which hunting rules never altered, governmental biologists would have a better understanding of the demographic dynamics of wildfowl. It was hoped that with this data the Fish and Wildlife Service would be able to determine which regulations would need tightening to enhance survival rates and future production, and which regulations could be liberalized to afford sportsmen even longer seasons and larger limits.

The trouble was that the five-year plan began on the eve of the worst series of mid-continental droughts in half a century. Besides that, abnormal winter weather forced many birds into unfamiliar territory where mortality levels were exceptionally high. In January 1981 I stood on a Virginia field and pass-shot ten-point pintail and wigeon from flocks that oldtimers in the area had never seen there before. That didn't stop them or me from exploiting the brief bonanza.

Three years later in Ohio, we reaped the meager fruits of our short-term delights. Not only were adult birds scarce, juveniles were practically nonexistent. Instead of tapping the interest provided by birds reared the previous summer, we were killing the principle in the form of older birds that hadn't reproduced at all. Instead of allowing potential breeders to live through another winter so they could re-nest the following spring, we pleaded with the adults to come closer and killed all we could. Throughout the flyway, tens of thousands of other hunters were doing the same, and for each additional week of overkill, one or two springs of optimum production would be needed to repair the damage.

My Ohio hosts were the founding fathers of the then moribund Canvasback Society. They were attorneys and businessmen without time or training in the fine art of promoting their concept beyond the initial news release and a lapel pin. Part of the reason I'd come to Ohio was to see if I could help them get beyond this formative stage. Unfortunately, for a lack of funding, the Canvasback Society went the way of all good intentions.

I'd also come to Ohio to visit two of the legendary hunting clubs of Sandusky Bay. Since there weren't many ducks about, Keith Russell volunteered to take me to the Winous Point Shooting Club after lunch. This venerable sporting fraternity was founded in 1856 and still operates under its original charter. Although New Orleans' Tally Ho Club is the oldest duck-hunting fraternity in North America (founded in 1815), it never owned any more land or marsh than the acre or so of high ground on which the clubhouse still stands. As a result, it never had the influence on wetland management that major marsh owners, but particularly Winous Point, have had. Several of Winous Point's nineteenth-century strictures—against dusking, for example—were adopted by the government after the management of migratory birds was federalized in 1918. Indeed, many of the conflicts in American wildfowling stem from those days when politically powerful shooting clubs used their influence to impose laws involving stiff sporting standards on subsistence hunters who mostly killed their ducks on the water and thought of the birds only as food. Whereas a generation of friendly persuasion and carrots would have been needed to convert market shooters into sportsmen, the clubs and the federal government tried doing the job with only the stick of legislation in less than a decade.

Some hunting-club rules are still more restrictive than those the federal government imposes. No member of any club is supposed to kill more birds than his personal limit and credit the surplus to his guide or another licensed hunter in the blind. This is technically illegal anywhere in North America, but the rule is rarely enforced because it's unenforceable. Yet it's one of those laws that might have become standard practice in North America had sporting clubs used their influence to educate the average hunter rather than sic federal wardens on him with threats of fines and imprisonment.

Several members of the Winous Point Shooting Club represent the fourth or fifth generation of families associated with the fraternity. Since the club has never had more than twenty-five members, dues run high—into tens of thousands of dollars annually. Such expensive recreation and the inherent exclusivity of the club have generated jealousy in outsiders, some of whom would give their eyeteeth to be on the inside looking out, but since they can't, object to the wealth and privilege they call "elitism."

While in Ohio, I heard several hunters describe Winous Point as a "racket" or, more sarcastically, a "charitable enterprise" able to deduct its "improvements." After the winter storms of 1972–1974, most local clubs had to repair their damaged levees without deductible funds. Still others couldn't afford to make repairs at all. The Winous Point Club had no trouble deducting the cost of its repairs. Some hunters even grumbled about getting the Winous Point nonprofit charter revoked. If that should happen, the principal losers—as always in brouhahas like this—would be the birds.

But how did this shooting fraternity qualify for a nonprofit charter?

Decades before other clubs began heeding the advice of wildlife professionals, Winous Point hired biologists to manage its marshes. In *Flyways,* John M. "Frosty" Anderson recalls how he was brought aboard at the end of World War II:

"I intended to explain to Windsor T. White [club president and president of White Motors Company in Cleveland] why I was not interested in the job as manager of the Winous Point Shooting Club. My reasons were that I was enroute to the Illinois Natural History Survey to resume my prewar job in waterfowl research with such characters as Art Hawkins and Frank Bellrose, and also that I considered marsh *management* a questionable concept since most of the information on which to base management was still buried in the marsh.

"On the subject of food habits, I explained my lack of confidence in the veteran hunters, guides, old Indians, outdoor writers, and other qualified experts. If I wanted to know what ducks ate in southwestern Lake Erie marshes, I would ask the ducks. Before I planted any more wild rice, I would try to figure out why it was disappearing and how valuable it was as duck food. I allowed as how age ratios determined in the fall migration could give us a handle on production rates, which, in turn, might provide a basis for hunting regulations.

"I took it for granted that the average duck hunter would say 'that's all very interesting, but I can't see how it would do much for our duck shooting.'

"Mr. White was not an average duck hunter. He listened intently with a faintly quizzical smile, which I was at a loss to interpret. I was about to reach for my hat when the old gentleman said, 'I first went to the Winous Point Club when I was eleven years old. The punters, the manager, and the club members were arguing about the very same questions you have raised. About sixty years later I became president of the club and I realized the same questions were still being debated. I now think it's time we got some answers.'"

Frosty Anderson spent the next twenty years at Winous Point, the first three as a consultant, then seventeen as manager before "retiring" to run the National Audubon Society's sanctuary program. Over the past thirty-five years, through association with the North American Wildlife Foundation and, since 1984, the Wildlife Management Institute, researchers at the Winous Point Shooting Club have contributed much to our understanding of freshwater ecology and the particular role played by the Sandusky marshes as staging areas for birds that move from central Canada toward the Atlantic Flyway—especially mallards, wigeon, and pintail—and for birds from eastern Canada (black ducks, in particular) that drift into the Mississippi Flyway.

Anderson insisted on aging and weighing every duck brought in by club members. He gradually learned that "Ohio mallards and blacks averaged about four ounces heavier than Illinois River birds, and about the same as Parker River Refuge (Massachusetts) black ducks. In some years, young of the year would concentrate along southwestern Lake Erie, giving an abnormally high age ratio. As more data from bag inspections, banding, periodic censuses, and harvest estimates accumulated, the basis for flyway management gradually became more stable. It became apparent that birds from the Mississippi and Atlantic flyways were crossing paths around western Lake Erie. Admittedly, there is still much to learn about the effect of various regulations on the longevity of the average duck, but we have come a long way since 1946."

Because of the exclusivity of the club's 4,500 acres, hunting pressure is a fraction of that found on state or federal refuges of comparable size that permit waterfowling. Indeed, well over half the human activity at Winous Point pertains to biological research, and some two dozen master's and doctoral theses have been written based on Winous Point ecology. Rather than pick at the tax-deductible status of the Winous Point Shooting Club, other clubs would be smart to seek educational alliances comparable to Winous Point's association with the federal Cooperative Wildlife Research Unit based at Ohio State University so that they, too, could make the protection of wetlands "a charitable enterprise."

Some people will always object to the concept of privately owned wetlands. They refuse to acknowledge that, as has been the case at Winous Point, privately-sponsored research is often more innovative and substantive than publicly sponsored research that receives approval only because it is uncontroversial and, hence, inconsequential. Privately-funded scientists have to spend less time selling and justifying their work than their public counterparts. Invertebrate research may seem to have little direct bearing on waterfowl management, for example, so state-supported researchers rarely have the opportunity to study snails. Yet snails are an essential component of any healthy marsh. While pausing to get pictures of Cyrus pulling his decoys at the end of our opening morning hunt, I found a three-inch snail shell in the shallows near the blind. At the landing I found another shell nearly as large and kept them both for identification. I had never before seen such hefty freshwater gastropods in North America's temperate zone, and I suspected they must be exotics.

When I mentioned the snails to Roy W. Kroll, the present manager of the Winous Point Shooting Club, he explained, "They're either *Viviparous japonicus* or *Viviparous malleatus*. They were introduced, probably by hobby aquarists, early in this century. Some texts insist they came in as channel catfish food about 1940, but oldtimers say they remember the snails from much further back than that, and they may have come in when goldfish became popular as pets around 1900. Since the Japanese breed these snails for food as well as for the pet trade, it's surprising no Sandusky entrepreneur has started selling the abundant local supply to the *escargot* market.

"Although these snails are gigantic by most standards," Kroll continued, "they represent the norm to local hunters who think such huge snails are found everywhere. When local hunters hear that canvasbacks, no longer able to find wild celery and other submerged aquatic grasses in the Chesapeake, are consuming large quantities of snails, they're incredulous. Children would have trouble swallowing these snails, even without their shells! How can a duck?"

Although Sandusky Bay was once a major staging area for diving ducks, I was intrigued to see that most of the decoys in the Winous Point clubhouse were Mason and Stevens factory mallards from the 1890s and early 1900s. The most curious lot of this waterfowlia is contained in a suitcase nearly a century old with a dozen mounted mallards on floating boards and the brand name: Decoys Deluxe, Whistler Bros., Morrison, Illinois.

While we were in the clubhouse, Keith Russell met an old acquaintance, Peter Hitchcock, whose morning's tally was a coot. We commiserated with him, but smiled, too, at the thought of what that coot must have cost Mr. Hitchcock. We also speculated about the decline of coots throughout the Mississippi Flyway, and I confirmed that their numbers were down in the Atlantic states as well.

"What will gunners do," I asked, "when they don't have coots to kick around anymore?"

Winous Point members not only have the good grace and humor to accept a single-coot day, they have the most modest club insignia in the sporting fraternity. Although the club's official emblem depicts a muskrat house bracketed by cattails and a great blue heron with a pair of ducks flying overhead—all this capped by the words "Heritage," "Habitat," and "Research"—the pin has nothing on it but a telephone pole on which is tacked a small sign with the initials: WPSC. This is all anyone passing on the highway outside sees of the club. Yet in that rarified realm where men sport hats gleaming with pins of leaping trout and flushing grouse, the understated Winous Point pin has a cachet equivalent to the Order of the Cincinnati. A wildfowler may wear holes in his sweater and patches on his waders, but so long as he also wears a WPSC pin, he "doth bestride the narrow world like a Colossus."

Members of the adjoining Ottawa Shooting Club—founded not

many years after the Civil War—stand nearly as tall. Winous Point and Ottawa have a long-standing rivalry, and there do seem to be essential differences between the two clubs. The right pedigree appears to be more important at Winous Point than at Ottawa. Ottawa members, by contrast, seem to have earned as much money as they've inherited. As I was shown about Ottawa's sleeping quarters, I was told not only the names of the members who went with each uniquely furnished room, but their working titles as well. That would have been considered gauche at Winous Point.

Equally unimaginable by Winous Point standards was the moment when an Ottawa guide charged up to Keith Russell, a former member, and hugged him like an old friend. Winous Point guides speak only when they're spoken to and never, ever hug club members.

The Winous Point facilities are taken over each summer by graduate students who work like monks on their research projects. Ottawa, by contrast, installed a launch ramp just so the members' families could come up on weekends to fish and water ski in the channels running through the marshes. Such year-round activity means Ottawa fledges fewer ducks than does Winous Point.

Going It Alone

Before I left Ohio, Oakley Andrews drove Keith Russell and myself to George Trenchard's place near the mouth of the Toussaint River to look at what one marsh owner was doing to combine the need to earn a living with a passion for duck hunting. The first thing we heard when we reached Trenchard's property was the roar of gigantic earth-movers behind his house. George was digging a 400-slip marina and hoping the income from this summer facility would enable him to survive during the fall and winter months without having to go to the nearest city for nine-to-five employment. Trenchard is aware of the trade-offs, but he figures that if the nuclear power plant across the river hasn't yet ruined local duck and goose shooting, his marina can't make matters much worse.

"My father and I hunted a lot of beautiful marshes when I was a kid," he recalled, "but it was amazing how the quality of these marshes varied according to the types and amount of food available. Unless you can control water levels in a marsh, you end up with cover too thick and better suited for pheasants, or with water too deep and filled with loosestrife and other plants that waterfowl won't eat. Managing water levels for natural bur-weeds, smart-weeds, and other desirable plants is tricky and expensive. It's easier to drain fields in the spring, grow crops on them, and flood them in the fall. A flooded field may not look as natural as a marsh, but the ducks get more food and I get more shooting."

I asked Trenchard about his preferred crops:

"All depends on how bad the blackbirds are," he said. "If you get huge roosting flocks, like those that congregate here along the shores of Lake Erie, forget millet or milo. Blackbirds will clean out a grain field long before the first duck can find it. Canadian farmers complain about duck depredations, but those farmers must never have seen blackbirds in action. They're feathered locusts!"

As if to underscore his words, clouds of grackles and starlings swirled in from the southwest to settle in the trees along the dikes fronting the lake not far from George's home. A few wood ducks sped between the flocks heading for his fields.

"Soybeans are my solution," Trenchard continued. "They ripen late enough so I can time my first water releases for the arrival of the first ducks. The soybean stalk is generally too delicate when green to support the weight of a blackbird, and the birds have trouble getting the beans out of the pods after the stalks ripen.

"When I begin flooding the fields, I release only enough water to attract ducks and discourage blackbirds. The ducks usually start with the lower bean pods. As I raise water levels, they work their way up the stalks. I release water only twice each fall and drain the fields in the spring."

A couple of local boys joined our group. Trenchard decided to organize a late afternoon jump-shoot by way of showing me his ducks. We split into two parties that came in from opposite sides of the property, and each party got a few shots at mallards, woodies, and black ducks. George took me around to where the early 1970s winter storms had turned the old high dike bordering the Touissant River into a series of rapidly eroding islands from which every year shooters make hit-and-run attacks on the waterfowl resting in his canals and flooded fields.

"The sooner the last of those islands is gone, the better. In addition to being used as commando bases, the islands are camouflaged platforms on which shooters sit and skybust every flock of passing geese. We could have some excellent pass shooting here, except the birds are already two hundred yards up by the time they cross my dikes."

George and several friends had each killed their one Canada goose limit that morning when the birds came in from the lake. Unfortunately, jealousy corrodes satisfaction. One of George's friends was angry about the fact that elsewhere in Ohio, hunters are legally entitled to two geese a day, while along the shores of Lake Erie, the gunners are limited to one.

"There must be a thousand birds in our local flock," this shooter declared, "and there's no way we could kill half that number at even three birds a day!"

"Are your chances of killing a goose elsewhere in Ohio as good as they are here?" I asked.

"No way!" said the hunter proudly.

"Perhaps, the reason your possibilities are better here is the one-bird-a-day limit. Over-shooting is driving Canadas away from many traditional wintering grounds. You're better off with one goose a day for the rest of your hunting life than with one or two seasons of go-for-broke shooting after which you'll be forced to spend your dotage talking about the 'good old days.'"

My words didn't change his opinion. The man was too absorbed in his envy of what other shooters could do to appreciate how much more blessed he was than they. Competition and ambition are said to be positive attributes. Yet personal ambition and self-centered competition are anathema to the cooperative needs of wildfowl conservation. The Winous Point Shooting Club is still influential, but George Trenchard's do-it-yourself waterfowl management is an increasingly important part of the future.

When the clubs finally fade, what wellsprings for sportsmanship and cooperative conservation will remain?

What will hunting become once all we have left is the shooting?

5

Arkansas

We Band of Brothers

Kaneaster Hodges, Charles Aubrey, and I had been college classmates, but we'd not been close friends. We knew of one another, since with only about 750 students in each class, it would have been difficult not to know of the others. But at the time, like all undergraduates, each of us was absorbed in his own ambition, and the realization we'd shared a powerful bonding experience only seeped into our consciousness later, after we'd wandered down 750 different trails.

The further we drew apart in our vocational years—Kaneaster as an attorney, land manager, and, for part of one term, a U.S. Senator; Charles as a businessman and developer of his own electronics firm before selling it to the 3M Corporation; and me looking for life's meaning in five different directions before accepting my fate as a writer—the closer the bonds of our youth, especially the hunting part of our youth, drew us back together again.

Kaneaster, Charles, and I feel little enthusiasm for crowds. We talked about going back for our twenty-fifth college reunion, but just Charles managed to get back, and then only for part of one day. Duck hunting offers a far more appealing basis for a reunion, and so in the fall of 1984, we put all our other projects on hold in order to stage a class gathering of sorts in the flooded pin-oak woods near Kaneaster's home in Newport, Arkansas.

Kaneaster had invited a Chicago business associate, Allen Turner, to join us. A sociologist examining our motley crew would have been hard pressed to discover how we all fit together. Three businessmen versus one law-school dropout (me); three WASPs versus one Jew (Allen); three people with vital interests in land versus one with no desire to own any more property than what his house sits on (Charles). Yet our common bond would have been obvious to other wildfowlers. We were assembled at Kaneaster's home to partake in an autumnal rite older than even the prehistoric clay bowls, figurines, and stone tools Kaneaster has collected from sites throughout eastern Arkansas.

For thousands of Octobers, mallards have traced the Mississippi watershed south to where streams like the Cache, Black, Yazoo, and the Mississippi itself overflow their banks and flood the rich alluvial plains and woods between Memphis and the sea. Nowhere else on earth do mallards concentrate in such vast wintering flocks. When the birds are scarce or missing elsewhere, they can still be found in Arkansas and Mississippi by the hundreds of thousands.

The first morning we hunted with Leonard Sitzer, a local farmer and longtime friend of Kaneaster's. Leonard has diked a huge tract of pin oaks and floods it each fall when the birds come south. He does this purely for the pleasure of catering to the ducks and his wildfowling guests. Like many other longtime duck hunters, he'd rather call the birds for other people than shoot them himself. Yet his gun is always ready to help secure a crippled mallard for a guest, be he a former President of the United States or a conservation writer from Virginia.

Leonard is a staunch Ducks Unlimited supporter and imposes a $25 fine, payable to DU, on anyone who shoots a hen of any species. Our first morning ended when Allen, filled with pride at his undeniable prowess, claimed two far-falling birds, one of which turned out to be a hen mallard. Allen has curly hair, large eyes, and a rubbery face like Harpo Marx. His quick transformation of expression from smug triumph to disbelief, bewilderment, and eventual embarrassment was worth the morning in the woods even had the shooting not also been memorable.

I learned much about hunting ducks in flooded timber that morning. Kaneaster and Leonard attracted the birds by kicking the water when the circling mallards had turned away. When the ducks came back over the forest opening, the water surface was rippled as though stirred by the decoys below.

I also learned you can't chase crippled ducks through knee-deep water concealing snags and fallen branches without eventually ending up stretched across its chilly surface. Since my field camera is waterproof, nothing was damaged but my pride, and that was a small price to pay for memories of Kaneaster's low warning whistle when he sighted ducks, Leonard's sweet-talking on the call, his Chesapeake's intense concentration, the click of Charles' safety as the mallards began to flutter down, and Allen's zany, tongue-out expression as a dozen birds settled in the ten yard space between us.

> We few, we happy few, we band of brothers;
> For he today that sheds his blood with me
> Shall be my brother . . .

War and wildfowling share many similarities: the nighttime hours of preparation, the pre-dawn sorties, the use of firearms, the camaraderie, and the killing, of course. Anti-hunters use this latter similarity to whip up public feeling against blood sportsmen. Yet the most important link between war and wildfowling is the fellowship and affection that grow between men who share intense moments that no one who wasn't there can comprehend.

On my way to Arkansas that November, I read an inflight copy of

Esquire featuring an article by William Broyles, Jr., who dared say something society doesn't like to hear: we who've been to war enjoyed being there. "That's why," wrote Broyles, "when we returned from Vietnam we moped around, listless, not interested in anything or anyone. Something had gone out of our lives forever, and our behavior on returning was inexplicable except as the behavior of men who had lost a great—perhaps the great—love of our lives, and had no way to tell anyone about it."

Many people like to imagine that veterans hate war as much as they should hate hunting. Some veterans do hate war—especially inconclusive wars where sacrifice is senseless. But for men of any generation, going is better than not going, for no other experience tells you as much about the enduring condition of man as war.

"Part of the love of war stems from its being an experience of great intensity," Broyles observes. "Its lure is the fundamental human passion to witness, to see things, what the Bible calls the lust of the eye. . . ." But the things the warrior or the wildfowler lusts to see are exceptional things. We seek experiences so intensely personal, they cannot be articulated or shared with anyone but fellow witnesses.

"War may be the only way in which most men touch the mythic domains in our soul," Broyles suggests. "It is, for men, at some terrible level the closest thing to what childbirth is for women; the initiation into the power of life and death."

"War stories inhabit the realm of myth because every war story is about death. And one of the most troubling reasons men love war is the love of destruction, the thrill of killing."

The power of war and the passion for wildfowling wells from deep within the human heart. Death is what gives life meaning, and a young hunter knows this from the moment he strikes down his first bird. The bird's living beauty is a kind of power, and part of that beauty and all of its power are transferred to the hunter at the instant of death.

Yet the greatest and most enduring emotion of wildfowling or war is comradeship. Wildfowling, like war, cloaks us in a costume that conceals the limits and inadequacies of our separate natures. It gives us, as Broyles writes, "an aura, a collective power, an almost animal force." Rather than wear the silly costumes of college reunions, Kaneaster, Charles, and I wore the camouflage patterns of warriors and wildfowlers. Instead of once-in-a-lifetime blazers, the four of us wore a kind of uniform that made Allen as much, if not more, of a classmate than any of the nonhunters with whom we'd gone to school.

In a society increasingly bounded by banality and second-hand experience, wildfowlers rejoin friends each autumn to relive the intensity, beauty, power, special knowledge, and fraternity of the hunt. This is the common property we share from the moment of that first dawn when birds glide out of the half-light as if to embrace us with their open wings. War is a youthful experience whose principal reward is survival; wildfowling is a lifetime affair whose many rewards include a recreated soul.

Totems

"I shot that duck!"

"The heck you did! You doubled the pair on the left, and I killed the drake on the right."

"That drake *is* the one that was on the left! The birds got turned around in the current, but I kept an eye on *my* ducks!"

"How could you keep your eye on 'em when you were starting the engine? I tell you, this is *my* bird!"

Kaneaster, Charles, Allen, and I had joined Pete Guinn and Jeff "Catfish" Ellis in a huge, boat-shaped blind built around the trunks of four enormous cypress trees above Kaneaster's property on the overflowing Cache. At least three others of us had fired at the birds, but Pete and Catfish weren't about to allow anyone else to stake a claim. They knew possession's nine points of the law. And the only question in their minds was whether possession went to the man who ran the boat or to the man who actually picked the duck from the water.

Why all this fuss over a single bird? Why would two of the most experienced duck hunters in Arkansas be fussing like a couple of kids over just one mallard?

The answer, of course, is that the mallard was banded. Pete and Catfish have three-quarters of a century of wildfowling between them, so mostly they're content to stand back and call ducks for others. But a banded mallard is another matter. No one ever gets so jaded with the sport that he's not electrified by the discovery that one of the birds he has just shot is carrying a code to its mysterious wanderings.

A band is frosting on the bird-shooter's cake. It makes the day, even the season, more memorable. Banded birds are so intriguing it's a wonder they only became an important adjunct to wildlife management in 1920, when the U.S. Biological Survey centralized the work of a growing number of amateur banders.

John James Audubon is frequently given credit for being the first person to band birds. In the March 10, 1985, issue of *The New York Times Magazine,* ornithologist Roger Tory Peterson noted that Audubon "performed an experiment that marked a first in the history of ornithology . . . he wrote that he placed 'silver threads' about the legs of a brood of young [phoebes] for identification, seeking to learn whether they would return the following year. Two of them did, building their own nests farther up the creek. Thus he became the first American bird bander."

First in America, perhaps, but certainly not the first. A kind of bird marking was practiced by the royalty of ancient Egypt and by the emperors of China. In more modern times, we know that after the restoration of the British monarchy in 1660, Charles II spent much time and treasure trying to learn more about the ways of wildfowl. He had a large duck trap—what the British call a "decoy"—built on one of the Crown estates (eventually St. James Park in downtown London). His aviary keeper, Edward Storey, did not trap ducks for food but in order to clip their wings, "ring" them (as the British describe banding), and feed them to induce them to stay and, it was hoped, breed in the park.

Between September 1660 and June 1670, Storey spent 248 pounds sterling, 18 shillings on "oatmeal, tares, hempseed, and other corn for the birds and fowls." By today's economic standards, this works out to thousands of dollars annually for duck fodder. Yet even this amount was probably insufficient to feed all the ducks kept by the king in the park, so courtiers, eager to show their respect to the Crown, supplemented the fare with donations of their own.

Charles II's successor, William III, had a blind built on Duck Island in the park's lake in which he spent long hours observing ducks, geese, and a particular favorite, the coot. William also issued stern edicts for the protection of these birds, one consequence of which is that we have few records of "royal waterfowl" that regrew their flight feathers and left the park. When a stray was found or captured, the fearful farmer or shepherd was more likely to wring the bird's neck and keep the silver or copper band than he was to turn it in and suffer the suspicion of having stolen the bird in the first place.

Unfortunately, such fearful reactions still haunt the banding business today. Many North American birds winter in Latin America, where a confrontation with authority has more dangerous connotations than it does in the United States or Canada. A good many Spanish-speaking farmers are reluctant to report the banded birds they shoot or find for fear they'll be accused of stealing someone's property.

Arnulfo Gomez Gonzales of Mexico was braver than many of his countrymen when he sent a bird band to Washington, D.C., with the following note:

"I wish to inform you that I hunted a duck. I am relating this to you with fear, as some of my friends have informed me that you blame our government, so that you may remove our arms. Actually, my gun is in very poor shape."

George Jonkel, who heads the U.S. Fish and Wildlife Service's bird-banding operations located in Laurel, Maryland, stresses, "It's very important that people understand that it's not *our* bird." He points out that the person who recovers a band is welcome to keep it. The only thing the Fish and Wildlife Service wants in exchange is information. If a wildfowler desires to make a totem of bands or wear them as a necklace with his duck and goose calls, that's fine. Jonkel despairs only when he thinks a hunter might add a band to his necklace without first using a postcard to print legibly and completely the band's number and the place and date it was recovered.

Information about bird bands recovered in overpopulated countries is often sent in with the expectation of a marvelous reward. The peasants may have watched too much satellite-transmitted TV and assume that everyone in America is either rich or wins a prize for merely being here.

"A lot of bands are recovered by poor people who think they've found the proverbial brass ring," observes Jonkel. "They even have visions of immigrating here. For many it's the great hope of their lives, and we hate to have to send them only a form Certificate of Appreciation, especially when the postage for sending in the band may represent a day's or a week's pay, plus whatever they paid someone to write the letter. We do whatever we can to personalize our thanks, but we're underfunded, understaffed, and the situation is getting worse."

A letter received from Renaldo Ellington of Guatemala capsulizes the tragi-comedy quality of such mail: "I am writing so that you can send me something for what I found. . . . That is all, Sir. I await your response. Greetings to your family, although I do not know them. I want to go there. I want to study mechanics, please."

Although Dr. Paul Bartsch of the Smithsonian Institution used the first numbered metal band in the United States in 1902, wildlife banding in North America didn't really get going until a reformed market hunter, amateur naturalist, and devout Christian from Kingsville, Ontario, got involved. Let Jack Miner tell you the story of his first banded duck.

"On August 5th, 1909, a wild black duck lit with my ducks in the north pond. I started cozening around her, not by going closer to her, but by letting her come closer to me. Finally she was eating out of the long-handled spoon that I had previously used for throwing a little feed over to her. The spoon, of course, was on the ground, gradually being drawn towards me until it came over my left hand that was lying flat on the ground, and on September 10th of the same year this duck actually ate out of my hand. We named her Katie. In a few months Katie got so tame she would follow us in the barn where we went after the feed. So I scraped around in my hunting-case drawer and found a piece of sheet aluminum about three-quarters of an inch wide and one-and-a-half inches long; I then took my sweetheart's best pair of scissors, and with the pointed blade I managed to scratch my post office address on it. Then I caught Katie and wrapped it around one of her hind legs. She disappeared on December 10th, and in January I received the following letter.

Anderson,
South Carolina
January 17th, 1910

Dear Sir,

On Friday evening, January the 14th, I was hunting on Rocky River, near this city, I killed a wild duck with a band on his leg, marked Box 48, Kingsville, Ontario. I suppose whoever sent him out wanted to hear from him, so I am writing to let you know where he came to his end. He was a very fine specimen. I must commend him for his judgment, for he came to the best County in the best State in America. If you will let me hear from you I will return the band I took from his leg. So hoping you will send me his pedigree I will close until I hear from you. . . .

Very respectfully,
W. E. Bray

"I at once wrote Mr. Bray and he kindly returned the tag, which is the centre . . . of my collection of tags. Mr. Bray made two distinct mistakes: one was when he called Katie 'him' and another, equally as big, was when he stated that the duck came to the best spot in America, for the fact is that Essex County, Ontario, this duck's summer home, is the best spot on this beautiful earth; this, of course, will include all of North America."

Because Jack Miner began inscribing brief religious messages inside his bands, they were considered the work of an eccentric and are today avidly collected by people interested in ornithological trivia. Miner's record-keeping, however, was detailed and precise, and no one could accuse him of being a careless researcher.

Miner made many friends through his bird banding. The Reverend J. W. Walton visited his home after recovering several Canada goose bands from Inuit living on the east coast of Hudson Bay, where Walton was a missionary.

Another time, a band bearing the message, "Get thee behind me, Satan," was recovered by a man living in the far North who confessed wrestling with his soul for many months before heeding the warning and returning the band to Miner.

Today 4,500 people are licensed to band birds with metal rings bearing the U.S. Fish and Wildlife Service code: AVISE BIRD BAND WRITE WASH. DC. Contrary to rumor, "Avise" is not a misengraving of "advise." This spelling was specifically selected because *avise* in French, Spanish, and Portuguese—the three other principal languages of the hemisphere—means "report" with a connotation of "send."

With such a carefully screened coterie of bird banders, the only problems arising from the reporting of birds should come at the recovery end. However, erroneous data sometimes gets into the computer when the bird is banded. For example, the banded redhead drake I shot in North Carolina was supposed to have been a *female* redhead banded two years earlier in upstate New York. A mistake like that might be understandable if you imagine half a dozen helping hands trying to make order out of the chaos of a large and crowded duck trap. A band slipped hastily onto a duck's leg might be credited to a hen rather than a drake of the same species. But the banded redhead drake killed by Art Carter that morning in Core Sound was supposed to have been a *hen pintail!* Unless the Good Lord never put a bubble in that particular bander's level, the only explanation is that someone pried a band from a dead pintail and put it on the leg of a crippled redhead he'd illegally brought from the marsh, but which later escaped carrying the bogus ID.

George Jonkel is somewhat fatalistic about the problem of misidentified birds. Furthermore, such bands have provided him with a considerable education in human nature over the years.

"Any band number that's mentioned in print is almost sure to be reported," he notes, "sometimes by several people. We have people reporting bands even before they've been issued to a bander, sometimes even before the bands have been manufactured!"

Yet the facts concerning certain band returns are far more amazing than the fictions created by publicity-crazed people. Bands have been recovered, for example, from polar bear feces. One was found embedded in the lower lip of a catfish caught in Alabama. My personal favorite, since I helped band the nesting colony in Virginia where the birds came from, were two royal terns that ended up in the stomach of a tiger shark. Their bands were recovered by a taxidermist in Fort Lauderdale, Florida.

Nearly forty million banded birds are on file at the Patuxent Bird Banding Laboratory. Most of these will never statistically reappear. Only a small percentage of even avidly hunted gamebirds have their bands reported. Using a variety of statistical checks, including reward bands—in January 1979 I killed a black duck in Virginia banded the year before on Prince Edward Island; the bird sported an aluminum band on each leg, one of which offered $15 to do what I would have done anyway: notify the Fish and Wildlife Service where and when I killed the bird—federal technicians have learned that well under half of all recovered goose and duck bands are reported. The rest are kept or thrown away by lazy or ignorant hunters.

"One problem we have," says Jonkel, "is the person who hunts in a prime wintering area and who actually reports the first few bands he recovers. Then, either because the novelty wears off or because he assumes that we have all the information we need about his area, he stops reporting recoveries. Since banding is one of the most important tools we have for determining the distribution and mortality of waterfowl, a single dropout can throw a wrench into the statistical profile for any one species. The next band you recover is just as important to us as the first one you reported five or fifty years ago."

Whenever a species raises questions about its range or relative abundance, banding is one of the most cost-effective tools for unlocking the answers. Bands confirmed the location of the Aleutian Canada goose's wintering area in California. Bands also taught wildfowl biologists that young female canvasbacks prefer nesting habitat on the fringe of this species' range. Most important, bands prove that ducks can survive well over ten years in the wild, and geese may live several decades. The management theory of "compensatory mortality"—that the dove or quail you don't shoot today is going to die of some other cause tomorrow—simply cannot be applied to waterfowl.

I shot a drake greater scaup on Long Island that had been banded as an adult seven years earlier and less than a mile from where I killed the bird. Think of the implications: that scaup had made at least eight annual round trips between breeding grounds in Canada and probably that one particular wintering ground in New York.

When I finally got a chance to hunt on the edge of the Merritt Island National Wildlife Refuge in Florida, I killed a banded green-winged teal that guide Dave Van Nest predicted would turn out to be from Labrador.

"How do you know?" I asked.

"Because we kill one or two banded teal a year here, and every one of them was banded in Labrador."

Sure enough, when Patuxent's computerized thank-you card came, it revealed that teal #644-39097 had been banded in Labrador as a hatchling in September 1985. Since I shot the bird in January 1987, she had survived one other round trip between the remote Labradorean pond where she was hatched and the mangrove-bordered estuary in Florida where she died. Biologists rarely consider such specialized programming when divvying up the ducks by genus and species.

Of course, not every migratory bird is as potentially predictable as most diving ducks or that green-winged hen. Of all waterfowl, shovelers and blue-winged teal make the longest regular annual journeys, which sometimes carry them into terra incognita. Pintail, although not normally as far-traveling as shovelers and blue-wings, are even more unpredictable. A pintail banded in eastern Canada is as liable to turn up in England as Louisiana; a pintail banded in Alaska is as likely to be found in Hawaii as southern California.

In October 1981, an Oregon hunter killed a pintail hen sporting a Japanese band. Russian bands show up from time to time in our Pacific Flyway, but this was the first time a Japanese band had been recovered in North America. The pintail had been banded two years earlier ten miles northwest of Tokyo on lands reserved exclusively for the use of His Imperial Highness, Prince Hitachi. Three centuries after Charles II and William III studied birds and banded them, another monarch on the other side of the world keeps alive this regal tradition.

——6——
Louisiana

A duck! No, a mosquito. I turn to face the insect hovering on the periphery of my vision and don't see a knot of blue-winged teal until they're over the decoys and gone again.

Where did they come from?! I turn about in the intricately woven one-man blind whose floor is a fiberglass pirogue and spot a huge flock of ibis over a distant petroleum pumping station.

I'm so absorbed by the spectacle, I start when wigeons whistle behind me. I whirl and flare the ducks a hundred yards out. Their call is so liquid clear, I think they must be hovering overhead.

Settle down, I counsel myself. You're hunting, not birding. Even as I mutter, a pair of gadwall appear. I point my gun at the drake and miss twice.

Come on, fellow! You know better than that. You don't need to swing so far ahead with steel shot, but you've still got to follow through.

A flock of green-winged teal comes from the right. I tumble out a hen just behind the target drake. Still not enough lead. She's crippled. I shoot again before she can orient herself and dive.

A pintail. A drake! He's wary and hanging high. If he'll only come a little closer . . . Now! He folds. A long fall into a geyser of water.

Two down. One to go. What should it be? Of all the candidates, green-winged teal suffered least from the drought last summer. Here's a drake. Flaps down, belly up. Pow! My limit.

The next ninety minutes are as satisfying as the first fifteen. I back the pirogue out of the blind, paddle around the pond picking up the dead birds and the decoys, return to the blind, get my camera ready, but watch more than I photograph. Film can't do justice to an ever-changing panorama of clouds, sun, and birds over the Louisiana marshes.

Anyone who can't find satisfaction in a three-duck limit is better off employed as the neck-nicker in a poultry plant than spending time in today's depleted wetlands. Although several thousand ducks gabbled and gammed in the sanctuary next to host Jessie Duet's tump-of-high-ground home in the middle of the marshes of LaFourche Parish, Jessie said that less than a decade ago, where we were seeing thousands, we would have seen tens of thousands.

Also, where we were seeing thousands of acres of marshland, we would have seen tens of thousands. No coastal wetlands in North America are disappearing faster than those of Louisiana—once 40 percent of the lower 48's total. In the time it takes you to read the rest of this chapter, another acre will vanish. The average rate of attrition is more than a hundred acres a day.

The rise of the Atlantic is more of a contributing than a causative factor. The ocean, after all, is not rising *that* fast. The main instigator of the crisis, as is true of wetlands misery throughout the South, is the U.S. Army Corps of Engineers. What ditching, draining, and water diverting the Corps hasn't done itself, it has encouraged agribusiness and the oil industry to do. Hundreds of thousands of acres of Louisiana's freshwater marshes are now scarred and drained by more than 8,000 miles of canals, which have turned once prime wetlands for wintering waterfowl into saltwater-intruded, grass-depleted, eroding muck. Gone not only are the great flocks of wildfowl, but the muskrats and crayfish (pronounced "crawfish") that once provided subsistence livings for hundreds of Cajun families, many of whom have split up so their men can find work in cities like Atlanta and Birmingham.

Although the Corps of Engineers has spent over $6 billion since 1928 to alter the natural filtration and land-building processes of the lower Mississippi, no amount of money can repair the damage now because too many lives and jobs depend on the degraded artificial system. Dr. Paul Templet, head of Louisiana's Department of Environmental Quality, estimates that only 14.6 million tons of the Mississippi's annual 183 million-ton sediment flow need be diverted through Louisiana's wetlands to stabilize and begin rebuilding the eroded marshes. But the people of New Orleans are too nervous about being below the level of the leveed river to want to risk diverting even a ton of upstream water and sediment.

Drought and drainage in the North, and channelization, erosion, and salt intrusion in the South have all played their corrosive roles in the decline of North American waterfowl. But Louisiana hunters have compounded these problems with shameful overshooting. Without the least thought for the future and reinforced by an ignorant fantasy about Canadians turning the eggs of prairie-nesting birds into glue, or what Louisianans don't shoot, the Mexicans will, Louisiana gunners made devastating inroads into continental duck populations.

Until a few years ago, the point system permitted Louisiana shooters to kill ten pintail, wigeon, and teal a day. The result was that Louisiana hunters were killing more ducks legally than the reported duck harvest of the entire Atlantic Flyway.

That, unfortunately, was not all of Louisiana's kill. Regional U.S. warden Dave Hall suspects that the illegal Louisiana kill was many times greater than the already excessively generous legal kill. A few shooters may have been more restrained and responsible than the majority, but for every thoughtful Louisiana sportsman there were a hundred gunners who didn't count it a good day unless they'd killed sixty ducks.

"Our goal was a hundred," reformed outlaw Dennis Treitler told me two days after the hunt at Jessie Duet's. "We came out of the swamp feeling bad if we got less than forty."

"Apiece?"

"Hell, yes, 'apiece!' The only way you could stop me from shooting was to take away my shells and throw them in deep water!"

"Hunters may have killed as many ducks illegally in this state as were being killed in all the other states of the Mississippi and Atlantic flyways combined," said Dave Hall from his side of Treitler's kitchen table. "For a long while, you couldn't do much about it. So many politicians were involved, all a poacher needed was to be a registered voter and have enough coins for a phone call, and he'd be off the hook.

"I chased one Coon-ass [pejorative for *Cajun*—unless, like Dave Hall, you regard yourself as one, in which case the term is used affectionately] whose pirogue was so full of birds, it swamped and sank. When I came up to the boy, he was standing waist-deep in water with a hundred birds floating around him. 'What's going on?' I asked. 'Too much duck,' he said. It was the first time I met a Coon-ass who regretted shooting more than his limit!"

I'd never been to Louisiana to hunt ducks before, precisely because of its reputation as an outlaw haven. All my previous invitations had been couched by promises that I'd have nothing to worry about: even if I got ticketed, I wouldn't have to pay the fine. My would-be hosts never understood that reassurances like that turn my blood to ice.

I'd agreed to come this time, not only because I'd be with a federal law enforcement agent throughout the trip, but because I wanted to learn just how sincere were the many born-again conservationists I'd heard about—people who Dave Hall had started down the straight and narrow path after arresting them with the evidence of videotapes he'd made of them in action. Dave's VCR films helped persuade federal judges to pass down stiffer sentences to compulsive violators—including time in prison, months of community service and, most onerous of all, years of lost hunting privileges.

Dave's movies had so riled up law-abiding wildfowlers in the Minnesota Waterfowl Association and the Izaak Walton League of America, that they'd spearheaded a national effort to purchase a helicopter for the law enforcement division of the U.S. Fish and Wildlife Service for assignment to Louisiana.

Helicopters may be the only practical way to put the fear of God into poachers working a vast marshy plain. A Cajun outlaw can hope to use his superior knowledge of the marsh to escape from a pursuing mud-boat, but, as Dennis Treitler puts it, "looking up at a helicopter is like seeing an electric chair hovering over your head!"

Helicopters are also the ideal way for a visiting outdoor writer and a Canadian biologist-friend, Norman Seymour, to get from the New Orleans airport across Lake Salvador to the Little Lake Club in Jefferson Parish where we hunted before helicoptering over to Jessie Duet's.

The Little Lake Club is a fraternity of New Orleans business and professional men founded around 1912. Just a few years ago, it was a den of iniquity so far as high-tone duck poaching was concerned, but I spent my first Louisiana sunrise in a pirogue blind with lawyer and reformed violator Garland Rolling, and chief club guide and former master baiter, Elmo Helmer. The shooting was spotty, giving us ample opportunity to talk about the bad old days.

"We figured everybody else in the world killed ducks the way we did," said Elmo. "Or they wanted to—except that nowhere else in the world had ducks like Louisiana."

"Was it fear of the consequences that made you stop?" I asked.

"That's part of it. When the feds began playing hardball, that made a big difference. But I think the biggest difference was the fact the ducks began disappearing."

They hadn't completely disappeared: Elmo crouched and began calling on his pipe-like wigeon whistle. A few moments later, he stood and knocked down a pair. I killed the crippled hen on the water. Garland hadn't yet taken his shotgun from its case.

"I think you've got to consider all the factors together," said Garland. "The big change came at the grass-roots level with the Bayou people. They're extremely honest and will give you a fair shake if you give them one. Wardens here used to do a lot of thin-pinching—looking for any little way to stick you. Dave Hall changed that. He spent more time visiting in the Bayous than he did staking them out. He explained to the local people about what fence-row to fence-row farming was doing to the ducks up north, and how in dry years, no ducks were being hatched at all. He persuaded some people that unless they stopped shooting the birds like they'd been doing, they'd eventually have none. Only after someone had heard Dave's talk and still wouldn't change did Dave come down on him with both boots. Then when the Bayou people saw that we in the clubs weren't getting away with our old tricks, they were more willing to stop their own over-shooting."

Garland uncased a grand old double-barrel in time to use it to scratch down a pair of mottled ducks. Both birds got into cover and appeared to have escaped. A cloud of disappointment hung over the blind; it wasn't the moment for me to suggest that going for marginal doubles in an era of three-bird limits and steel shot is irresponsible wild-fowling.

Garland saved the day with a Lab he borrowed from a nearby hunter. Since the Little Lake Club controls between 8,000 and 10,000 acres (at present rates of attrition, no one knows for sure anymore), every hunter in the marsh is a member or guest and perfectly happy to loan a dog to a needy colleague.

After figuring out what the three strangers wanted, the Lab burrowed into the grass next to the blind and came up with the first bird, the hen. Fifteen minutes later, and several hundred yards away, the dog came up with the second bird, the drake. We were all relieved and effusively praised the pooch. His dazzling display of scenting and tracking skills made our morning as well as his own.

A good retriever is like a good shooter in being a product of ample opportunity. Just as the borrowed black Lab at the Little Lake Club had obviously retrieved baskets of birds before, Jessie Duet's yellow Labs had also brought in more than their legal share of downed ducks. But their eagerness to hunt was not their only dimension. A sportsman is supposed to keep a dog or two. He can afford them. But a subsistence hunter like Jessie needs an additional rationale to justify a dog's expense. Jessie's Labs seem to sense this and volunteer their services as watch and patrol dogs. Nothing happens on or around Jessie's Shangri-la without them knowing and approving of it.

Like each member of the Little Lake Club I talked with, Jessie Duet never imagined his shooting would make a difference to duck populations. "We shot so many, but every year there were just as many. Then about five years ago, the flocks got smaller until today we don't have anything like what we had a decade ago."

Jessie didn't let up on the birds, even as they declined. He felt he had a superior right to them because he neither shot them "for fun," the way "sports" do, nor for the market, the way commercial gunners did. Besides, he believed the law doesn't apply to people whose ancestors have been trapping and shooting ducks on the Louisiana marshes for more than two centuries.

So long as the laws weren't being enforced on the big shots and the market shooters, the Bayou people were understandably bitter when a warden thin-pinched them. This is what Dave Hall changed, first, by eliminating the double standard, and, next, by singling out role models like Jessie and persuading them that conservation is not an anti-hunters' theory but a sensible way to ensure that there'll always be enough ducks.

Even with his broad understanding of the duck-poaching problem, Dave Hall would not have been half so successful were he not also completely empathetic with people who have traditionally earned their livings trapping muskrats, crayfish, and catfish. Dave cares deeply about others and although he denies it, he is an exceptional warden because of it.

"Dave saved my life," Jessie told me. "He had a doctor here who said I was gonna die unless I got a heart operation. Dave brought over a helicopter and got me to the hospital."

Jessie's brush with death may be part of the reason he no longer poaches ducks. The overall reason, however, is that he's grateful to and respects the man who gave him a new lease on life. When Dave Hall tells Jessie the old ways of killing ducks must change, Jessie listens. And because a man of Jessie's stature in the Bayou community listens and changes, other people change as well.

In addition to enjoying Jessie's dockside cooking and his invisible blind—Cajuns make wonderful blinds; unless you know where one is supposed to be, you'll pole or paddle past it, thinking it's part of the marsh—I also enjoyed learning a few Cajun names for waterfowl.

Some of the words are French translations of English colloquial names. Gadwall or "gray duck," for example, is *canard gris*. Scaup or "gray back" is *dos gris*. Canvasback or "horse duck" is *canard chevalin*. Pintail or "short straw" is *paille court*.

Few of the old French names for waterfowl are part of the Cajun vernacular. *Canard siffleur* or "whistling duck" is what French hunters call the European wigeon. But possibly because the Cajuns hunt a different kind of whistling duck, they call the American wigeon *zan-zan*—which has no meaning unless it's derived from the French word *zani,* describing a foolish merry-maker.

The favorite Cajun duck is the mallard, *canard français.* The modifier *t'* (short for *petit*) is used for little ducks. The ringneck, for example, is *t' canard noir,* "little black duck." And the littlest duck of all is named for the place where the littlest people, the pygmies, live. The green-winged teal is *t' congo.*

A number of waterbirds are identified by their beaks. Since ibises have decurved bills, they should logically be called *bec courbe* or "bent bills." Instead, they're called *bec-cros,* the Cajun variant of *bec-croisé* or "crossbill"—a completely different bird, of course, from the genuine crossbill of our northern forests.

Confusion over beaky names involves two other marsh birds. The shoveler, alias *becquin* (no particular meaning unless the word is derived from *becquée,* "beakful" or "full beak"), is also known as *bec-gros* meaning "gross-" or "big-beak." When the modifier is reversed, *gros-bec* (most commonly spelled "growbec") describes the yellow-crowned night heron, a popular subsistence species for Cajun shooters. (To add to the confusion, *gros-bec* in France refers to the hawfinch and in Quebec to the grosbeak.)

One of the convicted poachers we met was caught, not with a surplus of ducks, but with 645 "growbec." Robley "Baboy" Folse admits to having killed at night thousands of ducks over his crayfish ponds, but he was on his way to prison for killing growbec.

"I should't have put myself into a position to get caught," said Robley, twisting his hat in his hands. "I have too much at stake—too much position—to get caught."

"Why did you do it?" I asked.

"The growbec eat my crawfish. The government don't help me save crawfish. I do that. If I caught with ducks, I understand. Ducks in trouble. But they plenty growbec. They good eating. We always shoot growbec. I was so small I killed my first, the shot knock me down. My daddy laughed."

"Is it over now?"

"Yes, I was the caboose."

"Will you continue to hunt, but do it legally?"

"Hunting is none of my interest no more. My kids hunt deer. Shoot a wood duck or two. But no more sacks of mallard. No more sacks of woodcock. And no more sacks of growbec. Brings back bad memories."

"You'll go to camp in the swamps with your family, won't you?"

"No. It's dying out. Nobody go to camp anymore. The new world is here. Same everywhere. My brother Larry's in jail. Over in Lafitte. Roaches crawl in his ears at night. Murderers get out. My brother stays in. For what? For shooting growbec and too much duck. I go next."

Bitter as he was, Robley could not forget two centuries of Cajun hospitality. Before we shoved off that night, he insisted on boiling up one of the sacks of crayfish his men had just caught in the swamp. Dave Hall, Norman Seymour, and I stood across an improvised table from Robley and several members of his clan and ate crayfish and drank beer until we were sated.

On the third morning of my Louisiana visit, I shared a blind with Dave Hall and Kell McInnis, deputy secretary of the Louisiana's Department of Wildlife and Fisheries. Dave credits Kell with helping bring about a better working relationship between state and federal law enforcement officers.

We were hunting on Benny Cenac's Golden Ranch Farm, a huge corporate hunting club whose members are Shell Oil executives. Benny was another of Dave's reformed cooperators after an earlier career of hardcore poaching. Converted to the idea that you can have just as much fun doing things the right way, Benny had given us a tour of his 32,000-acre property (including an exhilirating mud-boat ride!) the afternoon we arrived.

Since Norman had had only makeshift hunting opportunities thus far on the trip, Benny kindly arranged for him to be in a hot spot with one of the club members. Norman proceeded to raise the executives' level of sportsmanship by insisting that each of them shoot only his limit and pursue any bird they downed (all ringnecks) until the ducks were recovered or definitely lost. Norman then suggested that lost birds be counted as part of the limit.

Benny gave Dave, Kell, and me a back-up blind at the edge of a marshy pond. Since we were set up before first light and well in advance of the official sunrise shooting time, I decided to practice calling. But what had been good enough for ducks elsewhere in my travels was apparently not good enough for Cajun birds, or at least so far as Kell and Dave were concerned. They said I could continue "playing" with my wigeon whistle, but insisted I put my mallard call away.

I have to admit my companions did sound better than I did—but still not good enough to persuade the few mallards and mottled ducks we saw to give us a fly-by. Thanks to Norman's research and that of his ever-changing guard of graduate students at St. Francis Xavier University in Nova Scotia, I didn't feel put down by my companions' criticism of my calling, nor let down by the refusal of the mottled ducks to give our spread a closer look.

Norman and his band of merry researchers have learned that the so-called "feeding chuckle" of black ducks, mallards, and mottled ducks is actually the hen's "inciting chuckle" to her mate. Generally given while approaching a flock of birds, the hen is warning her drake not to get any lecherous notions about other hens in the flock. This warning doesn't seem to do hen mallards much good. Drake mallards seem dedicated to courting every female, regardless of species, they find! But black ducks are more monogamous, and nonmigratory mottled ducks are completely so. As a result, when Dave or Kell let out with a lonesome hen holler, they tended to flare the mottled ducks—and understandably so when you consider the hen is probably petrified that the calling bird is competition. I told Dave and Kell about Norman's research so they could take pride in being able to call so well that they were scaring away the birds we wanted to shoot!

I doubt whether most Louisianans would accept Norman's observations. They believe the reason mottled ducks are so unresponsive to calling is because the birds are so smart. "They're here all year around," a member of the Little Lake Club explained. "They see exactly where we build our blinds, and they know exactly how far away to stay."

Maybe. But maybe, too, serious mottled-duck hunters would be better off hunting over pintail and ringneck decoys and keeping their calls—except pintail whistles and ringneck rattles—to themselves. About the only time mottled ducks come eagerly to decoys is when a recently widowed hen is looking for a new mate. This is equally true of late-season mallards and black ducks. A bird that comes low across the marsh and pitches to the decoys without circling almost invariably turns out to be a hen. Hunters who want to conserve mottled ducks and black ducks can use this knowledge and forego shooting such easy singles. On the other hand, having waited all morning for any kind of shot, they may rationalize that since it takes two to tango, expecially with permanently pair-bonded birds, the hen is no greater loss—and just as good to eat—than the drake.

Eleven teal of both species came in singles, pairs, and as a trio, before the 7:00 A.M. official sunrise shooting time. Eliminating half-hour-before-sunrise hunting has done more to save ducks—at least among law-abiding hunters—than all the other restrictions imposed as a result of the 1988 drought. But the operative word is "law-abiding." Had not Dave and Kell been there to reinforce my conscience, I wonder whether I might have shaved the official shooting time by a few minutes to salute birds so close and clearly lit I could count their toes when they lowered their webbed feet to land.

After 7:00 A.M. we had only a few ducks come to our decoys and managed to collect just two of them: Kell, a hen green-wing; me, a hen ringneck. Years ago when the debate over pre-sunrise shooting first began, retired Fish and Wildlife Service director John Gottschalk took a closure proponent down to the barge canal in Washington, D.C., for an early-morning hike. The proponent was an enthusiastic birder, and at the peak of one identification frenzy—while he was checking off chickadees, wrens, thrashers, and towhees galore—John asked him to check his watch. Fifteen minutes to go before official sunrise. John suggested that if it was clear enough to identify songbirds in the shrubbery, it was clear enough to identify ducks over a marsh.

Perhaps, when the ducks come back, we can once again hunt the wings of dawn when they're best hunted: at dawn, not half an hour later.

Dennis Treitler prides himself on being one of the few major Louisiana violators Dave Hall never busted. "He came close! I had a hundred ducks covered up by shrimp. If he'd looked under the shrimp, I'd still be in prison!"

When we drove into Dennis's place, his thirteen-year-old son, Christian—"I call him 'Baby,'" Dennis said, "but he wants to be called 'Ace'"—had just finished nailing the wings from the morning's hunt to the front of the decoy shack out back. Christian had only recently begun duck hunting.

"He killed his first bird, a blue-wing, with steel shot and at the legal time," Dennis boasted. "He waited for sunrise. In the old days, I'd have killed a hundred ducks by sunrise! I'm so proud of that boy! And you know, it makes me feel good just watching him do it right!"

Dennis's ebullience coupled with the passionate conviction of the convert makes him a marvelous missionary on behalf of ethical wildfowling. Every kid in the neighborhood stops by for duck-calling and decoy-carving lessons. Treitler also visits schools to talk about his conversion and the need for a higher regard for wildlife. In the spring of 1988, he went to Minnesota with Dave Hall to make a similar presentation at that state's annual Sportsman's Show.

"More than 125,000 people came to hear me speak and see Dave's video," recalls Dennis. "What a different world it is up there! Everything is save, save, save! Down here, it's kill, kill, kill! At least it used to be. I think it's changing. Only problem with people up north is they talk funny, don't know how to make blinds, and they can't call ducks worth a damn! They had a calling contest while we were there, and I thought they were joking when the first contestant got on stage. I had to borrow a call. Didn't have mine. Still had no trouble winning the contest. It was like taking candy from a baby!"

When Dennis's father, "Hooker Herbert," heard that Dennis was going up north with Dave, he bade his son farewell forever. He was convinced he'd never see his boy again once the Yankees got hold of him.

"My Daddy still shakes his head at how I've changed. When he hunts with me, I make him do it my way, and he's amazed that I'm having so much fun. He taught me everything I know about shooting. When he picks up a gun—even today at seventy—it's like watching a butterfly. He doesn't miss. When I was growing up, we cleaned ducks seven days a week. We shot blue-winged teal in September and we shot 'em again in March and April. The old-timers thought they were two different birds 'cause the drakes looked so different in the fall and the spring. My Daddy said we'd never see an end to the ducks, but we've seen an end to everything else. He and his two partners used to trap 16,000 to 18,000 muskrats a season, walking all day long in the marsh. Now we got nothing but a dollar nutria and a dollar-ten 'coon. We used to have crabs, shrimp, and oysters for the picking. Now you got to work all year to find enough to make a living. I told Daddy that the ducks are on the way out unless we stop treating 'em like we did years ago. So he does it my way, but he's not happy about it. He knows I'm going to Washington next June to speak at a big Ducks Unlimited conference. He figures the Yankees didn't get me in Minnesota 'cause they were saving me to be lynched in Washington! My Daddy thinks I'm that important!"

Treitler's laughter is contagious. He soon has out his favorite duck call—"I carved it aboard DD-732, the *Forest Royal,* when I was in the Navy"—and is giving us instructions. "My Daddy won the New Orleans Sportsman's League Duck Calling Contest seven or eight times in a row. Winning that title myself was the most important thing in my life. My boy practices his call an hour a night. I'm doing what I can to make sure he always has a reason to use that call."

I was skeptical when I went to Louisiana. I didn't believe that generations of excess could be curbed in one or two short years. Not all of it has, of course, but if wildfowling has a future in Louisiana, it's due to men like Dave Hall and Dennis Treitler, Garland Rolling and Elmo Helmer, Benny Cenac and Jessie Duet.

As Garland told me before I left the Little Lake Club, "I was over in Texas a while ago, and I saw a sign saying, 'Please Lord, give us another oil boom, and we promise not to piss this one away.' That's the way Louisianans have come to feel about ducks."

——7——

Mississippi

$\mathbb{A}$lthough I've hunted ducks in the State of Mississippi—three days of memorable mallard, wigeon, pintail, but mostly mallard shooting just outside the Yazoo National Wildlife Refuge before the U.S. Army Corps of Engineers made war on that exceptional wetland—this story concerns another kind of Mississippi wildfowl. Unlike most upland hunting in which shotgunners use dogs to find and flush birds, wild turkey—notice that the word *wild* is invariably used to modify *turkey*—are sought by solitary hunters who use calls and decoys to draw the wary Toms within range.

The following tale is true, but I've changed names, concentrated time, and created an additional character to protect the real players as well as my own future prospects for hunting in this sportsman's paradise. I've been warned that my hostess, Sally Worthington, sends out no more than three engraved invitations to any one guest in his lifetime. She provides no rain checks. That's why I always leave my spring schedule as tentative as possible with the hope that, this year, I'll be invited back again.

The Jake Bird

Once upon a time, there was a Southern gentleman who had such faith in land that he bought tens of thousands of acres. He mostly bought bottomland other people didn't want. When he died, he left each of his three daughters vast holdings and the homespun advice to "care for the land and the land will care for you."

The dissipated daughter sold all the timber on her property, leveled Indian mounds and filled swamp, and had the new landscape subdivided into "ranchettes." She put the profits into Swiss banks, moved to the Isle of Capri, and now spends most of each year flying between gambling resorts and recuperative spas.

The dull daughter cleared the timber and put down cattle. She lives in Natchez but visits her land once a year with an accountant to review the resident manager's receipts. Although the bear and the orchids are gone, along with the woods they once inhabited, her hedgerows and pastures produce satisfactory numbers of dove, quail, and grassland wildflowers.

The devoted daughter decided to keep her land as she inherited it and manage it for turkey and timber. She'd graduated from Mississippi State University with a major in wildlife science, and because she was active in alumnae affairs, when I went to MSU years later to give a speech, I was offered a turkey hunt at her estate in lieu of a speaker's fee. Thus I met the legendary Sally Worthington.

Kim Bradshaw, the MSU faculty member who'd arranged the hunt, told me the story of Sally and her sisters on the drive down to her camp. I assumed the camp would be only a variation on the deer and duck camps I'd known elsewhere. Kim had given me a cedar box with a hinged lid to practice calling in the car. Between my screech-yelping and his corrective comments and hunting anecdotes, we were soon enough at Ms. Worthington's turkey camp.

Some camp! The entrance ran through a tree-arched alley over six miles long. The last half mile wandered down by a river where the road was separated from the water by a line of immense bald cypress. Black servants in starched whites greeted us, and while two took our bags to separate rooms, each with its own bath, another servant took our drink orders.

Kim followed his luggage to change while I wandered and gawked. When I heard the bounce of a diving board, a splash, and some laughter and applause, I made my way through a long, high-ceilinged room with card tables and wildlife trophies on the wall and saw two young women swan-diving and jack-knifing off boards over a pool in the patio beyond. Other young women sat beneath an awning along one side of the pool and applauded what seemed to be a friendly competition between the divers. In the distance, two people were fishing from a Cadillac-like bass boat on a tiny lake.

One of the divers pulled herself up at the edge of the pool and saw me.

"Hello! You must be George," she called. "I'm Sally. If you don't have a swimsuit, it doesn't matter. I have dozens." She looked me over. "You'll wear a forty-two."

Without waiting for confirmation, she turned and called "William!"

A black man, who had been waiting quietly behind me with a glass, stepped forward.

"Show Mr. Reiger the changing room and bathing suits. No, leave your drink here," she said to me. "You'll have time for that when you come back. Hurry now! The sun will be down in an hour."

As I dutifully followed William to a changing room, I met my professor friend bouncing down the stairs in a bathing suit with a towel around his neck. "Ah, I see you've met Sally," he said.

"Yes, and I see you know the drill. Thanks for the warning!"

Kim laughed and strutted off to the patio. I changed, returned to the pool, dived in, swam across, met Sally's friends, had two mint juleps, changed again for dinner, and sat at a candlelit table not quite convinced I didn't begin dreaming the moment we left the highway.

"This is a hunting camp," I told myself as a servant reached over my right shoulder to pour white wine into one glass and red wine into another. The white wine was for the crayfish bisque and the red for the roast wild turkey.

"This is a hunting camp," I said to myself while Sally beamed on us from the head of the table where she was wearing a tulle gown that displayed her petite but amply proportioned figure to perfection. She was telling a witty story about the last time she'd shot driven grouse in Scotland.

Her friends were all comparably well traveled. Two of them were divorced, and the thought flickered in my mind that they'd been invited to the camp as company for Kim and me. With their ring-studded fingers and perfumed coiffures, I couldn't imagine they'd be hunting turkey.

At the far end of the table sat Sally's husband and a friend of his. They'd been the two people in the bass boat. I tried talking with them about hunting, but they acted bored. Only tournament bass fishing and televised football appeared to interest them. Since I knew little about the one and cared less about the other, my conversation was soon directed elsewhere. Although I'd met her only six hours earlier, I was surprised that a woman like Sally was tied to such a limited spouse. I asked the pretty divorcée on my right about the husband. She said Sally and he had met in college where he'd been a hotshot skeet and trap competitor, and she'd run the student council.

"I imagine they thought they were well suited for one another," said my companion who obviously shared my belief that they weren't.

"I'm surprised to hear about his clay target shooting." I said. "When I talked with him before dinner, he didn't seem very interested in hunting."

"He isn't," she said. "He's only interested in competition. He used to shoot quail and dove before they got married, but he never cared for turkey. He said that any sport where you got to fire your gun only once a day—if that—was dumb. The longer he and Sally have been married, the less shooting of any kind he's done."

"Do you like turkey hunting?" I asked.

"Mr. Reiger," she breathed, her voice suddenly going soft, "I adore it!"

After dinner, the husband and his friend cajoled Kim into joining them at one of the card tables. I demurred. I have indifferent luck at cards, but I was also enjoying the company of the women, and I saw no reason to sacrifice the rare evening.

Two of Sally's guests seemed to feel sorry for Kim and went to join the card game, much to the husband's annoyance. The rest of us sat close by a low fire in the center of the room and talked about remote lands we'd visited. My dinner companion's name was Megan, and I was pleased to find we had mutual friends in London. She told me that if I liked turkey hunting, she'd arrange a hunt with friends of hers in Virginia.

"It won't be like this, of course," she said, "but they are extremely nice people who have two beautiful mountains and a valley, and the views alone are worth a trip there."

Sally got up from the far end of the sofa, came over to my chair, and plumped down on one of its arms.

"I know you have dozens of questions," she said mischievously. "Ask me anything you like."

"Well, I do have one rather personal question."

Everyone near stopped talking to listen.

"Go on," said Sally, a little less confident.

"While Kim and I were driving down here," I said, "I saw a white-face bull with angus cows, and a Brahman bull with white-face cows. How do you control the purity of your stock if you allow cattle to mix like that?"

All the women laughed, and Sally put an arm around me. "You sound just like a Virginian," she said. "You're so concerned about thoroughbred thises and purebred thats—and thoroughbred people, of course—it makes us wonder what Virginians are trying to hide. Honey"—she leaned close to me, and her voice grew husky—"down here in Mississippi, we believe in hy-brid vigor."

My blush made the women cry with laughter, and as lightly as she had come, Sally was gone, this time to the card table where a debate had begun over who were better players: men or women. The opponents were divided along sexual lines with Kim attempting to serve as moderator.

"It depends on the type of card game," he suggested.

"You mean we're better at Hearts and Old Maid!" hooted one of the women.

"You said it!" roared Sally's husband.

"No!" said Sally, suddenly annoyed. "Skill at anything is based on interest and practice."

"That's what I meant," continued Kim. "More men than women

play poker; therefore, men are generally better at that game than women. More women than men play bridge; therefore, women are usually better bridge players."

"Bridge is a pussy game, not a card game," muttered the husband's friend.

"I don't think anyone here would contest the fact you're a good poker player," said Sally sweetly to her husband's friend. "Just as you can hardly contest the fact that any one of us women can outhunt you."

He might have said nothing except everyone but Sally's husband laughed at his sullen face.

"That's a lie!" he declared.

"Think so?" asked Sally. "Fine. Tomorrow we're going to have six women and four men out turkey hunting. Since two people are assigned to each sector, I'm going to make the pair in each sector a team. We'll have a contest to see who the turkey hunters are: men or women."

"That's unfair," complained the husband's friend. "There are six girls and only four men." He glanced Kim's way. "And I'm not sure half the men are men." He guffawed at his own terrific wit.

"Since I don't expect either you or my husband to do anything more remarkable than to get lost," Sally said, "Meg and I will shoot for the men. Even if we, and both Kim and George shoot turkeys, the contest will end in a draw since I expect my other guests to do just as well."

I looked around the room and saw that Sally's other guests were as puzzled as I. A hunting competition? That's an oxymoron. Shooting can be competitive, but hunting never. What was the real point of Sally's proposal?

Sally's husband spoke to the table over the top of the fan of his cards: "I'll agree to the contest, but only if I can hunt the sector I want."

"Which one?"

"The island," he said.

"Why?" she asked, suddenly suspicious. "You've been down there four days this week fishing and said you never saw a bird."

The husband's friend began to smirk.

"I've been getting the lay of the land," said the husband from behind his cards, "and I'm pretty sure I know where two Toms roost."

Sally looked from her husband to his friend and waited, but they said nothing more.

"All right," she agreed. "Wake-up call is at three-thirty." She left the room. The rest of us, except Sally's husband and his friend, soon followed.

A gentle tapping on the door woke me at precisely 3:30 A.M. As I slipped on my camouflage coveralls, I wondered whether Sally arranged to have servants with synchronized watches poised beside each guest-room door at the precise réveille second.

Breakfast featured omelettes cooked to order, but I was more impressed with the fact that all the women showed up. My latent chauvinism assumed that at least one or two would sleep in. Instead, hair tucked into camouflaged caps and faces streaked with green and brown paint, the ladies discussed tactics and strategy in earnest tones. Neither Sally's husband nor his friend appeared.

"They had their calls," said Sally. "I didn't expect them to make breakfast. They're after-nooners—when they bother to hunt at all."

We drew for sectors, and Sally reviewed the safety rules. She got a laugh when she said the no-show status of her husband and his friend indicated they'd thrown in the towel on the hunting challenge.

As we started to leave, however, Sally came to Kim and me. "It's up to you two," she said with a smile.

"And to you and Megan," Kim teased in return. "You can't go back to bed now that you've sent the rest of us out."

"I wouldn't dream of it! I know where a big Tom is roosted, and he'll be hanging on the rail by the time you two get back for brunch. By the way, you have the southwest sector down by the river. I want you to keep an ear tuned to the island."

"For shouts of help?" Kim asked.

"Something like that." She looked at me. "You know what a Jake is?"

"No," I replied.

"A young gobbler who thinks he's qualified for the major leagues, but isn't. I don't allow Jakes to be shot."

As we walked away, I asked Kim how I could tell a Jake from a mature gobbler.

"Jakes have short beards and are smaller than Toms. Their voices haven't changed yet, and they sound like a hen trying to be a Tom. They are easier to fool, too. If a not-very-big gobbler comes begging to be shot, don't do it; it's probably a Jake."

We drove for thirty minutes over logging roads through a dense and still-dark forest. Twice Kim stopped at a crossroads to study his map. We finally stopped at the edge of a field across which we could see thirty or more pairs of eyes reflected in the headlights.

"Deer," said Kim. "In the winter you'll see both the deer and turkey feeding together out there."

"Why only in the winter?" I asked.

"In the fall, the bucks are busy competing for the does just as now, the gobblers cherché hens. But put down some corn, and some gobblers will declare a spring truce just like it was winter. Let's go."

I eased out of the car and quietly opened the back door to get my over-and-under. I shucked its case and stealthily clicked the car door shut.

"Why are you being so quiet?" Kim asked from his side of the vehicle. "I always want to know where the Toms are before wandering into the woods." With that, he slammed his front door as hard as he could. Immediately, gobbling came from two different directions.

"There's got to be one closer than that," said Kim. He reopened the door and slammed it again. This time, three birds gobbled, including one that couldn't be more than a hundred yards away!

"That's my bird," whispered Kim, suddenly tense and quiet as he slid around the corner of the car. "Here, take one of these turkey decoys, a cushion, and this light. Follow the road along the edge of the field toward the river. Just before you get there, the road will fork. You'll find a clearing to the left of the fork. Put the decoy in the middle of it. Call just like you practiced yesterday, and I'll see you back here at ten o'clock with a gobbler."

I started to ask a question, but Kim shushed me and disappeared into the darkness.

I didn't have to use the flashlight since my eyes had become accustomed to the darkness. The twin sandy tracks of the road glowed faintly in the starlight, and I stayed between the black forest on my left and the grey field on my right.

I found the clearing and shoved the single spike leg of the decoy—a hollow plastic turkey hen—into the soft ground and took my seat thirty yards away behind a patch of brush and with my back to an enormous tulip poplar. As darkness gradually yielded to faint daylight, I made a few tentative yelps with my call.

As the dawn came up, the night silence was overwhelmed by a

rising tide of bird song. The murmur of water moving in the unseen river and the intermittent hoot of a barred owl a long distance away were gradually drowned by a symphony of warblers, wrens, thrushes, and thrashers. I was trying to distinguish the various species when I suddenly realized there was a turkey in the middle of the clearing.

I had neither seen nor heard him come. Like a mythical creature, the turkey had materialized out of thin air. My gun lay in my lap with the call box in my hands. Yet I felt strangely weak in the great bird's presence, as though, like Gulliver, I was bound to the tree and the ground where I sat.

Suddenly the clearing shuddered with the *shut-varoom!* of the gobbler's wings followed by a ferocious gobble. The maple box dropped from my startled fingers and clicked on the gun's barrels. Instantly the swollen bird shrank and froze. The turkey stood still for two minutes before tentatively stepping forward and bobbing his head rapidly up and down several times to aid his narrowly focused two-dimensional sight. I feared to look directly at the bird and concentrated my gaze on the decoy, watching the real bird from the periphery of my vision.

The suspense was intense, and my mind was delirious with the proximity of the gobbler's primitive majesty! When the turkey shuddered and lunged forward to gobble again, the hair crawled up the nape of my neck. It was then I noticed the beard as long as a Chinese lantern tassel trembling with passion on the bird's breast. I had my gun halfway to my shoulder when a shot sounded in the distance and my bird disappeared, followed a moment later by the roar of wings in the woods to my right.

I sat primed for a replay of the spectacular scene—a replay that, of course, would never come. Twice I put the gun to my shoulder and swung it over the vacant ground where the wild bird had been. Only after I got up to examine the faint tracks in the soft soil did I realize that low brush had screened the bird's coming and going from the clearing. Had I been able to anticipate its now-obvious route, I would have been sitting four yards to the right of the tree, and that would have made all the difference.

Or would it?

The bird came and went like a wraith. Like any magical creature, it probably would have picked some other, equally unexpected path.

Yet why hadn't I gone for the shot earlier? Was I really making sure the bird wasn't a Jake, or was I simply incapacitated by "Tom fever?"

I moved the cushion and resettled myself. At one point, and despite the increasing hum of mosquitoes, I must have dozed, for I came suddenly awake with the distant rapid fire of shotguns from across the river. The shots were overlapping and blurred but it sounded like eight of them. I glanced at my watch, 9:22. Time to be getting back anyway. I got stiffly to my feet, collected the cushion and the decoy and started for the car. Kim was waiting.

"How'd you do?" I asked.

"So-so," he replied. "Put your gun in the trunk, and let's go."

Since I hadn't had my gun in the trunk when we started, I guessed there was something for me to see there. When I raised the lid to look in, Kim's turkey scintillated with metallic hues.

"He's beautiful!" I said and ached with envy.

As we drove back to camp, I told Kim about my Tom, and he apologized for the bad luck of having fired just as I was getting ready to shoot.

"The first fact of turkey hunting," he observed, "is that by the time you develop enough skill to take advantage of the beginner's luck that sustained you during the initiation period, your luck runs out, and you're fortunate to see one bird in four outings."

"Your skill and luck certainly served you well today," I said.

Kim laughed. "Wrong! I didn't call that bird. To tell you the truth, I'd lost my bearings while trying to find the roost and was waiting to get reoriented when I realized there was a bird in the tree above me. I was partially hidden by the canopy, and after he flushed and I shot, I still didn't know whether I'd killed a Tom or a Jake. Thank God and blind luck it was a Tom!"

By the time we got back to camp, all the women were there. I retold my story while Kim hung his turkey. He said he preferred listening to the ladies sympathize with me than mocking him for the haphazard way in which he'd gotten his bird.

Sally had killed a Tom far larger than Kim's, but Meg had missed her shot. "I don't know how," she repeated sadly. "When I fired and he started running, I was so surprised I never thought to fire again."

Two of the other women had also killed Toms. Sally made much of the fact that although the rules of the contest meant there would now be a draw, the women had clearly carried the day.

We were eating brunch when Sally's husband and his friend swaggered in. They were dressed in well-pressed camouflage suits, and neither man had painted his face.

"There are some good-looking turkeys hanging outside," said the husband to his friend. "But only one of them looks bigger than the ones we got."

Sally's chair scraped back, and without a word she went out to look. By the time the rest of us got there, Sally was examining two huge gobblers hanging apart from the other birds.

"How'd you get these?" she asked without looking at her husband.

"With a shotgun," he replied. "We're not allowed to use rifles, remember?" He laughed at his own keen wit.

"Were you on the island?"

"That's where I said we'd be."

"What about it?" she asked Kim and me. "Did either of you hear shots?"

"I did," I said. "They were definitely on the island." The two men looked at one another and smiled. "But I wondered why they needed so many shots for just two birds."

"How's that?" Sally snapped, unable to suppress her emotions.

"I know I don't know much about turkey hunting," I continued, "but I think of it as a solitary sport. When I heard the shots from the island, I was surprised to hear so many. And I was puzzled that the guns would be shooting so close together and firing in the same direction. It sounded more like duck shooting over bait than turkey hunting."

"You son of a bitch!" began the husband's friend, but his words were drowned out by the husband's shouting as Sally ran to her Jeep.

"Do you think somebody should go with her?" I asked Kim.

"I think we should stay here," he said. And taking the husband by one arm and the husband's friend by the other, Kim steered them toward the dining room.

"We were just sitting down when you came in," he said. "You both must be famished."

Nobody ate much of anything while we stayed at the table waiting for Sally to come back. When she finally walked through the door, she went directly to her husband's friend.

"I'll give you fifteen minutes to clear out. If I ever see you here again, I'll shoot you." She turned to her husband. "You, come with me." The rest of us waited until we heard shouting from an upstairs room. Kim suggested we take our coffee down by the lake.

A breeze ruffled the water's surface and blew away the insects from under the pines where the servants brought us tea and coffee. One of the women began speculating about what happened, but Kim asked her to describe a recent wedding of a mutual friend.

We gradually broke up into small groups, and Kim followed Megan and me down to the lakeshore. "I suppose we'll be leaving in a little while," I said to him.

"Yes. We'll wait for things to quiet down inside. Will you be staying, Meg?"

"Yes, tonight anyway."

Not until we saw the husband drive away did we return to our rooms to pack.

My bags had just been taken to the car and I was sitting by the pool when Kim came out to join me. "Sally will be down in a minute to say goodbye." Then *sotto voce:* "They'd been baiting. They killed two other birds: a hen and a Jake. Sally found the spares stuffed up a hollow tree at the edge of the island."

Sally came through the door with her hand extended: "I'm sorry, George. Your first turkey hunt didn't result in a very good impression of the sport, but you must promise you'll come and hunt with us again."

To Kim she said, "I'll give you a call."

Five months later, I received this brief correspondence:
"Dear Colleague-in-Arms, Sally flew to Mexico last month to finalize her divorce. Her rednecked-Ex took her for some cash and stock, but she managed to hold onto the land. You must have impressed her, for she still talks about you and at one point wondered whether you'd be able to join us on a wingshooting safari abroad. I explained you were happily married and that your wife, whom I hope to meet one day, is insanely jealous. I also pointed out that I was as unhappily married as she'd been, and that I would have little trouble persuading the powers-that-be to give me a sabbatical, particularly one that might result in research reports on the field behavior of exotic gamebirds. So wish us well, George. I feel you had much to do with my current good fortune. Best regards, Kim."

The letter was postmarked Buenos Aires.

2

Abroad

—— 8 ——

Argentina

A Wingshooter's Shangri-la

We parked on a path between a corn field and a pasture and gawked at the shorebirds, ducks, swans, and even flamingoes flying close to us and in all directions.

"It'll be like shooting in a sanctuary!" one of my companions exclaimed.

"Is anybody ready?" asked our guide. "This flight of geese is in range."

I was furthest along since I had only a gunsock to slip off my over-and-under. I checked my coat pockets and found only one shell to shove into the chamber of my first barrel, but Sandy Wilson reached across my arm and shoved one of his shells into the second chamber.

"Go for it," he said.

My first shot started the nearest ashy-headed goose on a glide that would take the bird well out into the standing corn. My second shot folded the bird so it fell just a few rows in.

Sandy's gesture was typical, not only of him, but of each of my five companions. Yet not one of us had known more than one of the others before the trip began. Sandy was traveling with his sixty-seven-year-old father, Stan. Both Wilsons live in Thief River Falls, Minnesota, where they have an automotive parts distributorship. Oakley Andrews is an attorney from Cleveland, Ohio, and a longtime shooting compadre of Jeff Buford who is in the cable-TV business in Tyler, Texas. Oakley was our interpreter and diplomat. At one point during the trip his friendly but firm persuasion convinced an Argentine airline employee that unless he personally supervised the transfer of our luggage from one aircraft to another, where eighty increasingly impatient passengers were waiting, the airline would be held responsible for all our hotel and restaurant bills if and when we were forced to stay over with the luggage. Both our luggage and ourselves made the waiting flight.

By contrast, Jeff Buford is so laid back that not even the luggage incident and the possibility of missing a day of shooting ruffled him. He was far and away the best shot on the trip, firing in a loose-hipped manner that seemed like a combination of ballet and boxing. He moved like one of the ensemble in Copeland's "Billy the Kid."

Bob Ziemke and I had come without knowing anyone else on the trip. I was going to write about it, while Bob was making the one great wingshooting pilgrimage of his life after thirty years as a postal employee in Sauk City, Wisconsin. For economy's sake, he joined the party after the rest of us had already spent two days hunting geese. He was soon into the swing of things: flirting with stewardesses, telling us tales of previous hunts, practicing German he had picked up as Uncle Sam's guest in Europe in 1944-45, and scoring his share of doubles and triples.

Suppose you had saved for thirty years and wanted to splurge on the one great wingshooting trip of your life. Where would you go?

Some parts of North America still offer excellent bird hunting, but shooters may feel that restrictions on quantity affect quality. The best black-ducking left on the continent, for example, is in Nova Scotia. However, four blackies plus two teal, and you're done for the day. That may be a superb wildfowling experience, but it doesn't fall into the category of "wingshooting trip of a lifetime."

There are few limits on gamebirds in Europe, but you generally gear up there to hunt only one kind of bird at a time. If you've selected geese in Scotland, you may have scarce opportunity to shoot snipe. If you've selected mallards at dusk, you may be far from an area where you can also hunt teal at dawn.

Some nations in Asia and Africa offer a great variety of gamebirds, but, also, political instability and minimal comfort. Who wants to sleep on a hard pallet in a vermin-infested hut on "the wingshooting trip of a lifetime"? If a religious fanatic doesn't get you, the local drinking water will.

Does, in fact, a wingshooter's paradise exist? Is there a Shangri-la where you can shoot ducks and geese each morning to your heart's content, and pigeons and dove each afternoon, with side orders of partridge, snipe, and even parrots, if such bizarre fare appeals to you?

How would you like to ride to the shooting ground in an antique Buick convertible with running boards, feast on four-inch-thick steaks, goose breasts, and salt-fresh seafood washed down with delicious local wines, and sleep in complete comfort and security in towns filled with shopping bargains for the folks back home?

If all those things appeal to you, and you're able to pay roughly $2,000 a week to be there (including round-trip air fare), Argentina is your wingshooter's Shangri-la.

Being There

Although the Argentine economy continues to reel with triple-figure inflation, the unsuccessful war with Great Britain restored some measure of political sense as well as a grudging respect for U.S. currency. Whether your lady back home prefers gemstones or more practical things like cashmere sweaters, leather gloves, and stag-handled cutlery, you'll find lots to console her for not making the trip with you.

Bargaining is essential. The inflation rate was 568 percent the month we were there. The value of the peso dropped daily, so prices in the stores changed weekly. At one point, the government knocked four zeros off the currency and made the 10,000-peso note a one peso note. A souvenir bargain was the one million peso note. (Yes, *1,000,000 pesos.*) Worth only about $2.50 in U.S. currency, it made a nice gift for friends back home who had always yearned to be "millionaires."

Argentina's vast agricultural region and its rich, deep soils are reminiscent of America's fertile prairies. Yet topsoils are even deeper and darker in Argentina, possibly because they've been farmed for fewer decades. A drive through the countryside makes you wonder what our own late-nineteenth-century Midwest was like. The red-haired, blue-eyed, and freckle-faced *muchachos* who retrieved our birds in the Andean foothills came from a settlement of farmers whose Welsh grandfathers had pioneered the Esquel valley around 1910. By American historical standards, the last such settlements in similarly prime agricultural areas occurred at least thirty years earlier.

Although more varieties of all species are found in the tropics, huge flocks of a single species are more characteristic of the world's temperate zones. Nowhere are tropical seas fertile enough to sustain concentrations of many millions of herring, menhaden, or mackerel. Likewise, no tropical lands have soils fertile enough to sustain huge flocks of wildfowl. Argentina's subtropical northern zone provides niches for many different types of creatures so long as none of them are overly abundant. Only the well-watered grasslands to the south provide sufficient food and space for enormous flocks of grazing and seed-eating birds comparable to the great flocks of North American wildfowl. Thus, the seemingly endless flights of sheldgeese that funnel through the mountain passes of Patagonia are analogous to the great flocks of Canada and snow geese that pour down our own continental flyways.

South American wildfowl are familiar to us in some respects, but marvelously different in others. The five species of sheldgeese, for example, don't even have counterparts in North America. The general morphology and metallic-colored speculums of these birds suggest they're more closely related to ducks than geese, but their large sizes and small brantlike bills encourage laymen to look on them more as geese than ducks.

The Magellan goose (*Chloephaga picta*) is an especially striking bird. Males and females have completely different plumages. Although both share grey and white wings with green speculums, the male Magellan is basically a white bird with black-barred back and flanks and black legs, while the female is cinnamon with black-barred back and flanks and yellow legs. The closely related ashy-headed goose *(C. poliocephala)* has a more subtle beauty with finely barred chestnut markings on the breast and back shared by both sexes.

The marvelous colors and peculiar proportions of the sheldgeese, as well as the fact that the females make a stuttering caw vaguely like a crow, and the males whistle like a pintail, cause many North American visitors to stand astonished before the first few they encounter in the wild. The completely unrelated *bandurria (Theristicus caudatus),* a species of ibis, is occasionally shot by American visitors who find its flapping-gliding flight and eerie clanging call no more exotic than that of the *cauquen comun* and *cauquen cabeza gris.*

Sheldgeese prefer land to water. They swim when they must, but they are found along watercourses more for the lush grasses growing there than for any security offered by the streams. Preferred roosting sites are gravel islands in lakes and large rivers. The birds rarely roost on open water the way heavily hunted North American geese frequently do.

Before the turn of the century there were undoubtedly many millions of sheldgeese in Argentina. Magellans and ashy-heads poured down onto the Pampas from breeding grounds in the foothills of the Andes and in remote valleys of Patagonia and Tierra del Fuego. The local settlers made war on them in the belief, still largely held today, that several geese will consume as much grass as a sheep or a steer.

The most effective way to destroy wildfowl is to destroy their breeding habitat. If that is undesirable, or impossible as was the case with the sheldgeese, the birds' nests can be destroyed and the molting adults clubbed. In 1948, Admiral P. O. Casal wrote the International Committee for Bird Preservation that "one owner of an estancia destroyed last year 250,000 goose eggs."

Still, Admiral Casal was optimistic: "The greatest enemies of the *Chloephaga* were the Indians and the foxes, both great consumers of eggs and goslings; there are no Indians today [red men had been eradicated in southern South America by the end of the nineteenth century], and the foxes are fast diminishing because their hides are used for making imitations of finer furs. These two factors are in the favor of *Chloephaga.*

"Furthermore, the number of sheep farms has increased, thereby increasing the quantity of tender grass that is the food—almost exclusively—of the geese. We have therefore three favorable factors for their reproduction."

Favorable factors notwithstanding, sheldgeese populations have declined drastically since the Admiral wrote his letter. Even more discouraging, the Argentine government has no interest in waterfowl research, particularly concerning birds many landowners still regard as vermin and on which bounties were everywhere paid until recently.

A major reason for the inadequacy of Argentine wildlife management is that Argentina's best and brightest citizens regard themselves as Europeans. Their ancestors came only to exploit precious metals with the hope of returning to Europe once their fortunes had been made. The name "Argentina," and the name of the river separating Argentina from Uruguay, "Rio de la Plata," remind us of this early obsession with silver. Even after colonists realized that more substantial wealth was to be found in the fabulously fertile soils of the Pampas, the most successful landowners returned to Madrid, Rome, and Paris to live, supported by money sent to them by their estancia managers. Argentine absentee landlords maintain local citizenship to avoid European taxes and service in European armies, but they contribute little to Argentina's cultural or financial future.

Without the wealthiest Argentines exhibiting much interest in the indigenous fauna of their native land, most natural histories have been written by foreigners. Probably the best known of these inside-outsiders was William Henry Hudson, author of *A Naturalist in La Plata, Tales of the Pampas, Green Mansions,* and many other books with Argentine settings. Yet Hudson died in 1922, and most of the scientific work done since his day has more often been a matter of cataloging species than of studying them.

I was not sanguine about the long-term future of sheldgeese until I visited the Esquel Valley in the province of Chubut and shot under the auspices of Augustin Ichiro Nores Martinez. Born in Esquel in 1939 to an Argentine judge and a mother whose father had been Argentina's ambassador to Japan, Augustin traveled widely in his youth and learned excellent English as a student in Canada where his father was the Argentine ambassador. Despite his cosmopolitan upbringing, Augustin has turned his back on the superficial glamor of Buenos Aires to live for his dream of owning a large estancia in the Esquel Valley where he can host sheldgeese and foreign sportsmen to hunt them. He controls the shooting in this region on as nearly a sustainable basis as it is possible for any one man to manage.

He pays local landowners $20 per hunter per day, not because he has to—after all, his goose hunters are supposedly helping local sheepherders and cattlemen destroy vermin—but because he wants to impress on the landowners that the birds have economic value.

"If I can dissuade even a few sheepherders from sending their children out into the pastures to destroy goose nests, I feel the fee is worth it," he says.

Augustin has also established a local seasonal limit of 5,000 birds. Thus, the management of this major wildfowl resource may be unique in that one man with no greater credentials than the naturalist's knowledge and concern for the birds makes all the important decisions. Although Augustin has no idea how many sheldgeese there are, and no means to find out, he feels that a 5,000-bird limit provides him with a framework in which to detect local population trends. The seasonal limit is based on an average daily limit that fluctuates from year to year. In 1983, for example, the average daily limit was thirty birds per shooter. When this average quota was not reached, Augustin reduced the limit to twenty birds per shooter for the 1984 season.

"Average daily limit" means dividing the total daily kill by the number of shooters. Early in the three-month season and later, toward its end, gunners may average only six or eight birds per outing. Even during the height of the season, a poor shot may only kill ten geese per outing. But a skilled and determined shooter will kill over 100 geese a day in June, and Augustin feels his 5,000 total quota provides the birds with enough leeway to tolerate that kind of intensive gunning.

Unfortunately, Augustin does not keep records of age ratios among the harvested birds. Sheldgeese ganders are very aggressive during the breeding season, and they develop protruding "spurs" on their wings at an earlier age than Canada ganders develop comparably bony "knuckles." Our shooting party believed we could distinguish in-hand mature sheldgeese males from immature males, and we became concerned about the large percentage of older birds we killed.

In a well-managed system, the majority of slain birds should be young of the year. When the majority are adults, seasons or limits must be abbreviated to encourage an increased survival for mature birds. An arbitrary quota spread across a local wintering population of two species of geese simply doesn't provide a solid foundation for effective waterfowl management. On the other hand, with only Augustin to maintain the balance, and without any control over the birds' breeding areas, truly meaningful sheldgeese management is still just a future hope.

Moralists might argue that each hunter should be set a daily limit "on principle." However, we have enough arbitrary wildlife legislation in our own land without encouraging law for law's sake in other countries. Furthermore, such a restriction would dry up the market for American sheldgeese shooters, thereby eliminating the only economic factor currently offering the birds much protection. Argentina attracts North American gunners who want, at least once in their lives, to pull out the stops and not be breaking local laws in the process. Some visitors dream of a one-hundred-bird body count; most visitors are happy with half a dozen of the new-to-them birds.

If wintering sheldgeese continue to decline in Augustin's district, he might consider doing what the British do: discourage repeating shotguns. Augustin recalls one member of media-entrepreneur Ted Turner's party who, using an unplugged semi-automatic shotgun and reloading with shells stuck between his fingers, managed to kill eight geese with eight shots and still have a loaded gun after the flock's survivors were out of range. That's not hunting: that's strip-mining with firearms! No wonder the British call semi-automatics and pumps "gangster guns".

The word *double* implies a completeness to a shooting sequence that the words "triple," "quadruple," or, God forbid, "octuple" offend. Besides, birds shot two at a time are easier to keep track of than a deluge of feathered bodies. So far as I know, our party of six didn't lose one of the sheldgeese we downed. Not all of us were using doubles, but the birds came to us in small enough numbers so we were shooting game, not merely targets. High gun one morning took two dozen birds.

All the birds we killed were consumed. We ate some ourselves and found young sheldgeese, especially ashy-heads, to be delicious. The birds we didn't use began disappearing from the truck as soon as we parked for lunch. Little boys would stagger off with four or five each. Augustin assured us that even in June, when more than a thousand birds may be brought in each week, demand continues to exceed supply. "There are always people in the Esquel area who enjoy free food," he observed.

The Pampas

I knew it was wrong before I squeezed the trigger, but the temptation of incoming birds was too great. I had just knocked down into standing corn a *pato barcino* (what the Argentines call "speckled teal," but what is known elsewhere in South America as "Chilean teal"—a yellow-billed version of our North American green-winged teal). I should have marched directly there and searched for it. But four larger birds were approaching and from an angle that guaranteed any I killed would fall into the sparse, calf-high brush in front of the blind.

When I stood, I saw they were *pato overo* (Chiloe wigeon) and killed a bird with each barrel. I quickly found them, but I didn't so easily find the *pato barcino.* I had lost my precise bearing line to where the duck had fallen in the head-high corn, and I spent nearly fifteen minutes in a spiraling search pattern before locating the duck. Meanwhile, four hundred other ducks had come and gone over the decoys.

That first morning on the Pampas, I scored two Scotch doubles (two birds killed with one shot), but neither was intended. Such inadvertent doubling gives the sportsman little pleasure. It is the second duck's bad luck, and not the shooter's skill, that brings the bird down. The only time in Argentina I consciously attempted a Scotch double with a pair of ashy-headed geese, I missed both.

Ashy-heads are found on the Pampas, but they're strictly bonus birds among the waves of ducks flushed off distant ponds and sloughs by local outfitters rushing about in antique cars and honking continuously to stir the birds up. The ducks are ping ponged back and forth between ponds by the shooters and the rallying outfitter and his assistants. The cars swerve and slide wildly over the landscape because the tires have little tread and because local drivers seem unable to brake and steer at the same time.

Although much of the Pampas is given over to pasturage, a significant portion of the rich, flat soils is devoted to crops. Two of the three mornings we hunted ducks, the decoys were put on ponds well inside vast cornfields where ears were still two or three weeks from ripening. In order to recover fallen birds, I tried to ignore the temptation of second shots, marched directly to the spot where I thought my downed bird would be, tied a handkerchief to the nearest corn stalk, and began circling out from there.

Some of the downed birds were still moving when I reached them and were, therefore, easy to find. The most difficult to locate were those that had fallen stone dead. With perseverance and luck, I ended up losing only three of the three dozen ducks I downed in three mornings of shooting. One of these, a cripple, got down a rabbit burrow and would have escaped even from a dog.

Although the other shooters had *muchachos* to retrieve their birds, my percentage of finds was higher than theirs, partly because my one-bird-at-a-time rule focused my search effort. *Muchachos* dashing into the corn after a flurry of action were sometimes looking for five or six birds at once. They rarely came out with more than two or three of them.

I make much of this problem, because no wildfowler likes to lose half of what he kills. For this and other reasons, my companions rated our time spent with Augustin Nores as superior to the days we spent on the Pampas, even though the Pampas offered a greater variety of game. A friend and Accomack County neighbor, Steve Van Kesteren, solved this problem by flying to Argentina with his two *drahthaars,* combination retrievers and pointers. He rented a van and began driving west from Buenos Aires and soon found that because of the dogs, he had more invitations from landowners to hunt than he had days of vacation. Steve experienced a few logistical glitches, but on a previous visit he'd be-friended a young Chilean lady who later became his wife, served as his interpreter, and helped him over the hurdles. His overall cost for four weeks was less than that of the ten-day trips arranged by American outfit-ters. The only drawback to such do-it-yourself Argentine hunting is that you'll have no one to rally the birds off distant ponds. In Steve's case, that meant he saw only hundreds of ducks each morning, rather than thousands. He'd kill a dozen before breakfast before moving on to his preferred business of hunting *perdiz* with the dogs.

The most disturbing aspect of shooting under the auspices of a man who is not a naturalist, like our Pampas host, is that he has no con-ception of birds as anything other than feathered targets. Unlike Au-gustin Nores, who is curious about sheldgeese and very much concerned with their conservation, Chiche Bilo was concerned only that his clients knock down as many targets as they could. At one point, when he found me poking around looking for a fallen duck while dozens of others were zipping overhead, he yelled at me to "Stop wasting time! The sport is in the shooting!"

Bilo's urging us to shoot first and ask questions later led to a couple of unhappy incidents. Black-necked swans are protected even under Ar-gentina's casual conservation system. One morning I saw a pair approach-ing another hunter from the rear. I stood and shouted for him not to shoot. The wind must have blown most of my words away, for all he heard was the word *shoot*. Fortunately, the birds were high enough so the man's reflexive fire brought down only a few feathers. Nevertheless, the shooter and I were embarrassed and heartsick about the incident.

On another occasion while waiting for dove with Bilo at my elbow, a harrier-type hawk appeared over a row of eucalyptus trees and glided our way.

"Shoot! Shoot! Quick! Shoot that bird!" shouted Chiche.

"I don't want to shoot a hawk," I said.

"For me! Please! Shoot this bird for me!"

I thought Chiche must want the bird for mounting, so I shot it. Then Bilo told the nearest *muchacho* to take the hawk and jam its head between two strands of wire so the rancher would find it. "Hawks kill many chickens; the farmer will be glad to see we did this for him."

I was ashamed: I'd unwittingly helped reinforce an old and ignorant prejudice against rodent-eating harriers. I tried to explain this fact to Bilo, but he thought my science was sentimental claptrap. He was contemptuous of my dismay and suggested I was a hypocrite for feeling remorse at killing a hawk and only joy at killing a new (for me) species of duck. Such an episode and attitude would have been unimaginable with Augustin Nores.

Argentina may have enough productive wetlands to afford visiting shooters the luxury of treating all birds as targets for many years to come but I doubt it. North Americans don't have to look very far back into our own history to see the impact of over-shooting. All birds were devastated by go-for-broke market hunting before World War I, and many duck populations were knocked down to historic lows by over-shooting during America's stabilized regulations era of the early 1980s. It will take decades to repair the damage done in those few brief seasons, especially considering the ongoing loss of nesting habitat and wintering wetlands.

The most common duck in the Pampas south of Buenos Aires is *pato maicero,* one of three yellow-billed pintails found in South America or on South Atlantic islands. Its English common name is the "Chilean pintail," which, for diplomatic reasons, you don't translate into Spanish while hunting in Argentina. Like the Chiloe wigeon (named for an island in southern Chile and, hence, another bird for which you must use the local Argentine name, *overo*), both sexes of the yellow-billed pintail look alike and are similar to that of a hen northern pintail, except that the bills of southern pintails are bright yellow, not slate blue.

The white-cheeked or Bahama pintail *(pato gargantilla)* is also found on the Pampas, and I shot one of these distinctly marked birds with blended bright crimson and slate-blue bills the first morning. We shot far more *pato capuchino,* or silver teal, which some local landowners called *pato gargantilla.* However, silver teal have yellow bases to their upper mandible and are considerably smaller than any pintail variety. In addition, the snow-white face and neck of the Bahama pintail distinguishes it from the buffy-cheeked silver teal.

Yellow-billed pintail are slightly smaller than their North American counterpart, just as *pato overo* or Chiloe wigeon are slightly larger than the American and European wigeons. Indeed, the Chiloe wigeon was the largest of all the ducks we shot on the Pampas and seemed to be the preferred waterfowl for local consumption. Both sexes have similar plumage, including lovely green highlights in the head with a white "face," black-and-white barred breast, and rusty chestnut flanks. We asked Chiche to select some ducks for us to eat, and he had his boys pluck only wigeon. We enhanced this feast with a sampling of local wines.

Ducks evolved in the northern hemisphere, and almost every South American species is linked to a family found north of the equator. However, some relationships are more obvious than others. On our first morning on the Pampas, I shot a drake *pato colorado,* or cinnamon teal, identical in size and plumage pattern to our western species. Sandy Wilson wondered whether my bird could have wandered from Mexico through all of Latin America to Argentina. While nothing is impossible where wildfowl are concerned, the Argentine cinnamon teal is one of five closely related subspecies, each with its own distinctive range. The teal I shot was probably hatched not many hundred miles from where we hunted.

Another species with an obvious North American counterpart, but one so different in plumage that only the spatulate bill gives the kinship away, is *pato pico cuchara,* the red shoveler. Several were shot, but only one mature drake with his buff rather than green head and breast, and pale cinnamon flanks and belly with large oval black spots. His feet were bright orangish yellow, and both sexes sport a long pointed tail. The smelt-blue tertiaries and lesser coverts of this species' wings and its cinnamon body hint at *pato pico cuchara*'s evolutionary links with both the cinnamon teal and other shovelers. And as with all shovelers, the diet of *pato pico cuchara* is mostly invertebrates, and the bird's flesh is poorly flavored.

My favorite of all the Argentine ducks we shot—perhaps, because it's such a dapper little trapper, or maybe because my last memory of Argentine wildfowling was of one of these pint-sized blurs buzzing over the decoys—is *pato capuchino* (also known as *pato Argentino*), the silver teal. There are three subspecies of this uniquely South American duck with the northern silver teal (smaller than its southern and Puna cousins) being the most abundant on the southern Pampas ponds.

Unlike South American wigeon and pintail, which herald their approach by whistling, silver teal are mostly silent (the males have a low rattling call) and fly lower, just over the corn and reeds and are suddenly there and usually gone before the shooter can catch up with them. They are brownish overall with a green mirror between two white bars in the speculum, a dark cap and pale cheeks, and a pretty blue bill with yellow patches near the base.

Several genera of North American waterfowl are barely or not at all represented in Argentina. For example, there are no eiders, scoters, or goldeneyes in the southern hemisphere, and mergansers in South America are represented by a single rare species, *Mergus octosetaceus,* the Brazilian merganser.

Other genera, like *Oxyura* (the ruddy ducks), are well represented, but of little importance to the sportsman because they fly little, if at all, by day. *Pato rana* (also *pato zambullidor*), the Argentine ruddy duck, is widely distributed throughout the Pampas south of Buenos Aires and along the adjacent coast. However, we didn't see one on our trip, possibly because they are extremely secretive and prefer diving to flight when surprised by an intruder. *Pato fierro,* the closely related masked duck, moves about slightly more in the daytime, but usually in the half hour before dawn and after sunset, periods we were not afield.

In a genus all by itself is the puzzling *pato cabeza negra* (the black-headed duck). This brownish teal-like bird is of little interest to sportsmen because it prefers hiding to flight when disturbed. However, black-headed ducks are of particular interest to naturalists because this species, like the European cuckoo, is a reproductive parasite. It lays all of its inordinately large eggs in the nests of other waterbirds from ducks and coots to gulls and rails.

A favorite waterfowl group of North American sportsmen is

Aythyini, which includes the scaup, ringnecked duck, canvasback, and redhead. This tribe is represented by a single species on the Pampas: *pato picazo,* or the rosy-billed pochard. As with the drake canvasback, the drake *pato picazo* is a wildfowling trophy. Its plumage never goes through an eclipse, so it wears its dark purple and soft grey pattern set off by a large pink bill from the day it arrives on the Pampas until it leaves in the spring (October). Unfortunately, rosy-billed pochards don't begin appearing on their wintering grounds until June, and we never saw one. However, Chiche obtained a mounted specimen for me to examine and photograph, and while my heart still belongs to the canvasback, my next trip to the Pampas will coincide with the appearance of the splendid rosy-bill.

Isn't the greatest part of wildfowling the anticipation—never knowing what will appear next in the panorama of land and water? In this sense, hunting and birding on the Pampas is truly spectacular. *Cuervillo* (ibis) and *tero real* (pink-legged stilt) land in the shallows just a few yards from your hiding place. *Flamenco* (Chilean flamingo) and *cisne cuello negro* (black-necked swan) trade overhead, while everywhere there're hawks hovering, kites circling, and occasional eagles soaring. Since shooting involves little time, and the waiting and watching so much more, how glorious to have so much to watch while waiting!

Guns and Ammunition

Gas-operated semi-automatics were preferred by most of our party because their softer recoils take some of the soreness out of firing so many rounds per day. However, I did almost as much shooting as the others with a Browning over-and-under, including more than half a case of three-inch shells at ducks and geese, and never suffered the least pain. Some people might claim I'm too much of a lumnox to feel pain. That notwithstanding, the Invector model Citori gave me choke options no other manufacturer at the time provided. Even had I packed a semi-automatic shotgun with interchangeable barrels, spare barrels would have been too cumbersome to carry into the field. Fortunately, other major gun manufacturers have finally gotten aboard the choke-tube bandwagon, and American bird hunters won't be quite as burdened in the future with spare barrels as they've been in the past. Choke tubes are about an inch and a half long. Two tubes, plus their tiny wrench, weigh about two ounces, the same as an express 2 3/4-inch, 12-gauge shell. I kept several choke options in a shirt pocket and was well prepared for any eventuality.

Although the agent who handled my booking to Argentina advised me to take two shotguns, I got along fine with one. It's like the old debate concerning twin outboard engines: Does an extra engine provide an extra margin of safety or only twice as many headaches? Malfunctions are a threat in any frequently used weapon, but it seems to me that the simplicity of a double-barreled gun makes failure less likely than with complicated, gas-operated semi-automatics.

Furthermore, the Browning over-and-under design is acceptable in many parts of the world where semi-autos and pump-action shotguns are socially taboo. My only problem with the Browning is the perennial one with this particular weapon: the barrel selector switch is the same button as the safety, and in the excitement of a hunting moment, I sometimes jam the safety on the over-and-under track.

The Argentine government permits you to bring 1,000 rounds of ammunition (two cases) into the country, which most Americans divide between number 4s for sheldgeese and number 6s for ducks, buying local 7 1/2s for pigeon and dove at $10 per box. However, even when you purchase your shells in Miami and deliver them directly to the Aerolineas Argentinas ticketing agent, you and your Argentine co-conspirators are violating a nit-picking U.S. regulation by flying more than ten pounds of ammunition from a U.S. airport.

Since shells cost between $10 and $16 per box in Argentina, I know that some hunters ignore the U.S. statute and pack as many shells as they can distribute throughout their luggage. They especially do this when they want to shoot another gauge besides the customary 12. By disguising the shells as part of their luggage—stuffing a few boxes down hip waders, wrapping others in underwear, and even stashing spare rounds in a toilet kit—they pack almost a case of shells without attracting notice from ticketing agents. However, new gamma-ray detectors at airports have made spotting nitrogen-rich compounds like explosives in luggage a more certain matter. The age of terrorism has made carrying arms and ammunition by air aggravating enough without spending part of your vacation in prison!

9

South Africa

"Hurry up! This way! Go around! Take your time!"

These contradictory orders all came from one man, my South African host, Trevor Donald Comins. By this, the second day in our relationship, I was well used to the confusion and interpreted his instructions to mean only that he was as excited as I was.

Like an actor in a well-rehearsed play, I stepped up alongside Trevor's dogs, a pair of Swainson's francolin flushed, the Zulu dog handler and his animals crouched, and I watched the birds level out and begin to veer away from each other before bringing the borrowed Beretta over-and-under to my shoulder and killing them both.

There are two ways to have a perfect day afield. One is to be so relaxed that your reflexes work like a computerized guidance system. The other is to be so determined to do well that you *will* the birds dead as much as you kill them by shooting.

I was in the latter frame of mind because I was tensely aware of the very many strings that had been pulled to set up my V.I.P. hunt to South Africa—and because I had mostly fumbled the duck shooting the evening before.

Back in New York City, Peter Celliers, South Africa's tourism representative, had asked me whether I would like to shoot a kudu or nyala during my visit.

"Yes and no," I replied. "Yes, if I knew enough about those antelope to qualify me to hunt them. And no, because I don't. Heck, I didn't even know, until you made the distinction, that the female kudu is called a *cow* while the female nyala is called a *ewe*."

"Well, what would you like to hunt?"

"Birds."

"Birds? But nobody goes all the way to Africa just to hunt birds!"

"That clinches it. I must shoot birds if for no other reason than 'nobody goes all the way to Africa just to hunt them.' I'm a snob, I suppose, but I would rather shoot duck and francolin than nyala and kudu—particularly if you can find a South African with dogs who enjoys bird hunting as much as I do."

Of course, my preference for shooting birds rather than big game is more than a matter of snobbery. I suspected at the time, and I know now, that much of what passes for big-game hunting in Africa today is carefully staged theater rather than genuine sporting adventure. At a game reserve in Zululand, photographer Ken Garrett and I were taken right up to a trophy white rhino placidly browsing on a hillside. The game rancher told us he maintained a detailed stud book on all his rhinos, and that this particular animal—after producing X number of progeny and providing Y number of "photographic opportunities" for tourists and professional film-makers—was scheduled for slaughter by a "sportsman" in two months time.

"The brute is getting on in years," the rancher explained, "and I can't afford to keep him."

Big-game outfitters in the United States and Germany had been informed that a rhino of such-and-such dimensions would be available in the fall for a five-figure "trophy fee." After the bids came in and the outfitter was selected, his client would fly to South Africa. Since game ranchers know that most businessmen are reluctant to be away from their offices for more than a week at a time, four days are scheduled for the "hunting," with a day and a half each way for travel.

During the first day, the rancher or one of his "white hunter" assistants lets the client see the rhino. Then admidst much mumbo-jumbo about the dangers of the stalk, the guide leads the client away from where the guide knows the rhino is headed.

Excited by his glimpse of the beast, the client is taken to several other parts of the reserve over the next two days—but never allowed to see the fencing that encloses the reserve or the air-conditioned housing that makes life for the rancher and his family more comfortable than the "bush camp" in which the client stays. The client is encouraged to shoot an impala or a warthog for "camp food," but he is kept strictly away from the rhino until the fourth morning of his visit—about the time he begins to wonder whether he'll ever get a shot at the trophy he has come so far to obtain.

Early that morning, a derrick-equipped truck is taken behind a hill in front of which the rhino will be passing on his daily rounds. The kill is scheduled for 8:00 A.M. because, later, the heat of the day will make the skinners' job unpleasant and push the processing of paperwork and bill-paying too close to the client's scheduled departure time.

After a breakfast during which the white hunter sets the stage with much stimulating talk about having the right omens for a successful hunt, he takes the client out to where he knows the rhino is waiting. The two men "stalk" the animal, and the client kills it. The trackers and skinners surge around the client and congratulate him as the truck makes its unobtrusive entrance, cranks the rhino up onto its flatbed, and takes the beast back to the reserve's abattoir. In a dazed and euphoric state, the client tips everyone lavishly, thanks the rancher for a sensational hunt, and is on his way back to Houston or Hamburg immediately after lunch.

The world's zoos already have enough white rhinos, and truly wild habitat in Africa is increasingly a matter of memory. Old animals must die to make room for younger stock, and fees paid by foreign sportsmen help perpetuate rhinos. All this is true, but I still wish there were some other way than trumping up phony safaris that only serve to diminish the stature and achievement of bona-fide hunters. Spur-winged geese may not be as large or potentially dangerous as rhinos, but they at least are truly *wild* game.

So began a search for an outfitter, especially one with dogs who featured bird hunting rather than driven shooting. Telexes flashed between New York and Pretoria.

"Did you say *birds?*" government officials asked. "He wants to shoot *birds?*"

Part of my problem was the time of year. I didn't know it, but I would be going to South Africa a month before the various gamebird seasons actually opened. One can kill local dove and pigeon, classified as vermin, any time of the year in South Africa, but I wanted to hunt wildfowl. So a special permit was arranged for me to kill six each of duck, spur-winged geese, francolin, and guinea fowl. Had I known all this, I might have settled for a kudu!

I was traveling to South Africa to look at a broad range of conservation problems from the decline of jackass penguins near Cape Town to the overpopulation of elephants in Kruger National Park. Bird hunting would be a pleasant interlude, but it was not the point of the trip. Nevertheless, I got periodic updates on the proposed wildfowling excursion. When I learned that the best guide in Natal was scheduled for reserve military service, I concluded the hunting was off and left my shotgun and hunting clothes at home.

Nothing like *not* carrying an umbrella to induce rain! As soon as I stepped off the plane in Johannesburg, Brenda Bodde of the South African tourist office told me I would definitely be hunting birds. I was intrigued and excited, but disappointed I hadn't brought my own equipment. In addition, I also felt uneasy about being catered to in such a shameless fashion. I was no longer just a member of the press; I was now a Very Important Person for whom the South African government had pulled some heavy-duty strings with the hope of getting favorable publicity. South Africa is in a constant state of emergency, and I'm sure its army is not easily persuaded to reschedule an officer's reporting date. That such had been arranged merely to service the whims of an American outdoor writer with a penchant for wildfowling discomfitted me.

Land of the Zulu

Perhaps, I also felt a certain awe in visiting the area of South Africa where my hunting host lived. The past of no region or nation—not even our own—is touched by more sadness and glory than the land north and east of Durban. The confrontation there between white farmers and black warriors forever altered the course of world history. Seemingly insignificant incidents made all the difference.

I wondered what would have happened in North America had the Dutch in the mid-Atlantic region successfully staved off British hegemony even as their contemporaries did in South Africa. What changes would have occurred in America's concept of Manifest Destiny had shortly before white farmers begun pouring out across the Great Plains, an Indian chief with the authority and military skills of the Zulu Shaka been able to pull together all the western tribes under his single direction?

As our party drove up from the coast to Trevor's farm near Vryheid, I was keenly aware of the important events that had taken place all around me a century earlier. Not far to the south and west, a Zulu impi had wiped out two regiments of British regulars and several companies of irregulars at a place named Isandhlwana. Not far from there, fewer than 100 British troopers held off an attack by 4,000 Zulus at an outpost known as Rorke's Drift.

Even closer to Vryheid, an incident on June 2, 1879, forever altered the destiny of Europe. A young Frenchman trained and serving as a British artillery officer was cornered in a gully by seven Zulu warriors. Although the Prince Imperial fought courageously and without the benefit of his great-uncle Napoleon Bonaparte's sword, which had fallen from its scabbard, the once and future emperor of all France and her colonies was quickly slain.

The death of this twenty-two-year-old boy, whom even French Republicans had begun to accept as a probable Napoleon IV, ended the last hope for a French constitutional monarchy. A year later, the young prince's mother, Empress Eugénie, made a pilgrimage to Zululand. She met Zabanga, the man who had made the second spear thrust into her son. (Langalabalele, the man who had made the initial thrust, had been killed in battle against the British.) Zabanga told the Empress that her boy had fought like a lion and that "we would not have slain him had we known who he was."

The modern landscape of South Africa bears little testament to the wonder and tragedy of those times. Only as we Land-Rovered north over the red roads, crossing through a portion of Kwazulu, did the thatch-roofed rondavels and thorn kraals suggest what life must have been like there a century ago.

By contrast, Vryheid is a farming center much like farming centers in the American Southwest. At one point the road leads into a valley strangely reminiscent of Oklahoma; the next moment you pass a rocky outcropping called a "koppie" and spy a distant butte that stirs memories of New Mexico. Afrikaner farmers are thorough, and the only thing saving their vast grain fields from the monotony and game-sterility of comparable fields in Kansas or the Dakotas are the many geological anomalies that force the farmers to leave a hedgerow or an unplowed koppie here, and a small woods or a marsh there.

A Poor Start

We arrived late in the afternoon at Trevor's farm, and he immediately took me down to one of his marshes and installed me in a raised platform "hide" overlooking a little pothole. Behind me stood ranks of black and white spectators waiting for me to strut my stuff. Nobody else would be pointing a gun at the ducks and geese we hoped would visit Trevor's decoy spread of Italian-made (plastic) duck floaters and Trevor-made (wood) goose silhouettes. I felt like a batter in a World Series game in the bottom of the ninth with two outs.

Although the borrowed Beretta (with a stock too short) had skeet barrels loaded with number-7 shot, the first yellow-billed duck circled close enough for an easy kill. Trevor's black Lab retrieved the bird in elephant-high grass where even the ablest human tracker would have been lost.

But my limelight location and my less-than-ideal firepower soon contributed to a run of poorly hit birds and misses. The worse I did, well, the worse I did. My vanishing self-esteem was not restored by the painfully polite comments of the people behind me.

"It's all right, George. You must be tired from the long drive to-day."

"It's probably the gun. Would you like to try a side-by-side? I think we have one with a longer stock."

By the time several spur-winged geese appeared—at which I didn't fire because the range was too great for the loads and the chokes I had—I felt that the birds' being out of range was somehow my fault and that I had failed utterly in my commission as an American "ambassador of good kill."

Everyone was so kind to me at dinner that night, I thought I should step outside and commit suicide. Fortunately, an uninvited guest who had attached himself to our party that morning was less kind, and sparring with him kept my spirits up. He'd been a member of the Rhodesian national skeet and trap team and fancied himself an exceptional chap besides. His presence created a farcical situation in which Trevor thought he was a member of our entourage, and we thought he was an old friend of Trevor's.

Friendship or not, this man's *bon mots* to the effect that a conservation writer wasn't expected to be a decent shot since his job was to conserve game, not kill it, made me determined to shoot circles around him on the dove field the next day.

The man turned out to be a grim parody of white supremacy. He had come into camp with a black "boy" and left him sitting in the back of his vehicle for hours while he refreshed himself and shot the breeze. Almost as an afterthought, he made arrangements to put the man up with a local family.

At dinner, the uninvited guest, who made part of his living as a mercenary hunting black insurgents in Namibia, began talking about the "stupidity of the niggers" whom he and his men killed in Southwest Africa. He allowed, however, that as the insurgents had begun receiving arms and training from the East Germans and the "colored" Cubans in Angola, they were getting to be more of a challenge to find and kill—so much so that the mercenary was no longer sure he wanted to continue "nigger hunting" in Namibia.

"Why would a white man want to give aid to the niggers?" he asked. "Don't white people in other countries understand what we're trying to do here in South Africa?"

I thought photographer Ken Garrett was going to lunge across the table and strangle the man. Later in the privacy of our rondavel, Ken and I had an unhappy conversation in which we debated which was the greater hypocrisy: accepting South Africa's hospitality in the first place and then lecturing local people about the immorality of their racial policies, or remaining silent and letting Trevor and his family think we shared "his other guest's" bias against blacks. I chose silence but resolved to wipe the mercenary's eye on the killing field.

Redemption

By first light, I was crouched behind a grass panel below an irrigation pond waiting for several dozen ducks that had been flushed by Alfred's men to return down the valley. The Beretta now sported trap barrels, and I had some shells loaded with number-3 shot to go with the 7s. Most birds returned too wide, but one pair of yellow-billed ducks swung high overhead against the deep purple sky. *Pow! Pow!* Both fell dead.

"Reload!" yelled Trevor.

Another duck suddenly appeared low over the rim of the dam behind me. I snapped the barrels shut on the single shell I had managed to get in. *Pow!* The bird folded. I chuckled and did a little jig while reloading.

I missed only one bird during the next hour and even that one, flying fast and low from left to right, I overtook with my second shot. The duck flight was too soon done, and for the first time, some of the spectators would be armed when we moved to a freshly harvested maize field. Each of us was put into a small cornstalk blind tended by a youngster wearing a burlap serape for camouflage. Each blind was about eighty yards from the next with mine located between Trevor's and the mercenary's. I traded in the Beretta for a bore-choked British side-by-side and was soon averaging a dove or pigeon with every other shot. At one point I made three doubles in a row and killed a seventh bird before missing a cork-screwing pigeon with the second barrel.

"Still conserving 'em?!" shouted the mercenary.

Out of the next flight of Cape turtledove winging across the field, I managed to kill one with my right barrel and two with my left. I glanced over at the mercenary to see whether he'd noticed, but saw instead a puff of dust in front of his blind.

"Shooting them on the ground?" I called, thinking he must have fired at a low flyer.

"Killing a cripple!" he yelled defensively. His tone caught Trevor's attention. I was just learning to distinguish the more common Cape turtledove from the occasional red-eyed dove and laughing dove, and these three from the larger and faster speckled pigeon—a bird the size of our feral pigeon but prettier with a blood-red eye patch and, as it turned out, far tastier—when Trevor marched over to my blind.

"Is that man shooting birds on the ground?" he asked.

"I don't know," I replied. "I've been too busy to watch."

"I thought I saw him shoot one on the ground," said Trevor. Suddenly his eyes narrowed. "Why that son of a . . ." followed by an African expletive. I glanced over in time to see a cloud of dust just drifting away from a bird flopping on the ground twenty yards in front of the mercenary's blind. Another dove veered down and landed by the flapping bird. The mercenary shot it as well.

He evidently didn't know we'd observed him as Trevor marched his way. "How's the American doing?" he called. But as Trevor got close, the mercenary's expansive silhouette began to shrink. I couldn't hear their words, but Trevor was doing most of the talking, and he wasn't discussing the weather. He confiscated the mercenary's gun and marched back to my blind.

"Let's get to the francolin," he said, "before it's too hot for the dogs."

Trevor's pointers were big animals, but not inclined to range far ahead as their American cousins too often do. Whether this was because of their breeding, superior training, the increasing heat, or all of the above, it was pleasant to be able to hunt behind pointers while on foot, rather than have to chase the dogs with Jeeps or gallop after them with horses. It was pleasant, too, to watch the animals work out the contrary scents and to hear the commands given in Zulu by Alfred, the dog handler.

Depending on terrain and the individual bird, francolin behave like chukkar or pheasant. Some will run for the hills and flush wild the moment they sense a dog snuffling behind them. Others run only a short distance until they find cover, then sit so tight you have to tramp them out of hiding.

Like well-oiled machines, the dogs pinned down bird after bird. Also, like a well-oiled machine, I killed every one we flushed.

Trevor was disappointed that we'd not discovered any guineafowl in our francolin hunting, but no one was disappointed by the variety and quality of the shooting. Johan Erasmus, the National Tourist Bureau's regional director, was beaming: his charge (meaning me) was doing what I was expected to do, and Johan himself had fired a shotgun for the first time in his life. One empty box, one badly bruised shoulder later, and he had killed two dove.

"Bet you can't get close enough to kill the dove in that tree," challenged the ever-persistent mercenary, as our group headed back to the vehicles.

Still thinking the indomitable ass was Trevor's friend, I set off to maintain our nation's shotgunning honor. Fortunately, years of jump shooting have taught me the secret of successful bird stalking. Look nonchalant. Look as though the furthest thing from your mind is killing the bird you're approaching, obliquely, if possible. When the dove darted off the limb, I folded it as it came out from under the tree's canopy. At the shot, some thirty-five cackling mines exploded—*kek-kek-kek-krrrrrrr-kek-kek-kek!*— and went churning down the hill.

Guineafowl

"Alfred, take six men and block that corner! You"—meaning the mercenary—"run to the truck and let out the brown dog! You"—meaning me—"come this way, and hurry!"

Striding through the waist-high grass and issuing orders like a field marshal, Trevor was in his element. I trotted along behind until he commanded:

"Wait here! As the birds come over, kill two and mark where they fall until I send one of the boys to pick them up. Then run to where you see Alfred. And don't waste any time about it!" He strode away.

Hunting guinea fowl may seem like a joke to Americans—like hunting wild turkey seems to South Africans. In both cases, people base their attitude on their limited knowledge of the domestic counterpart of the wild species. Yet a wild-helmeted guineafowl bears no more resemblance to his domesticated kith and kin that a wild turkey does to the dull-witted creatures parading around barnyards under the name "turkey."

When the flock of guineafowl went into the air again, I was astonished by how quickly and how high they climbed. I had never seen an American-bred guineafowl fly more than a dozen feet off the ground, and here were some roaring by twenty-five yards up—more than enough altitude to stir the cockles of a pass-shooter's heart.

When the flock saw me, it veered, and I was able to kill only one bird before the others set their wings for the glide down the field.

"Hurry! *@#&*@%! Hurry!" came Trevor's distant voice.

I jogged down the field, trying to watch out for *dongas* (eroded gullies) and *mambas* (nasty snakes). I was supposed to be reassured by Trevor's estimate that he lost no more dogs to snakes than does the average Florida guide, but mambas and cobras strike more fear into my heart than the more familiar diamondback rattler.

I came out of a gully and was suddenly alongside Alfred and a tensely stalking dog.

"Run in!" yelled Trevor.

I charged ahead of the pointer, a guineafowl leaped into the air, and I killed it, although the gun wobbled with my panting.

"Hurry!" yelled Trevor. "You have four to go!"

The next twenty minutes were more like combat than bird hunting. We charged over hill and dale, sometimes firing on the run at flushing birds—as though I were a button-down version of Rambo—sometimes rushing into a tump of grass, only to find the bird had disappeared.

"Hurry! Hurry! Hurry!" yelled Trevor. "Don't let them escape!"

Most of the party hadn't even tried to follow us. After nearly two miles of broken-field running, my sixth and final guineafowl flushed within range, and I nailed it back to earth.

"*Ca! uyashaya lomlunga!*" exclaimed Alfred, and Trevor laughed.

"What does that mean?" I asked.

"Roughly translated: 'Wow! This white man can shoot!'"

Thank Heaven! My gunning could have no higher praise than Alfred's seal of approval. My meager reputation was mended, and I had restored honor to the escutcheon of American outdoor writers in Africa.

On the way back to the truck, we made a slight detour to round out my francolin limit. As this last bird attempted an evasion-and-escape maneuver at the head of a *donga,* I felt almost sorry for it. Guerrilla tactics used by francolin are just not in the same league with those employed by guineafowl. The francolin's tracking, flushing, and killing seemed almost anticlimactic after the workout I'd been through.

That evening, I commandeered the kitchen. South Africans follow two northern European traditions that have no place in a 90° Fahrenheit climate. They serve red wine at room temperature and insist on hanging fowl before plucking and eating them. When Trevor's lovely wife, Colette, refused to cook fresh duck, I herded her and everyone else away from the stove and prepared four large trays of split guineafowl, split francolin, plucked dove and pigeon, and plucked duck. I covered the skinless birds with bacon strips and squeezed oranges over the duck and dove and shoved the rinds into the ducks' cavities. I basted the birds with melted butter and their own juices, and I cooked everything at 375 degrees with the duck staying in the oven longest, perhaps, twenty-five minutes. The dove came out in fifteen minutes; the pigeon stayed in for another five.

The meal was a feast. Even Colette admitted that unhung game *was* tasty and she, along with most of the others, voted the duck "best of show." This was as fine a compliment as Alfred's admiration, for we'd already enjoyed several excellent meals cooked in Colette's kitchen, and her *melktert* (milk tart) will long live in my taste buds' memory.

How to Get There from Here

If you want to hunt South African birds, reservations can be made directly with Trevor Donald Comins, % Game Bird Safaris, P.O. Box 299, Vryheid 3100, Republic of South Africa. Bird hunting begins about the first of May and runs through August. There is no trouble about taking firearms to South Africa so long as arrangements are made in advance, and so long as you pass for Caucasian.

I won't dwell on South Africa's complex racial problems, except to point out that conflicts and killings are confined mostly to the cities and all-black townships. Large numbers of unemployed blacks, lesser numbers of whites dependent on black servants, and the catalytic presence of the press result in periodic eruptions of violence practically unknown in the countryside. If concern for personal safety is the only thing keeping you from visiting South Africa, you'll be safer at Comins's camp than on an American freeway.

Having said that, I cannot leave South Africa without relating the saddest and most unsettling incident of our three-week visit. Ken Garrett and I had gotten up early one morning to accompany one of the crews that check the shark nets protecting Durban's many miles of bathing beaches. Our host was a pimply-faced teenager who picked us up in a small truck at the Maharani Hotel at 4:30 A.M., after which we were taken to a train station to await the arrival of black laborers forbidden to live in the city. We three whites sat in the front with the engine idling while the young driver watched in the rear-view mirror as the truck filled with black men who ran from the trains, jostling and joking as they clambered aboard. There are more men than jobs, and would-be workers must rush from the incoming trains to get a place on a work crew.

On this morning, one man began to run after the truck after we'd already pulled away. In the side mirror, I could see the man straining to catch up, and I could see dark arms reaching out to haul him aboard. The driver was going just fast enough so the runner couldn't catch up. The runner stumbled once and began to give up. The driver slowed down. When the black man began to run again, the driver accelerated to keep ahead.

I glanced at the driver who was watching in the center mirror, without expression, the cat-and-mouse game he'd initiated. I heard shouts of encouragement from the men in the truck, and in the side mirror I could see the runner renewing his efforts. With a burst of speed, he nearly caught an outstretched hand. Then the driver suddenly accelerated, causing the men in back to fall over themselves, and the runner was left standing in the shadows of a street light.

The rest of the morning, the black men pulled nets in sullen silence and the white teenager said nothing and did nothing more than motor slowly from one net to the next. He sat at the console and stared into the sunrise until he was again needed to push the throttle forward.

"Sowing dragon's teeth," I thought, "to be harvested by people unable to understand where so much hatred has come from."

Trevor supplies all meals, accommodations, dogs and dog handlers, plus all the shells you can shoot for $600 a day. (At that price, you shouldn't have to share any part of your hunt with a braggart mercenary!) Trevor supplies 12-gauge shells only, so if you plan to bring your favorite 20-gauge gun for dove and francolin, plan also to pack a case or two of appropriate ammunition. If anyone in your family wants to share your adventures but not the shooting, his or her daily cost is $150.

Nyalaveld Safaris, based in Durban, offers bird shooting in the Orange Free State and Cape Province for less than $200 a day, shells and shotgun included. Or you can blend bird hunting in these same areas with pursuit of springbok (trophy fee: $100) or white-tailed gnu (trophy fee: $450). Many other game mammals are available in other provinces, with nyala and kudu featured in Zululand.

However, the advantage of Trevor Donald Comins's operation is that he can provide dogs on more than sixty leased properties located in prime farming country with ample waterfowl marshes and where francolin and guineafowl thrive on grain crops and find shelter on the many rocky ridges and outcroppings scattered over a magnificent landscape. If you'd rather hunt birds than big game, Comins is your man in South Africa.

When I arrived back in New York, a customs agent asked me what I'd been doing in South Africa.

"Hunting," I replied.

"That right? I've been saving my money to go down there for a crack at leopard or kudu. What'd you get?"

"Birds."

"Birds? But nobody goes all the way to Africa just to shoot birds!"

10

Europe and the UK

Africa springs to mind whenever we think of a continent that has undergone so many political changes that even the names of most of its countries are different from what we learned as twelve-year-old students of geography. Yet the continent of Europe has experienced even greater social upheavals since *Field & Stream*'s late, great roving editor, Van Campen Heilner, wandered there in the 1930s. And while Africa is today far easier to travel around and reach than it was fifty years ago, travel in eastern Europe is more tentative for a modern American wildfowler than it was for Heilner.

For some time I'd wanted to visit Hungary. My father's mother was born there. A wildfowling trip to Hungary would have given me time and opportunity to look up her limb of the family tree. I would also be following in Heilner's footsteps; he wrote some powerful prose about Hungary, beginning, "We came down out of the snow-clad passes of Czechoslovakia and it was Spring in Budapest." *Hortobagy* has been an alluring name for me from the moment I read Heilner's description of the plain in his *Book on Duck Shooting* as "one of the most romantic wildfowling spots on the face of the earth!"

Heilner introduced profile goose decoys to Hungary. The local guides had never heard of such things and because those guides, like local guides everywhere, thought they knew all there was to know about wildfowling, the Hungarians assured Heilner that his silhouettes wouldn't work. Naturally, because the greater and lesser whitefronts found on the plain, plus "a scattering of bean geese, an occasional greylag and very rarely some redbreasts," had never seen silhouette decoys before, they "worked like a charm."

Heilner concluded his chapter on Hungary with the observation that "all things pass, especially the years of one's life. And before it's too late I'm going back. Back to my Csarda, back to my gypsy music, back to my 'vast emptiness,' my Hortobagy!"

Heilner never went back. Nazi and Hungarian armies began dismembering Czechoslovakia even as he was departing. Yet even the Hungary Heilner knew was an illusion. The political winds that carried the make-shift nation into World War II and eventually behind the Iron Curtain had been blowing long before Heilner arrived on the Hortobagy Plain with his goose silhouettes. There is no present tense for Hungary; those who believe in Communism dream only of the future, while those who experience it dream only of the past.

When Heilner visited eastern Europe, he improvised his shooting opportunities by being there. Today all shooting is controlled and rigidly regulated by the state. My inquiries about hunting geese on the Hortobagy Plain were met with amusement or assurances that I didn't really want to try such "undependable" sport. Hungarian estate managers are geared up for *processing* bird *shooters,* not for *serving* wildfowl *hunters.*

Merely trying to get basic information about travel and accommodations in Hungary was a nightmare. The only person able to make decisions at the New York office of Hungarian Airlines was never in. During a single day, I was told by three different people that "she just stepped out for a minute," "she's at lunch," and "she's on vacation and won't be back for two weeks." I persisted and finally managed to reach her just before she did leave for a month-long holiday during the busy spring booking season. (Presumably nothing would be decided while she was gone.) She explained that there were three flights a week between London and Budapest, and that one of her staff could arrange ground transportation around Budapest. Then with a thickening of her accent, she told me that if I planned to travel outside the city, I would be strictly on my own; she would "not be held responsible."

"Responsible for what?" I asked.

"Getting lost," she said. "Some people come to Hungary and get lost."

She may not have meant that quite the way it sounded, but I felt an indefinable chill when I heard her say that I could "get lost" behind the Iron Curtain. After letting the lady's words worry me for a week, I decided I'd done things backwards. I would first get my visa and a gun permit from the Hungarian Embassy. (Mere formalities, surely.) With a visa in my hand, Hungarian officials would never allow me to get lost!

The Hungarian Embassy, however, was equally mysterious. No matter what time of the day or night I called, I heard the same recorded message advising me that the embassy's hours were 8:00 A.M. to 5:00 P.M., and that I should call back then. I called back at 8:30 in the morning, 10:00, noon, at 2:00 in the afternoon, and at 4:00. It made no difference. The recording was always polite but firm on the point that I must call back between 8:00 A.M. and 5:00 P.M.

Meanwhile, my ever-resourceful wife called a Hungarian tourist agent in New York and asked behind what unmarked door we might find someone who knew someone else who might be able to provide me with a visa and gun permit. The lady at the other end of the line gave my wife an obscure address in New Jersey and then, with a line right out of a 1940s film featuring Peter Lorre, warned that "dese tings somedimes dake avhile."

Clearly—my grandmother's connection notwithstanding—Hungary and I were not destined to see each other. My frustration with Slavic officialdom reminded me of Mexico—but with a difference. In Mexico, incompetence stems from corruption and laziness; in Hungary, it seems to result from a love of mystery coupled with a reluctance to accept responsibility for anything that might alter routine. I finally decided that entrusting my life and my Browning to a country whose embassy never answered its calls was not in my best interests, nor in the best interest of my family and my shotgun. So I switched my destination that fall to a friendlier and more familiar land, the United Kingdom. A shooting trip there is a pilgrimage to the "old country," a renewal of faith in the concept and traditions of sportsmanship.

Back to Britain

The only referee or judge in sport is the participant's *conscience.* You don't shoot a sitting bird because you're afraid of a man in a striped shirt yelling "Foul!" You don't shoot a sitting bird because sporting tradition dictates that a sitting bird is not "fair game," and because your conscience knows that you compound regret with each unethical kill.

Such traditions are unique to the English-speaking Union. Trevor Comins may have been born and brought up in Africa, but he takes his ideals of sportsmanship from Britain and the United States—not from Latin countries where killing, not sportsmanship, is the principal objective when you take your gun afield.

Where there are differences between the British and American sporting systems, they stem from our contrasting characterization of the renegade hunter. British poachers pit themselves against landowners, while American poachers pit themselves against the state. Since the U.S. government has formulated many shooting regulations irrelevant to the perpetuation of waterfowl, American sportsmen are somewhat schizophrenic in actively supporting state game agencies in their war on upland poachers, but in doing little to aid federal agents in their war on waterfowl poachers. Arbitrary waterfowling laws and their capricious enforcement by U.S. federal agents have effectively turned American waterfowling into a contest between them and us, with *us* defined as anyone not wearing a federal badge. The end result has been a gradual decline of sportsmanship due to the increasingly limited role that conscience is allowed to play in outdoor recreation.

Laws never work unless people in the situations for which the laws were designed want them to work. Once federal authority supplanted local custom and personal choice in such petty matters as the size of one's gun or shot, or the number of rounds to be fired at one loading, the government inspired the very people who derive satisfaction from subverting the law.

Every thoughtful person in the history of conservation has observed the same thing: higher authority is needed to establish seasons and limits based on the actual needs of game. Beyond that, in matters of moral behavior, the government has no role. Outdoor recreation is *re-creation*—a matter of fun and family tradition, not of governmental mandate. The feds legitimately tell us *what* and *when* we can hunt, but they must not tell us *how* if we hope to see shooting sports continue as something more than the killing of pen-raised birds.

Moonlighting in Scotland

I crouched behind a seawall and listened to the muttering of mallards and the whistling of wigeon and teal resting on the mud flats several hundred yards away. The sun had long since set, and my companions and I were waiting for the twilight to deepen and trigger the birds' impulse to fly to the darkening fields behind us. We hoped to pass-shoot the ducks when they whispered like shadows close overhead.

This is no poacher's confession, but the start of a legitimate outing I made one October on Scotland's Beauly River estuary. British wildfowlers operate under more moral personal standards than their American counterparts, so they feel less need for moralistic gunning laws. The time of day or night is unimportant to British hunters so long as the unwritten rules of fair chase are observed.

When I told my host, Lachie Smith, that in the United States we were prohibited from hunting waterfowl after sunset, he was astonished: "Why, you miss half the beauty of wildfowling!"

His friend and our companion for the evening, Edinburgh physician Ralph Pakenham, asked, "If you can't shoot after sunset, when does the ordinary working man have a chance to hunt wildfowl?"

It was an interesting question, for Scotland, like my adopted state of Virginia, has a blue law prohibiting Sunday shooting. Furthermore, many Scots, like my neighbors at home, work on Saturday mornings. If the Scots were unable to shoot the evening flights, they would be reduced, like many of my less fortunate Virginia neighbors, to half a day of hunting per week.

Another feature of British wildfowling that amazes moralistic, but frequently less moral, American hunters is the British refusal to ban certain kinds of guns and loads for wildfowling. If a shooter is convinced that the only proper way to bring down high-flying geese is with a 4-gauge cannon loaded with buckshot, that's his folly. He'll spend most of his time educating and not hitting the birds while developing a severe case of bursitis in the bargain.

Furthermore, if a chap decides to use an unplugged semi-automatic under the theory that if he puts enough lead into the air, a bird will eventually fall, there is no law to stop the heedless shooter. But there is widespread ethical censorship against using such warlike weapons. As a result, semi-automatics and pump guns are rarely encountered on the British foreshore.

On the other hand, if someone wants to try the generally fruitless pursuit of waterfowling with a punt gun capable of firing more than a pound of shot, he is perfectly free to have a go at this uncomfortable, rarely productive, often hazardous, but strangely rewarding sport.

Lachie Smith showed me a magnificent punt gun owned by Lord Lovat with the name "Iron Duke" inscribed on the barrel; it was stored in one corner of an eighteenth-century salmon smokehouse. Unlike American punt guns, which were made for market use and were, therefore, crudely wrought, British punt guns are works of master craftsmen. For that reason, as well as the romance of the sport, Lachie hoped to take the Iron Duke out for one last hurrah before hauling it up to Lord Lovat's castle overlooking the Beauly River for permanent display.

Puntgunning

In November 1985, I visited the headquarters of the British Association of Shooting and Conservation (BASC) where I picked up a brochure on "Puntgunning—A Fact Sheet About the Sport" and later visited its author, John Richards, at his home overlooking the Dee Estuary in northern Wales.

Although British puntgunning is often depicted as a sport of the past, dying out as the old-timers who still practice it die out, its most passionate proponents are young men—which makes sense when you consider that lying in an open boat on a winter estuary for many hours a day is hardly something that would appeal to older people increasingly aware of their own mortality.

John Richards is actually closer to middle age than youth, having been born in 1944, but he has a young man's energy and enthusiasm for the sport and served as the executive director of the Waterfowlers Association of Great Britain and Ireland (WAGBI) before it was absorbed into BASC several years ago.

John estimates there are between thirty and forty active puntgunners in the UK—"people who get out more than five or six times a year and another twenty or thirty people with some equipment who do so occasionally."

Tony Jackson, then editor of Britain's *Shooting Times*, had arranged my visit with Richards, with the understanding that if he decided I was acceptable company, I would go puntgunning with him. Unfortunately, with nothing definite, I allowed more certain prospects to fill my schedule. After Richards and I visited for several hours, he decided I probably wouldn't trip over my own boots, tip over his punt, or otherwise embarrass him, but by that time it was too late. I had to rejoin my shooting party elsewhere in Wales for an evening flight of mallard.

As I was leaving, we tarried at his front gate so that John could show me a flock of 9,000 pintail resting far out on the sands of the Dee estuary.

"That's what you'll be missing," he said.

"With my luck, I'd be missing them in any event," I replied.

Still, we'd talked, and I'd learned much about a sport I still hope to try one day.

"Puntgunners are the most passionate of wildfowlers," said John. "No person content with taking occasional shots from behind a seawall knows birds or the tides like we do. We sacrifice jobs, even marriages, to drink deeply of experiences that ordinary men can't even imagine."

Richards would not discuss any of his better days; he feels strongly that the less said or written about puntgunning the better.

"There'll be plenty of time to write memoirs when the sport's outlawed, as I fear it will be someday soon by bloody fools who have no idea what they're talking about!"

During the 1984-85 season, John was out in his punt forty times but fired its gun only five times. "You don't take a shot unless the number of targets equals or exceeds the number of ounces of lead you've loaded," he explained. "If I have a gun loaded with eight ounces of shot, I'll not fire at a flock smaller than eight birds. Since one of the guns I use loads thirty-two ounces of shot, there must be at least thirty-two birds in the flock, or I'll not aim at all.

"Puntgunning has a reputation for terrible slaughter," he continued, "but no puntgunner, no matter how dedicated, will kill as many ducks in a season as a frequent shoulder-gunner who kills his quarry only one bird at a time. No form of bird shooting is more truly a sport than puntgunning."

Nonetheless, everyone wants to hear about classic shots, and I urged John to give me some stories or figures. What is his average bag per season?

John would say nothing but referred me to his WAGBI brochure which states, rather dryly: "The report published in 1941 ['Facts Affecting the General Status of Wild Geese and Wild Ducks, Cambridge University Press] extracted information from a wide range of practicing puntsmen and found that the average bag per punt per year was as low as one in a bad season and up to fifteen wildfowl in a good season, for a wildfowler spending a reasonable proportion of the season afloat. But the report points out that when referring to 'a reasonable proportion of the season afloat,' the puntgunner has constraints imposed upon him that do not apply to the shoulder-gunner. The type of craft used places great restrictions on his sport; a gunning punt having only a few inches of free board can be positively dangerous afloat when the weather conditions are rough. In addition, the sport can only be pursued when the tides are at a certain height at a certain time. In general terms this means only two to three possible days during the fortnightly tide cycle when the puntgunner can go afloat in one particular coastal estuary.

"In 1967 the Wildfowlers Association of Great Britain and Ireland carried out an extensive analysis of bag records made by known puntgunners. Their survey took the form of sworn statements and revealed that an average of 8.6 ducks per shot were accounted for, but less than one shot was achieved per outing. Undoubtedly the publicity which has been given to the very rare large shot has led to the popular misconception that a puntgunner's bag is very considerably greater than the 1967 quoted figure."

The only hardcore information John would verbally share with me was that the best time to puntgun is during overcast, frigid weather when the birds sit shoulder to shoulder on the sands. On nice, bright days, the punt shows up too clearly, and the birds are alert and scattered.

The American puntgunner of yore sold everything he killed. By contrast, although wild ducks and shorebirds are legally sold in the UK, the ethics of British puntgunners forbid them from selling their game, as well as from hunting at night. So great is the British disdain for harassing birds on their roosting or resting grounds that some local clubs have rules against jump shooting—one of America's most popular ways to pursue ducks. As previously noted, night shooting is popular, but only for ducks and geese flighting from the sea to feed in fields. Once the birds return to the estuaries to roost and rest, they are protected, not by law, but by custom that recognizes it's in the wildfowlers' best interest to provide the birds with a sanctuary.

Management by Consent

All upland game is sold in the UK. It belongs to the landowner on whose property it's killed. By contrast, although ducks and shorebirds, including whimbrel and golden plover, are legal to sell, geese cannot be sold, because wildfowlers petitioned the government to take them off the poultry lists. Geese are regarded as trophies and jewels in the crown of wildfowling. They are also susceptible to great slaughter, especially under icy conditions, when thousands of birds for miles around flight to one of the few remaining food sources in a shire. When such conditions prevail, the wildfowlers themselves petition the government to close the season and rally fellow hunters to provide food for the starving birds. Nothing offends the sensibilities of British sportsmen more than to see a worthy quarry taken advantage of.

Since the waterfowl season along the coast of Scotland extends from the first of September to the middle of February, and since there are no daily or seasonal limits, I asked Lachie Smith and Dr. Pakenham whether they knew of any instances of overshooting. Yes, they were embarrassed to admit, there had been one incident several years previous involving a lad who killed over twenty geese in a single evening. Since an acceptable bag limit is determined by how many birds a hunter can comfortably carry across several miles of fields and mud flats to reach his car, two or three geese are all the average British sportsman aspires to in an outing. However, this greedy fellow came out asking for assistance to find and haul out more than twenty birds! He was treated to such scorn and anger (and maybe a little envy), he hasn't visited the area since.

In the USA, hunting ends too often justify killing means. American hunters will sometimes use every method within, and a few without, the law to get all the birds "they're entitled to"—as though duck stamps were food stamps. The result is that most hunters and all wardens seem to think that the successful duck or goose shooter is, *prima facie,* an illegal shooter.

The British feel that a few broadly based and enforceable laws work better than a mosaic of arbitrary and complicated ones. Indeed, the most revealing fact of British political life is that the UK does not have a written constitution. Not all the state and federal constitutions, and armies of lawyers and policemen, are enough to keep an intrinsically outlaw society like the United States in line, while a gentleman's agreement and a handshake are more than sufficient for the ordinary Englishman.

Of course there are scofflaws in Britain as well as the United States. But Americans are obsessed with surface morality in a way that makes a socially conscious people like the British uncomfortable. American hunters are always asking themselves, "Is this or that *legal?*" while British sportsmen ask whether or not it is *right.* Aware, and possibly ashamed, of the fact that many of our ancestors were the misfits and malcontents of Europe, we disguise our moral anxiety with a super-abundance of moralistic laws that have turned American society into one of the most legalistic on earth. Such a system invariably gives power to amoral people who know how to manipulate the law—the kind of people and the very system that our ancestors sought to escape when they came to America.

I have a non-wildfowling anecdote to illustrate this contrast in British and American legal attitudes. The morning that the director of UK Field & Stream Ltd. (no relation to the American magazine) and I were going to pick up some friends at Gatwick Airport, Richard overslept and tried to make up for lost time on the Motorway. The Motorway's speed limit is seventy miles per hour—at that time an astonishing limit for many Americans who believe fifty-five mph is fast enough. My host soon had his Range Rover up to more than one hundred miles per hour and only slowed to eighty when we whizzed past a police car. This, too, was astonishing. While American state troopers will allow you to hit sixty mph in a fifty-five-mph stretch of highway, they'll nail you with a hefty fine if their radar—how our cops love their radar!—determines you were driving sixty-five plus.

When we zipped past a third police car not seen in time for Richard to decelerate, my host predicted he'd be stopped. Sure enough, the cop car's blue "trouble bubble" flashed on, and we were soon pulled over at the side of the road. A policeman came back and proceeded to tongue-lash Richard, pointing out that one fatal accident had already occurred that morning on the Motorway and that Richard had been timed at better than thirty mph *over* the posted limit. The officer warned Richard to drive more slowly, returned to his vehicle, and left.

I gaped. Richard would have made an American state trooper's week, if not his career! Yet Richard got nothing more severe than a tongue-lashing. Why?

"I was driving too fast," Richard admitted, "but I was not driving recklessly. The policeman knew that. His job is to protect public safety, not to raise revenue by giving out tickets."

I was impressed. By reserving the full brunt of the law for matters of criminal intent and severe negligence, British enforcement officers leave more room for conscience and common sense to prevail. No one could condone Richard's excessive speed, but the police had decided they could better reform him without humiliating him.

And so with British wildfowling. You can kill as many ducks or geese, by day or night, and using most any size shotgun you like, but ethical good sense imposes a personal limit of whatever you can comfortably walk home with.

As the UK develops closer ties with continental Europe regarding a broad range of activities affecting resource management, I fear the British may let their wonderful common sense and irony be overwhelmed by more literal-minded tendencies to seek legalistic solutions for every wildlife problem. The compulsion to force some people to do what an uninformed but influential majority thinks is right tends to turn ethical molehills into moralistic mountains, many of which are impossibly steep.

A particularly sad case involves the long-billed curlew that was taken off the game list several years ago after bird protectionists persuaded a majority of the Members of Parliament that the species was "too pretty" to be shot. The decision is a triple slap at British wildfowlers. For one thing, curlew are wonderfully abundant in the British Isles, and there is not the least scientific reason for total protection. Second, complete protection implies that wildfowlers do not admire the elegance of the curlew as much as the preservationists do. Finally, and most important, whenever British birds were taken off the game list in the past, wildfowlers were always the ones to sponsor the move. Eiders, for example, have long been protected in the UK, not because they're rare, but because British wildfowlers agreed to protect the birds in order to protect the eider-down industries of Scandinavia and Iceland. In exchange, the Scandinavians and Icelanders agree to protect important British quarry species like the pinkfoot and greylag geese that breed in those northern lands.

The shelduck *(Tadorna tadorna)* has been protected for well over a century in Great Britain, not because of any legislation to that effect—nor even the view that the shelduck is not an edible species—but because the eggs of this cavity-nester were once an important source of food along the Dutch coast. Dutch watermen even created artificial nesting sites for the birds and took eggs from them as they laid them, but always leaving at least one egg per nest.

British fowlers respected the Dutch interest in shelducks and didn't shoot them. Sir Ralph Payne-Gallwey noted in 1875, "the shelducks are not, of course, allowed to be killed, and many times have they disappointed us of a [punt] shot by mixing with large numbers of other fowl, so that to fire at the mass would have proved fatal to some of the protected egg-supplying birds."

The important point is that the prohibition against killing shelduck was a matter of custom, not of law. The total protection of long-billed curlew, by contrast, is a purely moralistic gesture. And because it's a law without sense to British wildfowlers, it's a law they're not likely to uphold. One evening while sitting on the Scottish foreshore, I had several curlew come flighting from the west and pitch on the mud beside me. It was the first season of the closure, and while I regretted the timing, I honored the law and didn't shoot. When I rejoined my hosts an hour later at the seawall, two of the three said I should have killed one of the birds anyway. One man argued I should have done it "to spite the bastards who'd stop all wildfowling, if they could!" Such is the bitter fruit of moralistic legislation.

Sporting Mates

Despite the increasing appearance of slobs on the Slobs, and anti-hunters in politics, the UK is still a nation where sportsmanship prevails. Most of the dawns and dusks I have spent on British foreshores have been rewarded with a single duck or none. No matter. I've enjoyed my comrades with the brisk or burred accents and the opportunity to hunt bewitching times of day forbidden in the States. I also liked being in a land where sportsmen and naturalists are respected by their countrymen. I spent one memorable afternoon with Denys J. Watkins-Pitchford, better known to the readers of his outdoor books as "B.B." He has written or edited more than sixty books and illustrated many others. He lives with his daughter and a Canadian brother in a refurbished, circular toll house in the garden of which he raises endangered Iris butterflies and worries that the great blue herons that visit his pond are taking too many fish. To commemorate his eightieth birthday, the British Broadcasting Corporation did a television series on his many contributions to the public's understanding of nature and barely finished it in time for him to get away to join two gunning cronies for their annual goose hunt in Scotland.

While we were at lunch—roast beef and Yorkshire pudding, of course—B.B. paid two other British sportsmen (my friend, Arthur Cadman, and Douglas MacDougall, the author of *Goose Fever*) the highest compliment one wildfowler can give another. He noted they were experts at using the least amount of local cover for camouflage.

Cadman, with whom I've hunted greylags in Scotland, was at one time the manager of England's New Forest. In recognition of his innovative work there, he was awarded the Order of the British Empire (OBE), a significant honor personally bestowed by the Queen. In American society, comparable awards are usually reserved for the rich or influential in appreciation of their having shared their wealth or influence, or in anticipation of their doing so. An innovative naturalist who is not also wealthy or politically influential has little chance of receiving our society's thanks, at least not while he or she is alive. Although we have a Rachel Carson Council and a John Muir Institute for Environmental Studies, both these people were safely dead when the foundations bearing their names were started. It is unimaginable that any American who lives for wildlife—an equivalent of Britain's Sir Peter Scott or, decades ago, Canada's Sir Charles G. D. Roberts—should ever be honored with a national commendation comparable to knighthood.

Although I didn't see Sir Peter Scott on my last visit to England, I'd visited with him years before when he'd passed through Washington on a fund-raising tour on behalf of the World Wildlife Fund. I believe I annoyed him when, rather than show up with a copy of his autobiography, *The Eye of the Wind*—my copy being at the farm—I brought Van Campen Heilner's *A Book on Duck Shooting* and asked Scott to autograph the page showing him about to go puntgunning. He knew the book well enough so that after regarding the page a moment and commenting that "those were good days," he turned back to the photograph of him touching up one of the profile decoys that Heilner had brought from America.

Scott remarked as he wrote his name and date, "I'd rather be remembered this way."

Because I've hunted with Arthur Cadman, whose books include *Shouldergunning for Duck, Goose Shooting,* and *Tales of a Wildfowler,* I have especially fond memories as well as the highest regard for this excellent gentleman. He's a superb shot, a fact all the more remarkable for the cane he uses to hobble down to the foreshore. One morning I watched him from a less productive place of concealment half a mile down the dike kill four extremely high greylag geese with five shots. Unbeknownst to me, two wildfowling thieves were hiding near Arthur, and they stole two of his geese, calculating correctly that Cadman couldn't pursue them with an arthritic hip.

Arthur has a wonderful way of making his hunting lessons stick. An advocate of gloves for all wildfowling, regardless of weather, he dramatizes their importance by holding an imaginary pair of binoculars to his face and then wriggling his pale fingers: "Every time you move ungloved hands," he teaches, "you wave bye-bye to the birds."

When my hunting comrade and Canadian waterfowl biologist, Norman Seymour, went to Britain for a year to work and study I gave him Arthur's address with the hope they'd be able to share some dawns and dusks and that Norman would get the goose that eluded me on my last trip over to see Arthur. The two men shared several enviable days together, and Norman shot more than one greylag. He went on to hunt ducks and geese all over the UK and then traveled to the Continent to see what it offered. Since he now knows more about the contemporary western Europe wildfowling scene than anyone else, I'll simply quote one of his letters describing an excursion:

"Everything was *frozen* and especially cold in England where it seems houses are little more than a means of getting out of the wind! A friend picked me up at Heathrow and 1,700 miles (by car) and eight days later, dropped me back there. We did a whirlwind visit to Brussels to meet with the Secretary General of the Federation of Hunting Associations of the ECC—I'm now scientific advisor to the association—on to Brugge, Ghent, and then went into frozen Holland where we met with biologists and administrators of the Dutch hunting association. They were delightful!

"I had only two mornings that weren't burdened with business, but we made the most of them. My hosts took me hunting Siberian whitefronted geese about 50 miles from the Dutch city of Groningen in the north. There were 400,000 white-fronts, pinks, bean, and barnacle geese. All but the barnies were legal quarry. There were also good numbers of wigeon and mallard. The whole mass was agitated and on the move, looking for new feeding areas, since the snow had covered up so much of the habitat.

"A bit of background: There are no bag limits; all goose shooting ends at 10 AM; #5 (12 bore) is the maximum shot size allowed; live goose decoys are legal; season runs from September 1 through January 21 (though geese arrive no earlier than mid-December); sale of birds legal and limited market hunting prevails.

"The idea behind the restrictions on shot and gun sizes is to get the birds close before shooting. The idea behind the 10 AM closure is to minimize disturbance. What all this means to the shooter is that the birds are not at all spooky. We had literally hundreds of birds well within my idea of a good range that my host declined to shoot at!

"The greatest excitement for me was that we were using flying decoys. My host had raised the decoys (all white-fronts) from eggs, and he had four family groups. As you know, geese maintain very close family bonds. The male decoys are tethered in the field in front of the blind at a range where the shooting is to occur—20 to 25 yards, no more! The females and young are taken into the hide (alias, blind), and this is the stimulus for every bird to set up the most unbelievable clamor to try to locate one another. This certainly gets the attention of the wild birds which look, but usually continue on their way. That is, continue until the young birds in the hide are thrown into the air whereupon they fly about in search of their parents. Meanwhile the adult females are allowed to wander out of the hide. With all this activity, the wild birds come in as if on elastics!

"Our first morning was unsuccessful for some reason. We had, perhaps, 300 to 400 birds within 60 yards, but only one goose was shot. But the second morning was quite different. Snow had covered everything, and many birds had moved out. What flocks remained were really looking for food, and our decoys were just what they wanted to see. Every time my host lofted a bird, we had a little bunch come to us. We shot (two guns: a double and an o/u) ten birds in half an hour and decided that was quite enough—but we could have had 25 geese by 10 o'clock! Every bird was a clean kill at that close range, except for one runner which shouldn't have been touched."

Clearly, the Dutch have their wildfowling act together—except for one ingredient. Like their legalistic cousins in America, Dutch hunters want to codify certain aspects of the wildfowling experience, including maximum shot size. Indeed, the Dutch, Danes, and Swedes are currently debating whether the largest allowable shot should be number 4, 5, or 6. Once a number is selected and made law, local hunting clubs will find little point in teaching novice members the reasoning behind the customary use of small shot because the reasoning will no longer matter. What's law is law, and enforcement agents will not be concerned with how the laws got on the books—only that they're there and must be abided by.

What are the values of a wildfowling tradition controlled by conscience and not law?

Douglas MacDougall touched on them in *Goose Fever* when, after a successful salmon fishing trip to Scotland, he pondered why it was that wildfowling was still the most noble sport of all. Besides the fact that fishing is "hardly energetic and vigorous enough," MacDougall missed "the spacious freedom one enjoys when out after geese."

"On the Tweed," he said, "I was confined to the length of the river we had hired—a narrow ribbon of water perhaps a mile long. When wildfowling one feels almost as free and unrestricted as the geese themselves: all the coasts and estuaries below high-water mark are free, and one can often pursue the geese inland for the mere asking of permission from the local farmer. . . .

"This freedom in wildfowling applies to time as well as to place. One can chase geese at dawn and dusk throughout the day and even sometimes in the middle of the night under the moon. Salmon fishing seems to be much more regulated in every way."

Wildfowling in North America has become as regulated as salmon fishing in Britain. Yet American wildfowlers persist in believing that the cure for each new wildfowling problem is another law. We do not see that it's the very lack of complex hunting codes that gives the British wildfowler his freedom and, simultaneously, his greater responsibility to the game and to the unwritten rules of fair chase.

I pray the British never take their sporting traditions for granted and permit wildfowling to deteriorate into the pathetic game of "cops and hunters" it too often seems to be in the States. There may always be an England, but will there always be the grand unfettered sport of British wildfowling?

— 11 —
USSR

Hunting with the Cossacks

Wildfowlers have mixed feelings about low-flying jets booming over a marsh. On one hand, we dislike their noisy invasion of our privacy. On the other hand, we frequently benefit from the flocks of birds stirred up by their rolling thunder. But when the passing planes are MiG-23s, so close you can see the pilots as they bank slightly to see you, the concussion of their flight dramatizes the fact that you really are in Russia hunting ducks and geese.

The MiGs were paired, practicing low-level assaults from a base on the other side of the Sea of Azov, just the way F-14s periodically rip over my rooftop at home near the Chesapeake. But while my local F-14s generally stay above 200 feet, the MiGs were so low that had they barrel-rolled, their wingtips would have clipped half-mile furrows through the phragmites reeds surrounding us.

It seemed remarkable that no ducks or geese were killed when they flushed in fright from the roar of the passing jets. But the planes were almost out of sight by the time their sound exploded in the marsh behind them, and the wildfowl jumped into empty airspace. Familiar with what is probably a regular event over the flat terrain of Cossackland, most of the birds swirled around briefly before settling down elsewhere in the marsh.

A few flocks, however, stayed airborne. But then there were always a few flocks airborne somewhere over that marsh. A dozen birds were so far away downwind, I couldn't tell their species, only that they were ducks. My guide had already given up on them and was looking around the horizon for closer quarry.

Nothing ventured, nothing gained. I gave the distant ducks a hi-ball call. The birds must never before have heard a human imitate one of their kind, for in response to my less-than-perfect effort, three of the birds banked into such steep turns, they might have been using their feet to back-pedal as well as their wings.

With the trio turned, the other nine swung and followed. I called and chuckled to bring what I now saw were mallards closer, but I did as much for my own pleasure as to reassure birds already locked onto our combination of live and rubber decoys. As soon as the two live hen mallards on the water could see their wild kin over the reeds, they joined me in welcoming the free-flying birds. Our three live greylag geese decoys also got in the act with a crescendo of honks.

It was an irresistible invitation. Without even circling, the leading trio of mallards began slip-sliding into the stool. I killed the two drakes and left the hen to protest this insult to her love-life as she climbed out of range.

One of the dead drakes nearly landed on a live decoy. The hen squawked in surprise before indignantly pecking at the floating corpse.

The surviving ducks flared and disappeared over the phragmites. No matter. Three new groups of birds appeared on the horizon. I called the nearest bunch. I was working them around when a cluster of teal corkscrewed over the decoys and were gone so fast, I was still trembling with adrenalin when I straightened to kill a gadwall and miss another. You know it's a great day in the morning when you have the excuse of too many ducks to blame for less-than-perfect shooting!

Although it was 10:00 A.M., the birds were still trading on every horizon just as they had at dawn. I'd long since overcome my nervousness at being one of the first American writers to hunt ducks in the Soviet Union. But like the Russian naturalist, Mikhail Prishvin, when I first started, I'd imagined that "all my hunting stories were being put to the test. What if it turned out that I was just a fraud—a hunter on paper! What was more, if I was a fraud of a hunter I was sure to be a fraud of a writer as well."

Prishvin came through his trial by scrutiny with flying colors, and so had I. The Cossacks had never before seen or heard humans who could outcall their live decoys, and their on-going amazement at my calling fortunately obscured the fact that I missed some remarkably easy shots. I knew I'd finally passed muster when I killed a particularly long wigeon that spun out of the sky like a maple seed. The guides' collective "Ahhh!" was their seal of approval.

I never relished visiting a Communist country, especially Mother Russia. Indeed, the very idea reminded me of the joke about how many WASPs it takes to plan a trip to Israel. The answer is four: one to suggest it, and the other three to say "What?!" "Where?!" and "Why?!"

Communism does not favor individuals. It believes that ordinary people have little or no ability to make decisions for themselves. Everything is planned by committee and done in groups. When my companion, Bagley Walker, and I tried to see the Bolshoi Ballet, we couldn't get tickets because tickets are sold to foreigners only when they're part of a tour; or by scalpers at the theater, half of whom, we were warned, are government agents there to undermine the scalpers' enterprise by arresting anyone attempting to buy an unauthorized ticket.

Perestroika is no substitute for initiative. Another example: there are four doors at the main entrance of Moscow's famed, but pathetically stocked, Gum's Department Store. Bagley and I found only one door used with the result that dozens of people were lined up in the cold outside. I hate lines, especially senseless ones. I opened one of the other doors. The Russians glanced around nervously, perhaps thinking that the police would soon be there to take me away for questioning. Nothing happened. A few of the younger Moscovites tried the new door. Nothing happened to them. Most, however, continued waiting in the one tried-and-true line.

Not all Russians are as submissive as those Moscovites, and the nation's best wildfowling is found in the homeland of its most independent people. Indeed, one wonders if the wild spirit of the Cossacks was not inspired in part by the wildfowl that flock each fall to the wetland steppes lying between the Don and Kuban rivers.

The Cossacks first appear in history in the fifteenth century when no other Christian tribe in the region would stand against the invading Tartars. The Cossacks were part-farmers, part-horsemen who faced the enemy, not in pallisaded towns where the Tartars could have starved them into submission, but in cavalry units that harried the huge and unwieldy enemy army whenever it tried to move or rest.

The Cossacks became the principal reason the Moslem faith never spread north of the Black Sea. After Cossack cavalry smashed the Turks in two late-eighteenth-century wars, Catherine the Great curbed their self-sufficiency and corrupted their freedom by turning the Cossacks into Czarist Russia's privileged military caste. Vast plains of fertile land that had previously been held in common were privatized for the benefit of the ruling officers.

During the civil war of 1918–1920, the majority of Cossacks remained loyal to the Czar and fought the Soviet armies. Defeated and stripped of their privileges by Lenin, they were forcibly collectivized by Stalin. Had the conquering German armies of 1940 shown the slightest courtesy to the Cossacks and Ukrainians, the Germans would have been embraced as liberators. Instead, Nazi ruthlessness provoked a take-no-prisoner policy among many southern Russians who became fearsome enemies of the Wehrmacht.

The Cossacks may not boast of a Bolshoi or a Gum's, but they have something infinitely greater: some of the blackest and richest soil on earth. Only the pampas of Argentina and the prairies of North America can be compared with the tillable steppes of southern Russia. And just as the American prairies once boasted the greatest numbers of wildfowl in the world, Argentina and the steppes lying east of the Sea of Azov compete for that title today.

American sportsmen once made pilgrimages to Cairo, Illinois, and Stuttgart, Arkansas—not to tour local museums but to hunt seemingly endless flights of ducks and geese. Likewise today, no one goes to Rostov or Krasnodar to see the local war memorials. They go to see and share the last, best wildfowling in the northern hemisphere.

Clouds of primarily mallard *(krjakva)* pour across the marshes, but mixed with generous numbers of—in descending order of abundance— Eurasian teal *(chirok treskoonok)*, shoveler *(shirokonos)*, gadwall *(sivach)*, Eurasian wigeon *(krasnogolovaga)*, pintail *(shilofost)*, pochard *(nyroca)*, and even such exotica as ferruginous duck (also *nyroca*—and in this species' case, its correct scientific name; otherwise, *nyroca* means "diving duck" in Russian and is used generically for all members of the Tribe Aythyini).

Then there are the geese, streaming flocks of greater and lesser white-fronts *(kazarka)* and greylag (also, *kazarka*), and scattered families of the most beautiful goose of all, the red-breast.

My attempt to list all the names of local waterfowl was hobbled by my rudimentary Russian, and by the Cossacks' lack of scientific understanding of their different species. In the case of geese, for example, our guides thought that local birds (except the red-breast) represented just one species. Lesser white-fronts were believed to be young birds, while greylag geese were adult males and greater white-fronts, adult females. The fact that immature white-fronts of either race lack the speckle-bellies of the adults indicated to the Russians that the "babies" may vary in size (immature white-fronted geese of both races), but that some inherit more of their "papas'" (greylag) genes, while other "babies" (mature lesser white-fronts) inherit more of their "mamas'" (mature greater white-front) genes.

After thirty minutes of trying to get past the *kazarka* stage and being pitied by my hosts for my apparent feeble-mindedness, I gave up and used the more usual Russian forms of *goos* for one goose (regardless of species), and *gooséy* for geese. (One duck is an *ootka*, while two or more are *ootkéy*.)

I never did discover the Russian name for the red-breasted goose. The Cossacks, however, know one when they see one. And they know that no one should be seeing one of these rare and endangered birds in hand. A member of the Finnish party at the camp the week before Bagley and I were there mistakenly shot a red-breasted goose. The Russians made the man pay a fine and the cost of mounting the bird so the specimen could be kept at the camp for identification and as an object lesson to future wildfowlers.

To say that every Russian man or boy hunts ducks would be an exaggeration. It only seems that way. From the customs official who responded to the alarm set off by Bagley's and my double-barreled Brownings and our five hundred rounds of ammunition passing through the X-ray machine when we entered the country to the Intourist driver who took us to the airport for our return home, we met a surprising number of shotgun-owning Russians who try to find some time each fall to hunt ducks, principally *krjakva*.

The customs man characterized duck hunting as "very easy," which made me think he shot his birds on the water, but I was not about to argue the point since he held the fate of Bagley's and my expedition in his rubber-stamping hand. The Intourist driver was a more knowledge-able duck hunter and concerned about the Estonian situation, since that country's Baltic Coast had provided him with so many wildfowling memories. Bagley and I were sympathetic, but we suggested that with Aero-flot round-trip fares between Moscow and Krasnodar costing just $56 in roubles, it might be better to let the Estonians go their own way, while the driver confine his future hunting to marshes where he'd be more welcome.

Besides, we explained, the hunting in southern Russia is clearly better than along the Baltic. Why, otherwise, would so many Scandinavian and German wildfowlers from the Baltic region spend their hunting holidays in southern Russia?

Russians who hunt the top ten wildfowl management areas in the south of the USSR are limited to eight ducks and two geese a day—a generous enough limit by modern standards, but when the locals learn that foreigners (including visiting Americans) enjoy unrestricted shooting, some are understandably resentful, especially in a nation where first-class privileges of any kind are regarded as a bourgeois abomination. The fact that Russians pay nothing for their hunting privileges while foreigners pay generously for theirs does little to console local Russians who get little benefit from the infusions of foreign money.

The Soviet government is always looking for new sources of hard currency—not the funny money it allows its citizenry to play with and which has no exchange value outside Russia. Beginning about a decade ago with the Finns, Germans, and Italians, and in the past two years with Americans, Soviet authorities have discovered that there are a surprising number of Westerners willing to spend $350 a day (including airfare) to get to hunt Russian ducks and geese.

On the face of it, this would seem to be a good thing for all concerned. Our presence helps dispel some of the stereotypes the Russians have been taught about Americans, and vice versa. Furthermore, the swarms of wildfowl in southern Russia are comparable to what we North Americans once had before wetland drainage, drought, and the over-shooting of birds on ever-diminished habitat reduced our great clouds of ducks to scattered bands.

Unfortunately, a similar fate may be in store for Russia's birds. Farm machinery is getting better—meaning more thorough—with each passing year. Russian tractors now work all but the wettest areas, and Russian combine operators try to harvest every last grain of rice, wheat, corn, and milo. The use of highly toxic pesticides is widespread, and wildfowling is becoming popular with increasing numbers of tourists. The Kubanskoe Reserve, where Bagley and I hunted, could accommodate only six visitors at a time. Local authorities, however, are constructing an adjacent tourist facility, which, by the 1989 season, will accommodate more than two dozen hunters.

Although the Kubanskoe Reserve is a huge phragmites marsh at the center of a 500-kilometer circle of low-lying but deep-ditched farmland into which water from the surrounding fields is pumped; and although the fields still provide excellent opportunities for wildfowl feeding on grain missed by the combines; and although the canals and ponds cut into the marsh by local trappers—muskrats were introduced from the United States a century or so ago—provide roosts for tens of thousands of birds, there are indications that some species, especially geese, are declining.

Even generally trusting ducks, like shovelers (which the Russians very much wanted us to shoot), are being conditioned by the constant gunfire. On more than one occasion while working a bird toward the decoys, I lost the duck when it flinched and flared from the sound of Bagley's shooting more than a mile across the marsh.

Bagley and I each averaged fifteen ducks and four geese a day. On Bagley's best outing (Thanksgiving morning), he concentrated on teal and shovelers (for some reason—it can't be the flavor—the Russians were delighted when we shot shovelers), and by picking his shots and making two Scotch Doubles and one Scotch Triple (a Scotch anything is more than one bird with a single shot), he killed thirty ducks with forty rounds, including cripple-stoppers.

Since I love geese above all other wildfowl, my favorite outing was Thanksgiving evening when my guide, Sasha, put me in a curious, pulpit-type, iron blind in the middle of a large mud flat covered by a few inches of water. The sun set as a huge red disk on one horizon just as the full moon rose as a huge red disk on the other. While waiting for darkness and the geese to return, five fists of teal punched past, as always, from the opposite direction in which I was straining to see in the gathering dusk.

At last I heard the "wink-wink" cries of lesser white-fronts coming to the flats. Even with the moonlight, I could barely see their wings, so took my lead from the silhouette of their bodies against the deep purple sky. I had no perception of depth. When I fired, I couldn't tell for a moment whether my target was falling or flying on. Every one of my three shots, however, was followed by a long pause, then a resounding smack as the birds hit the shallow water. As I left the pulpit-blind to help Sasha locate my fallen geese, a tawny owl appeared and fluttered noiselessly and mysteriously about my head like a tethered wraith. When Sasha push-poled me back through the moonlit marsh, I knew at that hour there was no happier man on earth.

Since the birds we shot were welcome additions to local (and obviously lean) larders, Bagley and I were treated more as heroes than hogs for shooting so many. Furthermore, since we both batted better than .400, the Cossacks thought we were "professionals." They were amazed to learn that Bagley is an orthodontist in real life, and that I spend many more days indoors writing about duck hunting than out in a marsh doing it. We stressed that, by some American standards, we were only slightly better than average.

"Wait till you see our Big Billy Goat Gruffs," we told our Cossack hosts. "The shooting editor of *Field & Stream,* for example, hasn't missed a bird since 1973!" (The Russians can hardly wait to see you in action, Bob. I know you'll be able to handle the pressure, heh-heh!)

Our guides did little shooting. Sasha would put up his shotgun to blaze at the occasional hooded crow that drifted longingly over the windrows of fallen waterfowl on the downwind sides of the ponds we shot. And Vladimir would blast at any of the out-of-range geese Bagley and I let pass. Once he managed to break a wingtip with a stray BB pellet and bring the bird down. It wasn't a very satisfying shot—at least to us onlookers—but this meager success went to Vladimir's head. He boasted that if he had Super X, Double X shells, buffered Nitro Mag, or copper-plated Premium shot like us, he'd never miss! Bagley and I gave him an assortment, whereupon he promptly shot a hole in the side of a boat.

His colleagues were embarrassed by this folly because it reflected unfavorably on their overall competence, including Vladimir's. Make no mistake: Cossacks are excellent outdoorsmen. Both Bagley and I had been keen trappers in our youth, and we enjoy seeing how it's done in other parts of the world. The Cossacks were pleased we took time away from our shooting to run the traplines with them. I, for one, wouldn't have missed it for the world!

I was struck by Sasha's reluctance to kill the unwanted water rats he found alive in his muskrat traps. He'd release them with an admonition to stay away next time. His gesture and words weren't all sentimental, however, for he explained that if he killed the water rats, their niche would only be filled by "uneducated" ones that would have to learn (to Sasha's future annoyance) to avoid the trap sites. Sasha said he rarely recaught a previously trapped water rat. I found his explanation appropriate in the country where Pavlov conceived the theory of conditioned reflexes, but remarkable because I know of few American trappers who would take the time and risk of being bitten to do the same.

Hunting in a foreign land has as much to do with making new acquaintances as seeing and shooting new birds. We couldn't give the Cossacks a gift, whether it be a logoed T-shirt or a duck call, without them reciprocating with something of greater value—at least to us. Of all the souvenirs brought back from Russia, the accordian-doored muskrat traps and the rubber mallard decoys given to us by Sasha and Vladimir revive the most wonderful memories.

Perhaps it's my one-quarter Hungarian ancestry that allows me to be as openly emotional as the Russians. Whatever the reason, it was natural to exchange hugs with Sasha when it was time to go. Bagley, by contrast, has no Slavic blood. He's a thoroughbred Anglo-Saxon who went as stiff as a board when Vladimir approached with all the eagerness of a puppy. Respecting Bagley's reserve, but needing some way to express his intense emotion, Vladimir (whose Russian nickname of "Vulva" was something Bagley couldn't bring himself to say) ran to get his shotgun. As we were chauffeured through the compound's gate, Vladimir ran after us with tears in his eyes, firing his gun in a farewell salute.

For all the hassles of getting there and getting back, moments like that make a Russian wildfowling trip a sublime adventure.

Getting There

At the time Bagley and I went over, Klineburger Worldwide Travel in Seattle, Washington, was the exclusive American agent for Intourist, the only way you can travel around the Soviet Union. A curious feature of traveling with guns in Russia is that as soon as you clear Customs, you can go anywhere with a shotgun without provoking the kind of worried looks one usually gets when toting a shotgun through public places in the United States.

Bagley and I spent our first night with our guns and a case of ammunition in a hotel just half a block from Red Square. We wouldn't have been legally entitled to do that within a hundred blocks of Times Square!

The principal drawback to a Russian hunt is the number of days spent traveling compared to the number of days actually spent hunting. In our case, the ratio was nearly three to one. If more Americans make the trip, Russian officials say they'd consider other routes besides the now mandatory check-ins and outs through Moscow or Leningrad. (Since Krasnodar is the sister city of Tallahassee, Florida, we suggested a non-stop weekly flight during the fall season between the two cities.)

The principal advantage to hunting on a Russian trip is that the accommodations and food are the best you'll find in that otherwise bleakly provisioned country. Intourist supplied us with a professionally trained cook who made the most of locally grown vegetables, meat, and eggs, and the pike our guides netted in the marsh. As is true in many rural economies, the best Russian fare apparently never makes it to market in the cities. Bagley and I supplemented our tasty and imaginatively prepared menu with some of the ducks we killed. Bagley favored teal, while I preferred the larger but equally succulent pintail, split and roasted in one of Valentina's marvelous sauces.

Our quarters, although Spartan by American standards, were equivalent to a country dacha for a high-ranking Soviet official. In addition to having occasional hot water (when Sasha was there to make the heater work), we had a sauna that did double-duty as a place to dry wet clothes.

For optimum sport, plan your trip for mid-October. We were assured there were twice as many ducks then, even though Bagley and I wondered where in the sky more birds could find room to fly than those we saw. The drawback to hunting toward the end of November (when we were there) is that the weather has turned frisky. While this means only skim ice and a dusting of snow on the shooting grounds, it can mean blizzards in Moscow. Bagley and I arrived in a storm, and by the time we went back to Moscow for the trip home, there were sixteen inches of snow on the ground.

This reminded me that the Wehrmacht had been stopped in late November just eight miles short of Moscow (forty-eight years earlier). Midway between Moscow and its international airport is a huge war memorial honoring the millions of Russians who gave their lives there to defeat the Germans. Victory was attributed to fresh divisions of Siberian troops rushed from the East and superior Russian machinery. The Germans were confounded by the success of Russian tanks and trucks because the Germans believed that their more sophisticated machines had to be better because they were more sophisticated. Mechanical refinement, however, is not an advantage in extreme cold and crusted mud.

Bagley and I found that the Russians still make superior all-weather machines. Our trips across fields in hub-deep slurry were made in a Land-Rover look-alike called the Mountain Goat. "Water Horse" would have been a more appropriate name considering the terrain. Regardless of what it's called, the Mountain Goat is a fantastic machine. We never got stuck; we never came close to getting stuck—and in situations that would have jeopardized more refined American or Japanese four-wheel-drive vehicles.

We jokingly asked if we could buy and take one of the Mountain Goats back to the States with us. The Russians said that they'd be happy to trade all the Mountain Goats they make for a few thousand miles of our interstate highway system.

"We need our Mountain Goats," they said. "You don't."

I assured them that there were places and times when every outdoorsman needs a dependable Mountain Goat.

Decoys

For well over one hundred and fifty years, the Russians have used live decoys. These birds sometimes become highly personalized pets, riding on the bows of the boats as they're push-poled through the marsh. Mikhail Prishvin noted sixty-five years ago in his *Nature's Diary* that, "as for the mallard, they were all so different that you could always tell one from another just like human beings." (A serious flaw of many amateur decoy carvers is that they don't see such differences and hence carve and paint birds with all the individuality of department store mannequins.)

The Russians still enjoy using live decoys, and Bagley and I hunted over mildly talkative hen mallards and extremely talkative greylag geese. The latter comprised a family group split up and anchored separately around an open pocket in the marsh so they would call constantly to reassure one another that all was well.

Although lesser and greater white-fronted geese were more abundant than greylags, our live decoys had no effect at all on white-fronts, because the tame birds clearly lacked white-front genes. While a solitary greylag would periodically parachute down to join our semi-domestic birds on the water, the white-fronts rarely missed a wing-stroke as they mostly passed well out of range. It would have been instructive for those American hunters who insist that Canada goose decoys are general-purpose, able to pull white-fronts and snow geese about as well as they pull Canadas, to have seen the indifference of the wild white-fronts to tame greylags. If there is a generic goose, it's the greylag from which most breeds of domestic geese are descended. But even *live* greylag decoys had no noticeable appeal for wild geese of another species.

Our live mallard decoys quacked a lot at dawn when they were first put out, but as soon as the sun came up, the birds settled down to nibbling plants in the water, preening, and even sleeping. Fortunately, Bagley and I had brought calls with us. Since wild Russian ducks had never before heard artificial quacking, whistling, and grunting, we were able to pull birds our way so long as there were birds in the air to pull.

Before the Bolshevik Revolution, Russian waterfowlers used nothing but live decoys. That was when Russia still had an aristocracy that could afford servants to keep a flock of tame birds the year around for spring and fall shooting. In the 1920s, a former aristocrat asked Mikhail Prishvin to join him for a duck hunt with his one remaining decoy. Prishvin didn't think the bird looked very promising and was disgusted by the young man's dirty appearance. He told the man that "it is unseemly for a former nobleman to go about in such a state."

The young man replied that "nowadays one had to look like a worker if one wanted to get on."

Russian worker-guides today use rubber decoys to supplement their live birds. The artificial ducks are made from rubber because wood is both scarce and expensive, and because Russia's trade with its Asian client, Vietnam, seems to have resulted in a rubber surplus.

Like everything else in the Soviet Union, the manufactured decoys are standardized to a fault. Whether you're looking for birds in Moscow or the provincial city of Krasnodar, there is only one brand, one species, and except for a single drake with which our hosts presented us and which they acknowledged was extremely rare, one sex.

Based on the traditional use of hen mallards for live decoys, the Russians assume that the only artificial duck worth using is also a hen mallard. Dr. William F. Nickel, Jr.—who visited the Soviet Union on a medical tour in 1959—found that the Russians at that time made scaup as well as teal rubber decoys, but these other species are no longer obtainable. The pity is that a dearth of decoy diversity hurts Russian shooters even more than it does American souvenir seekers. While mallards are undoubtedly the most common duck in the Soviet Union, the overall numbers of other species we shot far exceeded the numbers of mallards we saw. Had we had pintail and wigeon decoys, I'm certain we would have had many more pintail and wigeon in our bags.

Despite standardization, the personality of the people who produce the Russian rubber ducks shows through in their painting. Some of the generic hen mallards had orangish feathering; others had gray. Some had orange bills; others had bluish ones. This attention to detail revealed much latent creativity. The one drake we acquired had separately molded wing tips and curly tail feathers, just like the real McCoy. It would be interesting to see what innovative vulcanizations the Russians would devise for pintail tails and shoveler bills!

Perhaps under *perestroika* the Russians will refine their decoys into something more truly collectable. In the meanwhile, we'll save what we brought back in the same spirit that we saved our cancelled museum tickets and the few kopeks we smuggled out. Russian decoys won't win any honors at the next Ward Brothers' competition, but they're grand souvenirs of a memorable expedition.

Rails, Geese, Sea Ducks, and Others

—12—

Rallidae

Coot

Despite the root *rallus* (Latin for rail), the Rallidae encompass coots and gallinules as well as rails. Coots are among my favorite waterfowl precisely because most hunters scorn them. I have tender feelings for any avian underdog (underbird?), and I also have wonderful childhood memories of coot shoots.

I recall my older brother and me sprawled port and starboard on the bow of a one-lunger skiff returning up a canal in Mexico from a morning of duck hunting. As we chugged along, coot would swim away from the banks ahead of us and suddenly lunge into a flapping dash across the water. Tony, barely eleven, and I, two years younger, would shoot at them with .22 rifles. Those we knocked down were scooped up in a net by our Mexican guide who enjoyed eating them—more, he said, than the ducks my father shot around the fringes of the lake. Later in Louisiana, I found Cajun shooters who killed *poule d'eau* (pronounced "pu-lu") for their enormous gizzards. To the Cajuns, throwing away the heart, liver, and gizzard of any bird is a crime punishable by ostracism within the malefactor's parish.

My first Mexican coot shoot took place in 1948, before mobs of middle-class American sportsmen, few of whom had ever tasted coot, taught Mexicans that only lower-caste people consumed such fare. As a result, when I visited Alta Vista in 1985, my guide would not even pick up the two coots I killed, driven to me along with ducks flushed off Lake Guerrero. That was annoying—first, because the coots had come downwind over the reeds at good speed and had provided as good sport as the bluebills and ringbills with which they flew; second, because sautéed coot breasts are as tasty as rare roasted bluebills and ringbills. I retrieved and dressed the coots myself, but I stopped shooting them. My guide would have lost face with the other guides had I continued.

Among other forms of corruption by Americans in Mexico, we seem to have undermined their common sense, at least where it pertains to food. As I dressed the coot, I thought of India where millions of people go hungry every day so that thousands of sacred cattle can wander over the countryside. Mexico's human population is already well beyond reasonable bounds, and countless people go hungry there every day. Meanwhile, most every lake and waterway resonates with the chuckling beeps, whistles, honks, and quacks of feeding coot. Few of these birds are shot or trapped by local people, less because there's a nationwide ten-*gallareta* daily limit than because Mexicans know that Gringos, whom they both admire and dislike, disdain such birds. Already-over-shot ducks continue to be over-shot while rarely shot coots continue to abound on marshes and lakes that the coots may one day have all to themselves.

Besides occasional food and sport, coots provide a happy alternative to swatting mosquitoes and waiting for ducks that may not appear. I remember winter afternoons in the 1950s when my younger brother John took his bolt-action 20-gauge Mossberg and pockets full of shells on circular stalks through the marshes surrounding our hyacinth-shrouded boat on Okeechobee. His double-purpose plan included shooting a limit of fifteen coot for himself and stirring up ducks for us that were lazing about in the bluebird weather. We tracked his progress by the periodic poppings of his gun.

Coots are a help to knowledgeable wildfowlers. They provided my companions and me with limits of ducks at Alta Vista when few other hunters were doing as well. This happened because most shooters obeyed the guides, who were generally more concerned with not losing their clients than with providing them with optimum sport. The drill was for the guides to drop off the hunters and a batch of nondescript decoys in a likely looking spot by the edge of the lake. Then the guides would go back out onto the lake and try to rally ducks over the clients. The only trouble was that by January, the ducks were decoy- and rally-shy. They were as likely to head for the middle of the lake as its marshy borders when flushed by the boats, and those few flying toward the hiding hunters would frequently flare from the decoys.

My companions, Mike Greata and Art Carter, and I could not persuade our guides to try anything they'd not been ordered to do. So we let them take us where they would. As soon as we were out of the boat, however, and the guides were poking their way back toward the open lake through the drowned timber, we'd leave our decoys and head for the nearest large flocks of coot.

The trick is to get downwind and close to the feeding fowl without alarming them. Coots (like all birds) are messy feeders, and they often eat only a portion of each weed they pull. Since grazing birds feed into the wind, concentrations of coot leave a banquet of scraps in their wake to which ducks will "decoy" more reliably than to anything but a baited pond.

It was exquisite shooting. Standing thigh-deep in the cool water next to a gnarled trunk with just enough of a skeletal canopy to disguise us, but not enough to handicap our shooting, we'd watch pintail and wigeon come our way and, at the right moment, step out to kill the drakes.

When pairs of gadwall hovered overhead, we'd kill both birds since we couldn't distinguish the brownish hen from the grayish drake against the winter sky. Occasionally, and completely out of place in the drowned timber, would appear a canvasback, most often a drake, rallied from the open water by the guides' pounding and whining boats.

Coot have a peculiar but successful defense against birds of prey. Unlike other water birds that dive or, if found on the wing, will fly into the water to escape the attentions of a falcon or eagle, coots will gang together in such numbers as to turn themselves into feathered mounds. The birds on top of the fluttering, squirming mass will roll on their backs, beaks agape, and jab their feet like roosters at the swooping predator. Such behavior must be effective in discouraging attacking eagles; it would otherwise have been purged from the species' programming eons ago.

Gallinule

Shooting is all a matter of context. Although I've shot only two gallinules (and one of those was for a museum display) on this side of the Atlantic, I was thrilled to kill a moorhen on the Scottish border of the United Kingdom. The American gallinule and the British moorhen are taxonomically the same bird: *Gallinula chloropus*. The British bird, however, is smaller and more colorful, and I regard my one and only as a distinct species for purposes of lifetime listing.

In the United States, the gallinule is not a traditional game species. It may be listed as game, but it is nowhere abundant and nowhere can you specifically hunt for gallinule as you can for coots. Furthermore, the state that has the greatest number of common gallinule also has the most purple gallinule *(Porphyrula martinica)*, and a reflexive shot at a flushing Florida bird might easily result in your killing one of the protected purple species.

Protection for the purple gallinule resulted from the fight to save Florida's Big Cypress swamp from land speculators. Conservationists had made an uncomfortable alliance with preservationists in order to save the vast periodic wetland, but preservationists were opposed to any human use of the area while conservationists wanted to continue hunting there. Johnny Jones, executive director of the Florida Wildlife Federation, proposed taking purple gallinule off the game list if preservationists would accept his organization's desire to keep other forms of hunting (particularly deer and pig) in the Big Cypress.

"It was no big deal for us to give the bird up," Johnny told me later. "No sportsman wants to shoot purple gallinule."

Although I'm happy the Big Cypress was saved, I'm unhappy the purple gallinule was stricken from the game list for no sound scientific reason. And I am further unhappy because it means I have been denied the opportunity to collect and mount one of the most beautiful of all water birds.

In the United Kingdom, moorhens make up part of the incidental kill on many a day of shooting lowland cover. It is not a fast flyer, and the one I shot was discussed in the following fashion as it flapped away:

"What is it?"

"A moorhen," my host replied.

"Fair game?"

"Oh, yes. The young ones are first-rate eating."

"You mind my killing it?"

"Not at all. Please do."

I did. And amidst all the driven pheasant and pen-raised duck shooting that day, the moorhen was the only truly *wild* fowl I killed.

Moorhens and gallinules differ from coots in not being so dependent on water sites for nesting. While a coot nest is invariably surrounded by water and sometimes floating in it, moorhens will occasionally pick a relatively lofty perch for nesting purposes, as high as fifteen feet from the ground. Indeed, this familiarity with trees may explain why moorhens do something that I've never seen or heard of in any other member of the family. On still days, they'll use their beaks and wings to help them climb to the top of a tall shrub or tree, much like a parrot, before launching themselves into flight.

A High Tide in September

Across the flooded marsh, we saw flotillas of clapper rail swimming toward the last clump of grass still above water. Two or three dozen marsh hens converged on the area while Shirley Belote push-poled the skiff closer.

"Get ready," he warned. "Looks like nothin's gone out the far side."

The scow barely nudged aside the first outlying grasses when a rail fluttered up, caught the breeze at our backs, and began to sail away downwind. I shot, and as the bird fell, other rails began flushing port, starboard, and dead ahead. I shot again, another rail fell, and I feverishly reloaded my 20-gauge double while birds continued getting up all around.

"Easy now," cautioned Shirley. "That makes a dozen. Three more'll do the limit."

The next shot dropped a bird, which dived. Shirley swung the scow toward where the bird disappeared and held us steady about ten yards off by shoving his push-pole into the muddy bottom. My golden retriever, Rocky, came back with the first rail, and I was giving him directions to the second when the cripple came up. A quick shot, and Rocky made that retrieve first.

By now all the rail had flown from the tiny island, or swum out the other side.

"Let's head in," Shirley suggested. "Tide's dropping, and I see a duck blind on the way back just above water. We should find a couple there to finish the limit."

I was reluctant to leave. We'd been out less than an hour, and the morning was crisp with that brilliant light seen only in the fall. Yet the tide had turned, and soon the vast bay Shirley was poling across would revert to a maze of salt marsh islands and creeks. The birds that had proved to be so vulnerable during the peak of the tide would soon be so elusive only their derisive cackling would provide some indication of how many hundreds were hiding in the grass around us.

Unlike shooting other types of water birds, the best sport with clapper rail has little to do with opening days. Unless there's a full moon tide under a strong northeast wind, you might as well stay home and rake leaves—that is, unless you enjoy swatting mosquitoes and slogging through soft mud with, perhaps, only the merest hope of seeing a flying bird or two at extreme range. However, for a few days each month in September, October, and November—and occasionally when an offshore storm threatens the coast—high tides will drive clapper rail to any structures or grassy tumps standing above the water. If you're at one of these places at the right time, the birds will provide some of the fastest legal shooting left in the United States.

Splendid settings, comfortable shooting, fifteen-bird limits, pre-season practice for ducks, and superb eating are just a few reasons for being on a flooding coastal marsh in September. A strong breeze at your back keeps the biting flies and mosquitoes at bay, and you share your keen anticipation with a partner poling in the stern who gets his turn to shoot on alternate flurries.

John Krider and H. Milnor Knapp were among the first to describe this uniquely American pastime. The rules of the game have changed little in the past century and a half:

> The post of the pusher is in the stern; that of the shooter a little abaft the bow. Each pusher is stripped to his shirt and pantaloons, and holds in his sinewy hands a pine [or more often today, a cedar] pole fifteen feet long, and weighing about four pounds. It is his arduous task to flush and retrieve the game; the sportsman has nothing to do but to load and shoot.

What has changed greatly since 1853 are the number of places you can hunt rail. Krider and Knapp shot sora rail on the once-extensive brackish tidal marshes of Delaware, largely sacrificed to industrial development today. A similarly sad tale can be told of coastal New Jersey, Long Island, and Connecticut, where boundless home construction has led to the filling and bulkheading of hundreds of thousands of acres of prime salt and riverine marshes since the 1930s. The story is even more tragic in California where the western clapper rail is as threatened with extinction as the salt marshes that sustain it.

Yet starting in Maryland and running just inside the barrier islands of Virginia, down through the Carolinas and into the 350,000 acres of salt marshes of Georgia, skipping across to the Gulf Coast, particularly portions of the Florida panhandle and Louisiana, there still exists the opportunity to hunt rail on a par with what our nineteenth-century predecessors knew.

Although the vast majority of salt-marsh rail will be clappers, every autumn I shoot a few Virginia rail and brackish-loving soras that come to the edge of the sea. Twice I've flushed, but never shot at, the tiny and elusive black rail. Curiously, after twenty seasons of rail hunting, I've shot only one possible king rail. This larger and rusty-colored edition of the clapper is so devoted to freshwater environments that even though king rail breed on the Delmarva peninsula, they rarely, unless driven there by exceptional winds, visit the fringing coast.

Except for S. Dillon Ripley's monumental tome on the *Rails of the World* (1977) and Brooke Meanley's research on *The Marsh Hen* (1985), little modern writing has been done on any of the rails. This may be because rails are classified as gamebirds and hence spurned by many non-hunting ornithologists who probably suppose there are more than enough "gamebird biologists" studying the family. Yet rails are little regarded and rarely studied by state or federal wildlife biologists, some of whom think their careers would be stunted by specializing in such out-of-the-mainstream gamebirds. Such biologists forget that George Bird Grinnell, long-time editor of *Forest and Stream,* founder of the first Audubon Society, and author of the first great book on *American Duck Shooting,* did his doctoral work on the roadrunner—hardly a mainstream species. Success has always been within the man and not in what he studies.

In the International Association of Fish and Wildlife Agencies' *Management of Migratory Shore and Upland Game Birds in North America* (1977), you sense the desperation of wildlife biologists trying to say something new about rails that nineteenth-century observers didn't already know. In the section on "Current and Potential Harvest" of Virginia rail, we learn that biologists working in Alabama, Iowa, Maryland, Ontario, Rhode Island, South Dakota, and Texas believe that "additional hunting potential for this species" exists, and that Colorado biologists "estimated that there are fewer than 500 hunters shooting Virginia rails and that fewer than 1,000 birds were killed."

For sora rails, "no accurate harvest figures are available." Only Nebraska, in all the United States, came up with a firm estimate of an annual kill, and the hat from which that state's biologists plucked the number 5,680 remains a mystery.

The yellow rail is practically unknown and represents very fertile ground for amateur ornithologists since, as the International Association's book stresses, "at present, no state or province feels justified in devoting management efforts to the yellow rail."

Estimates for clapper rail are more generous. Approximately 3,000 hunters kill about 15,000 clappers in New Jersey each year, and about 4,000 hunters kill approximately 50,000 to 75,000 clappers in Georgia. Obviously, as the summary warns, "the greatest need is for research projects." From 1955 to 1972, fewer than 4,000 clapper rails were banded. Since then the effort has diminished toward zero as limited funds available for waterbird banding in the eastern United States and Canada are now devoted to snow geese, Canada geese, black ducks, green-winged teal, and common eider.

Despite the fact that clapper rails and laughing gulls were for three centuries the principal source of fresh eggs for people living along the southeastern coast of the western Atlantic, and that John James Audubon once observed "it was not unusual for an 'egger' to gather a hundred dozen [clapper] eggs in one day," little is known about the hatching success of marsh hens. Ornithologists know that the clapper hen produces an average of eight eggs, that incubation lasts twenty to twenty-four days, and that all hatching normally occurs within twenty-four to forty-eight hours. Practically nothing is known about first-year mortality, and what percentages of attrition are due to predation, storms, disease, and pollution.

A recent South Carolina study indicates that the raccoon is the rail's principal predator in that state, killing up to 74 percent of all birds killed by mammals—including man. Crows and hawks are traditional predators, and in coastal Maryland and Virginia, clapper rail production has declined even as the numbers of nesting herring and greater black-backed gulls have increased. The worst destruction of nesting rails, however, is caused by spring storms. While high water alone cannot hurt the eggs, wave action breaks up the nests and drowns some adults.

Thanks to work done by Vic Schmidt and Pete McLain in New Jersey in 1951 and Warren Blandin in South Carolina in 1963, we know that clapper rails will re-nest if they lose their first clutch of eggs, and some will even re-nest after they rear their first brood. But we still don't know the average success of nesting rails, even if we define success as a single hatched egg.

It comes as a shock to the novice rail shooter that these birds are excellent divers and swimmers. Even fully fledged birds seem to prefer swimming to flying. Early in the season they'll frequently continue swimming after you've push-poled up alongside them and tried to shoo them into flight. Such birds are sometimes clobbered and collected by the push-poler. By the second month of the season, surviving rail rarely let you get that close. They secretively swim away and take to the air after they're well out of range.

Unlike crippled ducks, which generally dive and swim as far as possible before coming up again, a crippled clapper does not swim a great distance underwater. This is probably because he has less strength and stamina than a duck and is less able to push aside submerged reeds. Perhaps, too, rail intuitively know that grass stems moving above the surface give a predator—man or marsh hawk—a fix on where a rail is going. When a crippled rail dives, scrutinize the area where the bird went down. It'll frequently come up precisely where it went under. Look carefully, however; you may only see the bill close by a reed.

My golden retriever loved rail hunting, and it was comic sometimes to watch the bird bob to the surface just behind the dog while Rocky was staring intently where the bird had dived in front of him. I'd call out, the dog would whirl around, the bird would dive again, and the routine would be repeated, sometimes two or three times, before the dog finally saw or calculated where the bird was swimming, plunged his head under, and came up with a mouthful of reeds—and the rail.

The clapper rail is an indicator species for the environmental quality for any salt marsh. If birds are abundant, the fiddler crabs and other invertebrates on which the birds feed must also be abundant. And if the invertebrates are abundant, the marsh is healthy.

Unfortunately, birds shot in the Turtle River-Brunswick area of Georgia, north of the Sidney Lanier Bridge, have been found to have as much as eleven parts per million of mercury in their flesh. Since the U.S. Food and Drug Administration specifies that foods containing an excess of 0.5 parts per million of mercury are unsafe for human consumption, clapper rail from this zone are not only dangerous to eat, they're an indication of severe environmental stress. Like canaries kept in coal mines, these Brunswick, Georgia, birds notify local human residents that all is not well with their world. And since at least some of those birds migrate from Virginia or New Jersey, our Atlantic coastal marshes may appear healthier than they are.

A number of traditional rail-hunting ports still exist along the coast where experienced guides can be hired by the tide. The Wachapreague Hotel & Marina on Virginia's Eastern Shore has been providing this service for about a century. However, do-it-yourself hunting is the prevailing theme of modern American sport, and all you really need are a friend who shares your enthusiasm and a lightweight, preferably flat-bottomed, boat.

You may use a small outboard to run from the dock and get upwind of the hunting grounds. But when the poling or paddling begins, be sure to get that engine out of the water. On October 14, 1985, a former Assistant Secretary of the Interior was arrested and later convicted for "taking or attempting to take migratory game birds by aid of a motorboat under power." The shooter alleged he was only pursuing cripples, but the conviction will pursue his reputation for the rest of his life.

A field-grade 20 or 28-gauge double loaded with 8s is ideal for rail shooting, though I have one friend who insists on express 7½s in a 12-gauge pump and still another friend who says that a .410 loaded with 9s is more than adequate. They're both right. Since rail are fragile birds and can't carry much shot, a .410 can be a lot of fun on close shots early in the season. By October, however, you may need express 7½s in a 12-gauge gun or have to pass up a lot of long targets.

Two words about preparing rail: *skin them*. The skin tears easily, and much of the marshy flavor, to say nothing of chemical contaminants, will come away with the skin. I used to save the giblets (heart, liver, and gizzard), dice them, and add them to side-servings of rice. Unfortunately, such organs concentrate carcinogenic compounds, and I now sadly, but wisely, discard them with the skin, head, and feet.

Unlike his sora and Virginia cousins, the clapper rail is a good-sized bird, containing about the same quantity of meat as a green-winged teal. Like teal, rails roast deliciously. Wrap the birds in bacon, cook no more than fifteen or twenty minutes at 350° Fahrenheit, and—*voilá,* just eating them has turned some rail hunters into trenchermen, and some trenchermen into shooters!

13

Geese

Taxonomic Games

Where ducks themselves are not declining in North America, the quality of most duck shooting is. Some species of geese, however, are doing well, and Canadas even constitute a nuisance so far as some farmers, groundskeepers, and a few other kinds of land managers are concerned. So long as snow geese and Canadas were making a comeback from early-twentieth-century population lows, state and federal game agencies were happy to take credit for the return. Now that both snows and Canadas are superabundant, biologists are ready to admit the birds' comeback was mostly a matter of birdy initiative beyond technical control. This confession, however, has not prevented biologists from busying themselves with the captive breeding of certain rare races of geese and with abolishing the scientific subdivisions that distinguish other rare races.

Half a century ago, when Francis H. Kortright wrote *Ducks, Geese and Swans of North America,* he included more than a dozen species, subspecies, and races of waterfowl that are no longer found on the official list of the American Ornithological Union (AOU). The "extinction" of such beings as the blue goose and Richardson's goose has had nothing to do with diminished habitat or overshooting. They were extinguished by scientific decree.

All taxonomy hinges on a fundamental definition of *species* as "a population of actually or potentially interbreeding organisms sharing a common gene pool." While the European and American green-winged teals, for example, obviously share a common gene pool, they just as obviously do little interbreeding—just as little as the American and European wigeons. Nonetheless, European and American green-winged teals are now regarded as the same species, while American and Eurasian wigeon are still two different birds.

Likewise, the blue goose is only a color phase (it has become taboo to use the word "race") of the snow goose, while the Richardson's goose is only a "geographic variant" of the Canada goose. However, this is where scientific censorship steps on its own feet. If all other subspecies and races of the Canada goose have been abolished, why single out the Aleutian Canada goose, as the U.S. Fish and Wildlife Service has done, for special treatment as an endangered species? Almost all geographic variants of the Canada goose can and do interbreed. Hence, they are supposedly all the same species and managed equally—except that the Aleutian Canada goose is managed more equally than others.

Why single out this one variant for special treatment? Biologists tend to mumble their answer because it's riddled with political considerations. Bureaucratic careers can be built on the successful breeding of an endangered species, and the Aleutian Canada goose has everything going for it that an endangered species program administrator desires.

First, whereas most of us cannot tell a diminutive cackling goose from a giant Canada goose, except by the now allegedly unimportant factor of size, most Aleutian Canada geese have distinctive white throat bands that make them recognizably different from other geographic variants. And what looks different—despite the fact that superficial characteristics are supposed to be inconsequential today—makes this bird more acceptable as a *unique* creature deserving special endangered species treatment.

Second, because it is a Canada goose, *Branta canadensis lencopareia* is a cooperative breeder, and the odds of saving this supposed subspecies are excellent. Hence, the Aleutian Canada goose becomes an ideal show-and-tell item for a federal endangered species program continually harried by tight-fisted politicians looking for quick results.

Third, because the Aleutian Canada goose is being re-established on remote islands of the remote Alaskan archipelago, it is an uncontroversial species. This is no endangered snail darter holding up a pork barrel project, or a pupfish preventing the suburbanization of the desert. The Aleutian Canada goose is a politically safe bird to rehabilitate.

Rehabilitate in the Aleutians, that is. What happens once flocks of Aleutian Canada geese begin migrating again to California, their ancestral wintering home, is another question. Have endangered species program managers looked down the road to the problems they're hatching for their successors?

I'm referring not only to the fact that Aleutian Canada geese wintering in California will meet other "geographic variants" and possibly cross-breed with them, thereby diluting the Aleutian Canada goose gene pool. I'm referring to a politically explosive situation in which Aleutian geese will be shot by California hunters who will assume (correctly, by scientific standards) that they have killed only a slightly different color phase of the Canada goose.

Will California have to stop all Canada goose hunting once flocks of Aleutian Canada geese begin wintering again in that state?

Not likely. As natural historian Stephen Jay Gould remarked in an essay on racism and recapitulation, "scientists tend to behave in a conservative way by providing 'objectivity' for what society at large wants to hear."

In other words, only after such a crisis occurs will wildlife administrators suddenly determine that the classification of the Aleutian Canada goose was in error. The bird's status will either be downgraded to "threatened"—which means it can be hunted—or it will be declared a nonspecies as has already happened to most of its taxonomic cousins.

How can I speak with such certainty of the future? Because California hunters are already shooting a subspecies of geese that is in far greater danger of extinction than the Aleutian Canada goose: the tule goose.

Right now, there exist over 5,000 Aleutian Canada geese, yet fewer than 500 tules. The tule is a larger, darker version of the white-fronted goose. What makes it as much of a subspecies as the Aleutian Canada goose is its distinctive behavior—even though the concept of *behavior* gives most bone-oriented taxonomists apoplexy! California waterfowlers have known for nearly ninety years that tule—or "timber geese," as they are sometimes called—prefer the more secluded areas of a marsh where ponds and sloughs are surrounded by tules and willow trees. Hunters have to make special efforts to get where the tule geese "use," but once there, the birds fly generally lower and less warily than white-fronts.

Even before it became a scientifically acknowledged subspecies in 1917, the tule goose was a superior trophy for California waterfowlers due to its larger size and the difficulty of reaching its preferred habitat. The tule is even more of a trophy today due to its increasing scarcity and despite the fact that state biologists do not manage it as a distinct subspecies. Ornithologists would probably have scrubbed the last traces of the tule goose from the AOU roster by now except for a study published by Bruce Krogman in the March 1978 issue of *American Birds.* The study was an annoyance to scientific administrators on several counts. Krogman revived the idea of the tule as a separate subspecies and warned that it was barely hanging on in California's Central Valley. Had Krogman been supported by a state or federal endangered species program, such a claim would have been understandable. But Krogman's work was largely funded by sportsmen who hunt in the Central Valley. Why would they pay for research that might result in them losing their hunting privileges? Doesn't the fact that sportsmen funded Krogman's work give it credibility?

Neither question is being answered directly. Instead, state biologists claim that closing the goose season in Central Valley would not guarantee that tule and white-fronted geese wouldn't interbreed. So the biocrats have "solved" their problem by rejecting Krogman's work as politically motivated (!) and declaring the tule goose a mere geographic variant of the white-front. They then hurried back to breed more "endangered" Aleutian Canada geese.

The Sea Goose

Another goose plagued by questions of race and subspecies is the brant. In addition to the Pacific "geographic variant," there are "light-bellied" and "dark-bellied" races—whoops! "sub-geographic variants"—of the Atlantic geographic variant. Although the dark-bellied version winters principally in the British Isles, I've shot dark-bellied brant in New York and Virginia and seen a fair seasoning of some western Atlantic (light-bellied) flocks with darker-bellied birds in Britain. That notwithstanding, British ornithologists insist that the dark-bellied bird is a unique eastern Atlantic variant whose limited gene pool must be protected. As a result, and despite the presence of tens of thousands of brant—or, as the Brits call them, "brent"—along the UK and Irish coasts, dark-bellied brant, including a sprinkling of light-bellied strays from this side of the ocean, are protected everywhere in the British Isles and Ireland.

A similar point of view nearly resulted in a permanently closed hunting season for brant on this side of the Atlantic. The debate peaked in the mid-1970s when brant were recovering from a disastrous overkill during the winter of 1972–73. Two unproductive breeding years in the Arctic preceded a hunting season in which perfect weather conditions and human desire combined to put unexpected numbers of shooters onto the coastal bays where the birds were wintering. An estimated 73,000 light-bellied brant were legally shot under a six-birds-a-day limit, and the western Atlantic population plummeted from a peak of 213,500 birds during the winter of 1967–68 to a record low of 41,900 at the end of the 1972–73 season.

Brant are nesters of the high Arctic and, as such, beyond the effective range of any form of wildlife management except season lengths and daily limits. Long before the first Inuit or European began hunting them, brant populations varied according to late spring or early autumn snow storms on the birds' breeding grounds. Brant broods require a minimum of seventy-one days to fledge; high Arctic weather normally provides no more than eighty days of snow-free summer. That's cutting it close.

State wildlife administrators in the Atlantic Flyway traditionally push for open seasons on brant whenever the fall migration has been predicted to exceed 75,000 birds. Fortunately, federal administrators have the final say in migratory bird management, and they've established 100,000 as the minimum for an Atlantic brant season. In the spring of 1975, less than three years after the great overkill, brant had perfect Arctic breeding conditions. Just over 100,000 birds started down the western Atlantic Coast that fall. The federal government cautiously agreed to a two-birds-a-day, thirty-days season, with its fingers crossed that the spring of 1976 would be just as productive. It wasn't. But lower limits meant brant populations were not devastated. Indeed, by the natural process of two steps forward and one back, brant gradually increased, and populations today sometimes match the highs of the mid-1960s.

Once burned, twice learned, however, and the federal government will hopefully never again allow more than two brant in a daily limit. The years of six, seven, and eight brant per day are gone, and rightly so, for the brant is a wildfowling trophy whose meaning is only diminished by additional killing.

One winter I hosted wildfowl biologist Norman Seymour to a brant hunt on the Virginia coast. He enjoyed shooting black ducks and snow geese with me, but these were familiar game to a southeastern Canadian. Brant were not. As the first flock of several hundred swung low over the decoys carved by our guide, Grayson Chesser, Jr., I heard Norman murmer above the sound of the wind and distant surf, "My God, they're beautiful!" Later I helped him skin several we killed, including a dark-bellied specimen, and the best of the lot is now flying around his office at St. Francis Xavier University where he helps stimulate a younger generation's appreciation for the wonders of wildfowl.

Black Brant

Along the Pacific Coast, the brant is becoming a rare prize for wildfowlers not because black brant are declining overall, but because this "species," "subspecies," or "geographic variant" can no longer abide the intensely settled coastal region between southern British Columbia and southern California. Although black brant (what some biologists still call *Branta bernicla nigricans*) have had an average population of between 125,000 and 150,000 birds for the past four decades, wintering numbers in the United States have fallen drastically.

In the 1940s, Washington State hosted about 25,000 brant each fall; by the early 1980s, only 6,450 brant were there. In the 1940s, Oregon hosted roughly 7,000 birds; in the early 1980s, there were just 700. And in the 1940s, California hosted 40,000 to 50,000 brant; in the early 1980s, that state's total averaged 485.

The draining of coastal marshes, the conversion of bays to marinas, and the innocent impact of weekend boaters have driven brant on to Mexico where wintering populations have grown from 80,000 in the early 1950s to as many as 130,000 today. Unfortunately, Mexico's capacity to sustain brant is being exceeded. Although neither of the two Baja coastal lagoons where the birds winter faces imminent development, the west coast of Mexico, where most of the spillover has flown, is of growing interest to both mineral prospectors and resort developers.

The last hurrah for Pacific brant hunters occurs each fall at Cold and Izembek bays near the western tip of the Alaska Peninsula. These bays contain some of the largest eelgrass beds (*Zostera*) on earth, and every fall the world's entire black brant population, as well as tens of thousands of snow, Canada, and emperor geese resort there to feast on this important marine grass. At Izembek, shooting pressure once fell on the now protected emperor goose. Today, the superbly flavored brant is the principal target.

A Matter of Taste

The reputation of the black brant for wariness and excellent flavor puzzles many western Atlantic coastal shooters who consider its light-bellied cousin easy to decoy, but not worth eating. Yet at the turn of the century, Atlantic brant were rated as the most delicious waterfowl, after canvasbacks, to be found in eastern U.S. markets. Of course, Atlantic brant once fed exclusively on eelgrass just as their delicious Pacific cousins do today. As for Canada geese, ugh!, you didn't know what fare those birds had picked up while poking about the mud flats. Consequently, their market value was never as great as the brant's, even though Canadas are twice to three times larger than the smaller sea geese.

How times change! In the 1930s, eelgrass vanished along both sides of the Atlantic (and to a lesser degree in the Pacific) possibly due to a mycetozoan called *labyrinthula*. Serious declines were noted for a variety of fishes, birds, and animals dependent on eelgrass, but no decline was more dramatic than that of the light-bellied and dark-bellied variants of the brant. At one point, our western Atlantic population may have had fewer than 10,000 birds. These survivors resorted to any kind of sea weeds, especially the alga called sea lettuce (*Ulva*), to survive. This alga gave the birds most essential nutrients, but *Ulva* was and is the source of the rank smell and flavor associated with brant after hunting seasons were restored in 1951. Indeed, because Atlantic brant weren't hunted hard due to their unflavorable reputation, the U.S. Fish and Wildlife Service allowed generous daily limits and long seasons throughout the 1960s. That's why the tremendous harvest of 1972 caught the Service by surprise. Had it been more thoughtfully monitoring the decline of broadbill and black ducks along the Atlantic Coast, the Service might have anticipated increased pressure on brant.

Adaptability

Some time in the early 1970s, brant on both sides of the Atlantic began feeding in fields of winter wheat, rye, and barley. They initiated this behavior about the same time greater snow geese began using upland fields, but decades after Canada geese had improved their numbers and flavor by field feeding. Although brant are the most maritime of all geese (save the emperor), a flock of brant may have followed some snow geese from the salt marsh one day, and the rest is (natural) history. During severe winters, brant can be found feeding in seaside fields in Maryland, Virginia, and Ireland. The quality of their flavor and overall survival rates have improved, thanks to the food value of the upland grasses. Yet one facet of this recently acquired behavior rekindles the old debate concerning the alleged stupidity of birds.

In bygone days, when brant fed exclusively on eelgrass, they did so according to the tide: resting when water covered the grass beds, flighting about when the beds were exposed or close enough to the surface for the brant to tip up and feed. Today, even though tide has no effect on the availability of winter wheat and barley, brant still adhere to tidal schedules when feeding in fields.

At high water, the birds sit on bars or rest in rafts, sleeping and preening and waiting for the falling tide to trigger their feeding urge. Suddenly, their biological clock strikes the magic hour, and hundreds, then thousands, of brant sweep up and fly inland with rapid wingbeats, making them appear like a cloud of mallards until, with a unified bank and turn, the entire flock reverses direction with the breathtaking speed and grace that only brant possess.

Muttering, the birds sweep low over a grain field, looking as though they are about to land. Suddenly they rise, turn, and sweep on for another quarter-mile before beginning to settle down when, perhaps, they swirl up and on to still another location, but always one within a mile of open water. After the first birds pitch, others quickly surround them.

After fifteen minutes or half an hour of feeding, the brant abruptly sweep into the wind again and turn wide around the field, banking and twisting amidst constant babbling, until they precipitously land again, often within a few yards of where they were just feeding. This time, however, the birds at the rear of the flock are now nearer the front, and they get first opportunity at the tender wheat tips. Such nervous and apparently random behavior reconcentrates the flock, drawing in birds that have gotten too far from the safety of the group.

After several hours of such activity, the brant's biological clock tells the birds that the tide is rising and that it is again time to find gravel bars and calm water. With one last swing around the field, the birds sweep low over a hedgerow bordering the bay and fly to a watery sanctuary of shallow flats.

Such behavior would appear to be stupid, except that it's so successful. The truth is that no creature that has survived tens of millions of years can be called "stupid." (The genus *Homo* has been around for only a few million years, and some wonder whether we'll survive another century!) If their genes and the exigencies of winter survival persuade brant to come readily to decoys, this is because the greatest survival potential for this particular species lies in its flocking behavior. Furthermore, brant pair-bonds are marvelously strong, and adult birds will defend their young from predators with greater vigor than almost any other waterfowl. Even young brant from the previous year have been known to help drive off an Arctic fox from their parents' new nest.

The alleged stupidity of brant is probably nothing more than the bird's difficulty in adjusting to man's on-again, off-again role as predator. Obviously, if one or more seasons pass without a gun being fired at them, brant may decide that men, like the seals on their breeding grounds, are no threat. And since in most years when hunting is allowed, 20 to 30 percent of the total population are juveniles who have never before had to reckon with hunters, it's not surprising that the seven-month-old birds respond enthusiastically to the sight of several dozen decoys, particularly if their appeal is reinforced with good calling.

Brant have the habit, shared with the equally maritime emperor goose, of trading around low over the marsh and water. Such birds may have no intention of pitching to a spread of decoys. Their curiosity lures them over, and their low altitude makes them vulnerable. By contrast, snow geese and Canadas are usually coming in to land when shot over decoys—hence, the need to "work" them in and their resulting reputation for wariness when the "working" proves difficult. Brant shot over decoys are often only looking the situation over. Since successive flocks check the spread out in the same low-flying manner—behavior intrinsic to their search for submerged vegetation and company—many gunners call brant "stupid." Yet calling these birds "stupid" is less an indictment of brant intelligence than of the slanderer's ability to comprehend anything of nature beyond his fingertips.

Knowledge of a creature's habits enables you to hunt it with greater success than that of the casual shooter. Brant respond well to decoys—perhaps, even those you've made yourself, because those of commercial manufacture are no longer available. Brant respond well to calling made by vibrating the tongue against the roof of your mouth with a rising guttural inflexion. Such personal ingredients help make brant hunting among the most satisfying forms of wildfowling. Perhaps this is also true because you find them flighting low over white-capped seas or through the overwash passes in barrier dunes, and you love their environment as much as you love the little sea geese.

Snow Geese

John James Audubon was a careful observer of wildlife. Yet he characterized snow geese as silent birds, "rarely emitting any cries unless when pursued or being wounded." Where in the New World did he hunt such silent snows, and under what circumstances?! About the only time I find snows to be silent is when they sense they're being stalked, or after they've been wounded and are hiding in the grass, trying to escape detection.

You normally hear flocks of snow geese long before you see their black wing tips twinkling in the winter sky. The sound is less melodious than the call of Canada geese, and some say it's like the yapping of dogs. Yet its harshness contains a certain wild beauty, and you shiver to hear it, remembering that the old scientific name for the bird, *hyperborea,* means "from beyond the north wind."

Snow goose hunting has changed enormously since the flocks began increasing exponentially in the 1960s. The most dramatic example involves the greater "geographic variant" in the Atlantic Flyway. In 1902, fewer than 3,000 greater snow geese existed, according to ornithologists E. F. G. White and Harrison F. Lewis. In 1931, greater snows still numbered fewer than 10,000 individuals. By the 1960s, however, greater snows numbered 100,000, and state and federal agencies began considering an open season.

By the time political and legal obstacles were overcome, the greater snow goose population was about 200,000. An important factor in the 1975 federal district court's decision to allow an Atlantic Flyway snow goose season was Canadian biologist Hugh Boyd's estimation of the annual adult mortality of greater snows compared with that of the Mississippi and western flyways' lesser snow geese, that were already being hunted. The lesser snow's annual adult mortality rate is about 27 percent, while the *unhunted* greater snows was 23 percent. Carefully regulated exploitation by hunters would be a negligible factor in the overall annual mortality of the Arctic-island-breeding birds.

So an Atlantic Flyway season was opened amid dire predictions by wildlife protectionists of wholesale extermination. The first year, the birds—particularly gray, young-of-the-year snows—were remarkably easy to attract with half-a-dozen, lifelike decoys supplemented by two dozen bleach bottles, diapers, or even old newspapers. Yet fewer than 3,000 greater snows were killed—less than 2 percent of the estimated population.

The following year, the birds were already more inclined to move around in large flocks. Decoyable family groups became the exception, and susceptible singles were downright rare. Atlantic coastal gunners looked to Louisiana and Texas for tips about how to hunt snows, and the word came back, "try kite decoys and lots and lots of white objects on the ground." The season after that, word came back, "use super-sized realistic decoys supplemented by lots and lots and *lots* of white objects on the ground." By 1980, if you weren't using *hundreds* of realistic snow goose decoys, about the only creatures to show much interest in your spread were gulls and curious cattle.

Today, the most successful snow-goose hunters from North Carolina to Texas put out more than a thousand decoys. Even if most of these are of the handkerchief and wind-sock varieties, they take more time to put out and pick up than the hunters spend hunting. If the birds come well, shooters will kill a limit within a few minutes from one or two huge flocks. If the birds don't come at all, picking up a spread of a thousand decoys seems to take all day!

As snow geese have continued to proliferate, wintering concentrations have taken on some of the behavioral characteristics of densely schooling fish, and with the same result: a relatively few individuals on the fringe of the school or flock are taken by predators, but short of surrounding the entire school or flock with a net, the overall mass continues to expand beyond local carrying capacities. As soon as one habitat's food supply is exhausted, or predators (including man) become too numerous, the snows move on.

Some rough winters, however, the birds will do reckless things. In January 1988, a flock of 4,000 snow geese (including approximately twenty blues) fed in a field next to a major north-south artery (Route 13) in Accomack County, Virginia. The birds had doubtlessly been attracted to the area by the hundreds of ring-billed gulls hanging around the Perdue chicken slaughtering plant adjacent to the field. The geese were being watched and photographed by people in cars pulled up to the side of the road when a truck-load of rednecks pulled up and blazed into the flock with shotguns and rifles. The shooters killed over thirty birds and crippled another fifteen. They were caught and fined, but not before many of the horrified watching nonhunters had been converted into *anti-*hunters.

Since snow geese are relentlessly persecuted whenever they leave the relatively few national wildlife refuges adequate to their behavior and numbers, individual snows are far warier than they were a decade ago, and their collective, or flock, savvy becomes practically impenetrable due to the multiplicity of wary eyes. But "wariness" is a relative term. The same goose can appear both wary and foolish within a single minute. Consistent hunting success depends less on hoping for a few consistently foolish geese than on consistently being able to anticipate what an established flock will do according to the vagaries of weather or time of day.

All wintering geese have a routine that includes a daily (sometimes twice daily) flight from a resting area to obtain food, grit, and water. Greater snow geese don't seem to need fresh water the way Canadas do, and this makes them less predictable than Canadas.

Another difference is that snows fly generally earlier and higher than Canada geese. One December on the border of Bombay Hook National

Wildlife Refuge in Delaware, I listened to what sounded like half the snows in creation leave the refuge before first light!

When the weather is foggy or snow-stormy, geese avoid flying at all. I've watched snow geese in Virginia and North Carolina pick a living from the salt marshes behind a coastal barrier island three days in a row rather than risk poor visibility to reach preferred feeding grounds some miles away on the mainland. When snow geese move on a foggy morning, they generally do in one vast flock. If they hear you calling or one flies low enough to spot your spread, you'll suddenly have all the geese for miles around in your decoys. Regardless of what you decide to do about it, you won't see another snow goose the rest of the day once that visit is over.

One misty dawn several seasons back, I was sitting in a blind built into a ditch with three companions when wave after wave of greater snow geese suddenly began coming through the fog and landing in our decoys. We were hoping for Canadas. Only two of us wanted to kill any of the less flavorful snow geese, and, unfortunately, the man who was supposed to call the shot didn't like to shoot snow geese at all. As a result, the optimum moment passed in which the two of us who wanted snow geese could have killed a bird each and flared off the rest of the flock without unduly alarming the other birds.

The shot-caller told us to wait because he thought he saw some Canadas mixed in with the next wave of snows coming out of the mist. These darker birds turned out to be juvenile snow geese, but by the time they were on the ground, the shot-caller saw several more gray birds in the next phalanx—which also turned out to be juvenile snow geese. By this time, there were three hundred birds on the ground, some only a few yards from the edge of the ditch and scrutinizing the screen of cedars through which we peered.

One of our non-snow-goose-shooters suddenly changed his mind. That decision as well as the argument over why the shot-caller had delayed giving the go-ahead was hard to hear above the clamor of birds. By the time the three of us who wanted to kill a snow goose each had convinced our nonshooting companion that none of the birds out front were Canadas, or would be Canadas, some six hundred geese were on the ground and more were arriving with every passing second.

When we three shooters finally yelled to get the birds airborne, our shouts could barely be heard above the cacophony of babbling geese. I picked out a target, made an easy kill, but didn't fire again when I saw a bird behind the one I shot fall out as well. One of my companions fired three shots, and the third man fired twice. In all, we fired six rounds, but birds continued to drop out of the retreating flock like sacks of flour. The man who'd fired twice looked at the carnage, sat back down, and put his face in his hands.

"God, I feel sick," he said.

There was no time for such emotion, for all four of us had to scramble from the ditch and begin chasing cripples. Ironically, the fellow who'd delayed calling the shot and, by doing so, inadvertently set the stage for the unwanted slaughter ended up firing thirteen times at running birds when he'd never intended to fire a round. We picked up twenty-one geese and lost two others in the woods and marsh.

Compare that unhappy misadventure with this, more satisfying story:

Punt-Hunting

"On this shore the tide runs out for many miles and the creeks drain into leads and the leads into channels, until the whole estuary is a network of waterways amongst the mud and sand.

"To go there the wildfowler must have a boat, in which he can drop down with the ebb-tide and come back again with the flood, a lovely, silent progress. Down on the sands far from the shore he finds the mallards and wigeon asleep in great companies, and, if it is the time of full moon, he may also see the geese. They have fed all through the night, and now are resting far away from the haunts of man."

Sir Peter Scott wrote *Morning Flight* in 1935 when the east coast of England still resembled the mid-Atlantic shore of the United States. Sir Peter's beloved "brown land," however, lacked the extensive cordgrass cover of North America's salt muds, and perhaps for that reason the British never had the cordgrass-eating hordes of greater snow geese that winter on barrier islands from New Jersey to the Outer Banks of North Carolina.

Stray greater snows do visit the British Isles every winter—most often Ireland—and British wildfowlers who seek this uncommon trophy sometimes do so from a low-profiled punt. Punt-hunting requires a keen knowledge of such ever-changing variables as wind direction, tide, the sun and, at one time in the United Kingdom, the moon at night. (Although puntgunning in the UK is still legal at night, by common agreement, puntgunners no longer hunt at night so as not to disturb human residents in homes around the shore or birds resting on the estuary.) The supreme experience of puntgunning involves geese. The bird's ungainly—hence, less sporting—takeoff is more than compensated for by their wariness.

In southern New England, there is little public land. Flocks of Canada geese are found in abundance on private golf courses and industrial park lawns, but golfers and industrial executives object to people dressed in commando camouflage wriggling across a manicured landscape with shotguns cradled in their arms. Fortunately, Canada geese are also found on coastal estuaries, which, although developed and polluted, offer punt-hunters possibilities denied their shore-based colleagues.

Years ago, Tom Lomas and Jim Malone learned to use maps, their imaginations, and Lomas's punt to hunt Canada geese in some surprisingly urban areas of Connecticut. Inevitably, the boys wanted to take on a rarer quarry, the snow goose. They studied bird books and flyway maps and found that their best chance in the Atlantic Flyway lay along the coast between southern Maryland and North Carolina. They decided to invest their out-of-state license money in Virginia, even though neither boy was familiar with the area.

They planned their visit for January. A great freeze had locked up the Northeast, and fleeing waterfowl had concentrated in marshes behind barrier islands all along the Eastern Shore. Tom and Jim launched their outboard-powered punt at public ramps and for the first two days anchored in tidal guts and channels and hunted ducks in the mornings and afternoons. In the middle of each day, they explored the network of marshes and waterways for geese. They saw skeins moving everywhere, but they were unable to locate any place the birds could be stalked with a punt.

On the third afternoon the boys decided to look for a roost. After two hours of exploring, they found a flight path where several dozen birds flew low across a channel on their way to the beach. The boys knew that if they tried to jump the geese on the beach, they'd not only spook them before getting within range, they'd ruin the barrier island as a sanctuary. So they located a marsh drain under the birds' flight path, tucked their boat and themselves into it, and prayed that a few birds would eventually come in lower than the rest.

The wait was long. The snows seemed to know that if they stayed a hundred yards high, they'd be safe from enemies below. A couple of small flocks flew over at extreme range, but the boys didn't shoot. They thought they might only cripple the birds and lose a better opportunity later. The rim of the sun had just kissed the horizon when a straggler, eager to join the squadrons already on the sands ahead of him, ventured low enough for a killing shot.

Tom was jubilant! His first greater snow goose! It was all the more of a trophy because it had been earned with planning and patience. Jim was now more keen than ever to shoot a snow goose of his own.

The next morning, the two boys passed up black-ducking to scout the marshes and bays within a five-mile radius of the launch ramp they used. Although a thorough search eventually would have involved exploring dozens of miles of channels and guts, the boys got lucky about noon when they ran into decoy carver Mark McNair and me. We knew where an enormous flock of snow geese had come out of a rye field to rest and take grit in a shallow bay.

As the boys motored slowly ahead of us into the upper end of the bay, they were overwhelmed by the sight of so many birds. The area had not been hunted yet that season, and the waterfowl were comparatively tame. Or perhaps—like the greylags and barnacle geese Sir Peter once described—"the birds were tired after the buffetings of the wind the day before." Flocks of brant and black ducks got up and flew only a few hundred yards before settling down again. Tom got out his camera and exposed film as fast as he could advance it.

Then the hunt began in earnest. Moving ashore, we helped the boys divest themselves of everything not absolutely essential to their stalk. The punt's engine and gas tank were removed and replaced with a sculling oar. The boys removed their decoys, extra life preservers, anchor, even their spare clothes and shells. After throwing some grass on the bow to make the low boat look like a floating island, Jim lay forward and Tom, the sculler, lay in the stern. They pushed off for the main body of snow geese more than half a mile away.

Imperceptible movement is the key to successful sculling. Still, it's difficult to avoid trembling when you hear birds by the thousands all around you.

The bowman must stay out of sight and reject any temptation to take a peek at the ever-watchful birds—even when you're surrounded by a once-in-a-lifetime panorama.

Slowly, ever so slowly, the artificial island moved closer to the geese. The snows did not seem to notice that a grassy tump was moving against the current. Even more curious, the narrowest end of the tump was always pointed toward the densest concentration of geese.

When Tom and Jim were within a hundred yards of the birds, they told us later, it was impossible to communicate without shouting. The din of geese reverberated from the very thwarts upon which the boys lay.

Suddenly, a hush fell over the bay. The silence was so profound, Mark and I, waiting by the discarded gear, could hear a song sparrow in a hedgerow more than a mile away. Tom knew what the hush presaged, and he propelled the boat more swiftly toward the nearest group of birds. With a deafening roar, like a moonship straining to leave the earth, the geese began to rise. Pinions on the water and in the air flailed like a hurricane as the two boys sat up quickly and selected targets. Mark and I never heard the shots.

"We picked birds on the fringe of the flock," said Jim, "so we wouldn't kill more than two apiece. But I'm amazed we didn't!"

Had the boys killed more than one bird with each shot, their otherwise perfect stalk would have been marred, even though each boy was entitled by law to four snows. A punt-hunting expedition is successful when hunters are able to get off a shot. Beyond that, triumph is two different matters depending on whether you're using a shoulder gun or a cannon. In the case of cannons, the more birds killed, the greater your proof that luck and skill combined to provide an optimum shot. In the case of shoulder guns, however, a right and a left are perfection. This subtle distinction is difficult to explain to nonhunters, and even a sportsman must be a wildfowler to comprehend it.

A Glut of Geese?

Are there too many geese for the good of the geese and the good of wildfowling? Will familiarity breed diseases as well as contempt? Will the vast flocks now concentrated in a few prime wintering areas increasingly suffer from epizootics due to overcrowding? And have Canada geese, in particular, lost some of their luster as the traditional *ne plus ultra* wildfowling trophy due to local abundance and the increasing lack of wariness that goes with living in sanctuaries?

The general public doesn't understand that geese in a refuge—be it an official federal haven or a golf course pond—know the precise boundaries of that sanctuary better than any human. The average person cannot comprehend that the very same goose so willing to take food from his hand by a park pond can be a cautious customer a few miles away while being cajoled from a field pit.

Consider how many times this past season you worked a string of geese, turned them time and again with your calling, finally got them locked up for a landing, when along came another, larger flock that pulled every one of "your birds" away. Consider how many more times this past season you sat in a blind and watched the flocks and family groups fly toward a distant refuge without once missing a wingbeat on behalf of your decoys.

The only way to guarantee goose hunting today is to use a great number of realistic decoys (often economically or logistically impossible), adopt hit-and-run tactics (useful for occasional success, but no way to sustain a ninety-day season), buy or lease land surrounding a goose sanctuary so you can pass-shoot birds coming out to feed (sport of a sort, but not real hunting), or you can spend enough time studying the birds to become that all-too-rare phenomenon: a hunter who knows how to anticipate what wild geese will do.

Have you ever noticed that Canadas behave differently over decoys than do snow geese? Snows characteristically hang high in the wind, murmuring, seeming to discuss the situation below. Canadas, by contrast, tend to circle a decoy spread or work their way upwind from side to side until ready to lock up for landing. Canadas will occasionally hover, but not like snows. This suggests that silhouettes may not be as effective as half or full-bodied decoys for snow geese, but possibly as effective as half or full-bodied decoys for Canadas. If a snow-goose spread is composed only of silhouettes, most of those decoys mysteriously disappear from the perspective of hovering birds. On the other hand, silhouettes may be even better than shell or full-bodied decoys for Canada goose hunting, because as the constantly shifting Canadas scrutinize the flock below, the silhouettes seem to move—appearing, disappearing, and reappearing—in the circling birds' cone of vision.

Have you ever noticed how geese stop calling when they hear gunfire? By continuing to call birds when shots sound from a nearby field, you're not only wasting your breath, you'll spook geese that might otherwise have come to you.

Have you ever asked a guide whether he leaves his decoys out in the same place for the entire season? If he does, odds are his clients will see half the action, or less, of the guide in the next field who takes up his decoys after every hunt. Permanent decoys warn wary birds, and only storm-battered or late arrivals will show much interest in a fixed stool. Permanent decoys end up facing the wrong way on many days, and half of them end up falling over or are encrusted by snow on the best morning of the season. Farmers wanting to protect their winter crops from geese depredations can't do better than to set out decoys in each of their fields, gun those fields the first week of the season, and then let the "scare-geese" keep birds at bay for the rest of the winter.

Do you realize that so long as geese have open water and snow-free feeding, they'll remain on a favorite wintering ground throughout the coldest weather? Francis Howard of Easton, Maryland, uses a road grader to scrape the snow away from in front of his field pits.

"A tractor with a big blade would do just as well," admits Howard, "but since one of my friends owns a grader, there's no sense in not going First Class.

"Given a patch of snow-free dirt," he continues, "a Canada goose will survive by eating it for its grit and minerals. It's only when birds can no longer reach grass or dirt through a layer of ice or deep snow that they'll move farther south. Federal law says I can't bait waterfowl, but until a federal judge rules that snow removal constitutes baiting, I'm going to pray for blizzards and the good health of my friend with the grader!"

A significant and growing proportion of the nearly two million Canada geese in the Atlantic and Mississippi flyways spend their winters north of the Mason-Dixon Line. It's touching and even a little sad to what lengths state resource agencies will go in their efforts to give resident hunters the impression that the agencies can do something about this trend. In the 1960s, North Carolina had an average wintering population of 232,000 Canada geese. By 1986, the number had dropped to 22,000 birds. In 1987, the state general assembly agreed to spend $100,000 to begin transporting thousands of geese from northern states to six relocation sites in coastal North Carolina counties. Yet if North Carolina's experiment follows the pattern of earlier attempts by Florida and Louisiana, the transplanted geese will make every effort to rejoin the main concentrations of birds to the north—even when they're pinioned so they can't fly back. While some small North Carolina flocks may develop after a decade of this costly program, the birds will be largely nonmigratory in behavior—hence, defeating one purpose of their being brought south in the first place, which is for most of the transplants to return north to recruit other birds to winter in North Carolina. We wish the state well, but we'll believe the success of North Carolina's effort when we see it.

A growing source of frustration for Mississippi Flyway hunters results from the widespread re-introduction of the largely nonmigratory giant Canada goose. These big birds sometimes weigh more than twenty pounds, more than three times the average size of the ordinary honker. Long believed extinct, a flock of giant Canadas was rediscovered in Minnesota in 1962. Rumors of similarly huge Canada geese nesting on the cliffs above the Missouri River west of St. Louis began circulating in the late 1960s, and in 1971, a team from the Missouri Department of Conservation confirmed the rumors. By 1979, waterfowl technicians estimated there were 70,000 giant Canada geese in the flyway.

Today that figure is 170,000 and still rising. Since the birds winter not far from where they breed, they have ample time throughout the year to discover the best localities for food and the safest flight paths to and from equally safe roosting areas. The core of the Minnesota flock, for example, winters in downtown Rochester where convalescing patients from the Mayo Clinic keep the birds well provisioned with bread and crackers.

When the rest of the Mississippi Flyway's population of Canadas comes south from their breeding grounds near James and Hudson bays, many attach themselves to families of giant Canadas and, thereby, gain the immunity from gunfire that the local, larger birds have acquired through their knowledge of safe flight paths and feeding grounds. The huge *maxima* subspecies seems to attract the newly arrived smaller birds the way super-sized decoys do—except these super-sized decoys call, fly about, and know all the best places for food, water, and safety.

Canadas that once used the Mississippi and Missouri rivers as flight paths south now winter on the chain of lakes these rivers have become. From 1953 through 1965, peak winter counts along just that stretch of the Missouri flowing through South Dakota averaged 32,300 Canada geese. From 1976 through 1984, peak winter counts averaged more than 177,000, and in December 1980, more than 259,000 Canadas were found roosting on South Dakota's portion of the Missouri alone.

Significantly, each time an impoundment is created to the north of another impoundment already holding geese, the new reservoir acts as a magnet for the wintering flocks. After South Dakota's Fort Randall Reservoir was created in 1952, it began pulling the Hutchinson's race of the

Tall Grass Prairie population of Canada geese away from their less well-watered, but traditional migration path to the east. Sand Lake National Wildlife Refuge in northeastern South Dakota had formerly been a major concentration and staging area for the little Hutchies. Yet from the late 1950s, counts at Sand Lake declined steadily, while Hutchinson's band returns from the Missouri River increased. After two additional dams were built upstream of Fort Randall (Oahe in 1958 and Big Bend in 1963), the Hutchies, along with other Prairie and Great Plains Canada geese, shifted their wintering bases to the more northerly reservoirs.

In an attempt to prevent the birds from leaving the Fort Randall area, local landowners lobbied the South Dakota legislature to make "their" impoundment a statutory waterfowl refuge. This was done in 1961, and for a few years, this seemed to help goose hunters on lands adjoining Fort Randall.

Then the decline began all over again in the mid-1960s, about the time Oahe reached its full potential as a reservoir and roosting refuge. In 1959, Fort Randall accounted for 80 percent of all the Canadas wintering along the Missouri in South Dakota. By 1978, Fort Randall accounted for only 20 percent. That same year, 80 percent of the Canada geese killed along South Dakota's portion of the Missouri were shot around Lake Oahe to the north.

In 1970, I went to South Dakota to shoot under the auspices of a Lake Oahe farmer and goose guide who, besides his own sizeable holdings, rented lakeside lands from the Indians. His clients shot from trenches overlooking the Missouri River, and the geese flew up and out of the long shadows cast by the bluffs into the blinding sunrise behind us. Although the birds were several hundred feet above the lake, some of them were only a few yards above our heads. The setting was magnificent but the pass-shooting was mechanical and verged on slaughter.

Despite a one-goose daily limit designed to enhance the hunting experience and to reduce shooting pressure, brigades of expectant hunters were fed into trenches overlooking the reservoir. All guns fired on one whistle signal and were silenced on the next. Each shooter then grabbed a goose—any goose would do—and hightailed it for the opposite end of the trench where trucks waited to take the first fire teams back to the farmhouse where other platoons of shooters were waiting to fill the trenches. Each pulse of shots sounded more like an execution than hunting. One trench might serve a hundred shooters a morning. Canadas flighting off Oahe were enduring the equivalent of assembly-line slaughter and some of the most intense shooting pressure anywhere in North America.

North Dakotan and Canadian landowners looked south and coveted the financial gravy. The money being spent by goose hunters in South Dakota exceeded what some local farmers could hope to earn by growing grain. North Dakotans and Canadians decided to enhance their own wintering areas for geese by eliminating afternoon shooting. Whether the geese needed that inducement, or whether, as South Dakota waterfowl biologist Gay Simpson suggests, "geese fly no further south than necessary to meet their biological needs," flocks soon began building on impoundments in North Dakota and Saskatchewan where some of the best goose shooting on the continent is found today. Ultimately irrelevant, the sanctuary status of Fort Randall Reservoir was repealed in 1981.

Whereas shooting pressure is probably contributing to short-stopping in the western flyways, it's almost certainly the principal cause in the Atlantic Flyway. How else can we explain the birds' ongoing abandonment of the earthly paradise of Maryland's Eastern Shore for the congested landscapes and polluted waters of New Jersey, southern New York, and coastal New England?

In March 1986, Osbourn Owings—owner of Jamaica Point Farm, once the best private goose-hunting property in Maryland's Talbot County and the place where Kip *(The Ducks Came Back)* Farrington shot many of his Canadas—sent a letter to his regional waterfowl advisory committee:

"It appears we have a problem with our declining goose population. . . . Twenty-seven years ago, I leased Jamaica Point Farm and twenty-five years ago, I purchased the farm. There were many ducks but very few geese on the Shore at that time. The first year I hunted at Jamaica Point was 1957–58, and we bagged five geese. In the season of 1958–59, nine geese were bagged. It was during this period that I set aside an area of land approximately one-half square mile with water on two sides, as a sanctuary, and began feeding birds in that area. I fed from the day the first goose arrived until the last goose left in the spring. The season of 1959–60 we bagged 206 geese, and the [average in succeeding years] increased to over 400. . . . I shot only two one-half days per week (Fridays and Saturdays), plus holidays.

"In 1975 the farm adjoining Jamaica Point was leased to commercial hunters. They did everything possible to kill geese. They shot six days a week—daylight until dark. . . . Year by year Jamaica Point's success went down to as few as 124 birds in 1979–80. We are now back to 400. [The reason is that] six years ago, Dave Pyles bought the [overshot] farm, Cherry Grove. He ceased hunting rights [but] *it was only during the last half of this season, five years later, that geese again began to use Cherry Grove. . . .* This suggests to me that hunting pressure in Maryland has become so great that we are driving geese out of the state. I blame 90 percent of the pressure on the commercial guides. There must be restrictions on commercial hunting."

Owings goes on to suggest that the daily goose limit be reduced from three birds to two, and that legal shooting be restricted to Fridays, Saturdays, Mondays, and holidays. He also suggests "shooting hours for Canada geese be from sunrise to 3:00 P.M. to give birds an opportunity to find a quiet roosting place for the night." In addition, "we should encourage landowners to provide refuges, to plant green crops, leave standing corn and to feed after the season closes."

Some changes were made for the 1988–89 hunting year. The length of the Delmarva season was reduced and the daily Canada goose limit dropped to two birds. Any more changes, however, seem unlikely. The enormous undeclared income stemming from hunting leases and guide fees and the availability of ducks, make serious re-evaluation of Maryland shooting hours practically impossible, despite the example of a noon closure in North Dakota that has resulted in more birds taken per hunter, rather than less. If Maryland sportsmen could curb the commercial hunting lobby and persuade Delaware to cooperate, they'd shoot many more ducks and geese under Os's suggested 3:00 P.M. daily closure and encourage more birds to winter on the upper Delmarva peninsula than happens now when the birds are shot at from sunrise to sunset. Although the golden-egg-laying goose will continue dying unless the northerly drift of wintering flocks is stopped, the majority of commercial guides and property owners are more concerned with cash today than flocks tomorrow.

The future of all goose hunting is more a matter of smart planning than smart shooting. The most crucial ingredient will be restraint. By reducing limits to one or two birds, and by not shooting a productive location more than once a week, hunters will end up with more satisfying seasons than if they went for broke every time they went out. The expectation of seeing and working birds is what makes for world-class wildfowling, and nothing is more desolate than fields and bays once filled with the choruses of ducks and geese now bereft of all sound but the sighing of wind.

—14—

Sea Ducks

Alaska

The settings were spectacular, but the dog work was more so. Some blinds were located high on the sides of schist-sharp cliffs and barely in range of the decoys at low tide, but the

Labs—Katie and Blue—jumped from rock to rock like melanistic goats, made the retrieves, and clambered back into the blinds without any whimpering for assistance.

Other blinds were two-man rafts dressed with netting and spruce boughs. The impatient dogs would sometimes try to charge through the netting when a bird was down; but once the rafts were lifted off the mud flats by the more than twenty-foot tides and swung about in the wind and current so that all downed birds drifted past the open gate, the dogs figured out the pattern and were so dependable that you'd be reliving a shot and for the moment forgetting about the birds when you'd look back and here came Katie, barely making way against the swift current, with the last of the ducks in her mouth.

Each member of our four-man party had a favorite day and place of duck hunting in and around Kachemak Bay, Alaska. Dick Graham will think of the Pipeline that he likened to a three-dimensional Space Invaders computer game in which each cartridge was a quarter and the phalanxes of Barrow's goldeneye were endlessly attacking aliens. Birds came from two directions at once while the racing, rising tide seemed to swirl up from everywhere. Dick swore at himself and laughed at himself, dropping shells and dropping birds, and retreating up the cobblestone beach a dozen yards after every volley.

Mel Baughman will remember the flooded timber at sunset with clouds of super-sized mallards and an anomalous pair of gadwall settling around him like the feathered fallout from a nuclear explosion. The puny sound of his shots could barely be heard above the cacophony of wildfowl. After killing a double, he hung up his gun to try to capture the scene on film, but no camera was adequate to the wonder of being there.

Paul Wirth's best day was on the rocks at Peterson Bay with pairs, trios, and an occasional Barrow's dozen of goldeneye, harlequins, surf scoters, and red-breasted mergansers whirling by on 20-knot gusts, only briefly in range above the crest of a wave before dropping out of sight in its trough and reappearing at the next crest a hundred yards down the line. Exhilarated by the setting and the weather, and inspired by the challenge of the shooting, Paul has never been more deadly; few birds escaped his tracking gun unless he wanted them to.

My favorite memory was the afternoon we crouched like outcroppings on a black sand spit and rose suddenly when scoters appeared over the crest, fired, and heard their bodies thud on the sand, whirled to fire at their companions lost in the sun and, temporarily blinded, unable to see those birds fall, heard their splashes in the water beyond the beach.

The best memories involve tension and triumph. For that reason, one very special afternoon will be etched in the minds of Dick Graham and myself so long as we both shall live. We were hunting harlequins and scoters from the top of a tiny islet where we'd been left by our host, Mike McBride, while he rode off in his Boston Whaler to tend Mel and Paul on another rock on the other side of Cohen Island. Mike had left Blue to retrieve our ducks, but at first I didn't see how a dog would be much use. There were only two ways off the islet: a flying leap from the top and a tortuous path down one side ending above a surf-swept ledge.

Yet Blue's first round trip seemed as though he had springs, not muscles, in his legs. He flung himself off the top near where I stood, dropped more than a dozen feet to the water below, and swam quickly away from the islet to keep from being swept back in against the rocks. On his return he bounded from the water to the first ledge like a dog-faced penguin.

By his third and fourth retrieves, however, he'd stand on the surf-swept ledge a moment, contemplating the last hurdle. He'd brace himself against the surge and psych himself for the supreme effort. He never put down the bird to suck in more oxygen, and he never took his eyes off the landing above, as though willing it closer.

Our fifth duck nearly killed him. The scoter was hard-hit but, also, hard-swimming. Dick and I fired a dozen follow-up shots but stopped when Blue neared the circle of our distant patterns. The dog pursued the crippled duck for five hundred yards out into Kachemak Bay while all my frantic signaling with a bright orange life vest to Mike in his boat went unnoticed.

The duck and the dog were so far away by the time Blue caught the scoter, we couldn't be sure that the miraculous event had occurred except that the dog appeared to be swimming back.

"He's got it! I think he's got it!" shouted Dick.

Minute by minute crawled by without the dog seeming to get closer. Our jubilation turned to anxiety when we thought the current might be too strong for him. Several flocks of sea ducks came and went over the decoys without Dick or me firing for fear we'd compound the crisis by dropping more ducks into the water.

I tried again to signal Mike. I climbed to the top of the islet and swung the life vest back and forth, slapping its straps on the rocks on either side of me in frantic sweeps. Mike slowly motored out of sight around the headland where he was tending Mel and Paul.

When I got down, I thought Blue might be closer. Dick, who'd been watching the dog intently, doubted it. But when another five minutes passed, we were certain the dog was making some headway.

"Come on, Blue! You can make it! Come on, boy!"

Fifteen minutes later, Blue swam into the eddies downstream of the islet. Ten minutes after that, he stood on the now-exposed threshold rock, and Dick and I swarmed over him in affection and admiration. We didn't even mind when, with the still-living bird in his mouth, he suddenly shook salt water over our guns and cameras.

Blue allowed me to take the bird and then climbed laboriously to his old position. He sat, looking out over the decoys and waiting for our next shots. But there weren't going to be any. Dick and I unloaded our guns and took pictures of the dog and of the ducks flying over the decoys until Mike came back an hour later.

Most everything about Alaskan wildfowling is majestic. Bald eagles drift high over your blinds, and some may even be drawn by the shooting the way vultures hunt over rural roads at dawn, looking for whatever man's technology provides in the way of a meal. Although the eagles are omnipresent, they are also discreet, and we lost only one crippled bird, a goldeneye, to an eagle—a duck we probably would have lost in any event.

Sea otters rolled and dived among the decoys the day we hunted with Blue on the islet. The sound of gunfire and the periodic presence of the dog didn't seem to alarm the animals. Once, after we thought we'd frightened them away, a sea otter surfaced among the decoys, swam about as though looking for something it had forgotten, then drifted off with the tide.

When the four of us told friends we were going all the way to Alaska to hunt ducks, they thought we were kidding. When we came back full of enthusiasm for what we'd done, they *knew* we were crazy.

Some of these skeptics were hunters and fishermen like ourselves. A few would even spend more money on a trip to the Carribbean in search of billfish, to New Zealand for trout, or even to Alaska to hunt big game than we had on our duck hunt. Yet they were baffled that four seemingly sensible people would fly thousands of miles to hunt ducks—and *sea* ducks at that!

A $60 non-resident Alaskan small-game license entitles a hunter to seven "game ducks" a day, including goldeneye, mallard, bufflehead, gadwall, teal, and pintail in that order of abundance; plus fifteen "non-game ducks," including surf and common (black) scoters, harlequins, red-breasted mergansers, old squaw, white-winged scoters, and various eiders, also in that order of abundance.

Although none of us killed a twenty-two-bird daily limit, it wasn't for lack of opportunity. Had we wanted to "go for it," we could have been out at first light—which means 8:30 A.M. at China Poot Bay in late November—and not come back until midafternoon. Instead, we slept late, hunted only about four hours, and hardly hunted at all on Thanksgiving Day. Yet we never averaged less than a dozen birds per gun per outing, which is hardly shabby shooting.

So the four of us weren't worried about what others might think about a sea-duck hunting expedition to Alaska. The four of us have hunted and fished together long enough to know that our concept of a trophy outdoor experience fits no clichéd ideal of proper sport. We want the best, but we learned long ago that the "best" is a total experience that has little to do with piles of dead game.

How does one define the total wildfowling experience?

Some critics of our trip were hung up on the sea duck angle. Had we gone to Homer specifically to hunt the giant coastal mallards found near there—3½-pounders—that would have made the trip more comprehensible to them.

Yet must a total hunt be concerned only with the largest of something? Surely birds as rare and exquisite as harlequin and mature Barrow's goldeneye drakes qualify as memorable prizes.

"But you can't eat such birds," other critics complained.

Really? We ate every one of the birds we didn't bring home for mounting, and these included a good many more scoters than super-sized mallards. By the time the birds had been breasted, the breasts brushed with Diane McBride's secret mustard sauce, and grilled for a few minutes over an open fire, you could not distinguish the succulent flavor of the scoter from the equally succulent mallard.

Even the guts, skins, wings, and legs of the sea ducks we shot weren't wasted. They were used as bait in traps from which we pulled the most delicious Dungeness crabs.

But before allowing ourselves to be boxed into a corner with further considerations of sea ducks as food, just who, pray tell, considers meat alone as the foundation of the total hunt?

A moose hunter might come home with several hundred pounds of prime steaks and chops, but that's not the reason he goes to Maine or Alaska to get such game. A total experience is a product of time, place, and especially effort. If you haven't *earned* the bird, beast, or fish you capture, you're unsatisfied—no matter how big or rare it is. For true sportsmen, effort always counts for more than end result.

A friend of mine gauges the success of his offshore fishing trips by the size of lunch he eats. If he finishes everything, that's evidence there was so little action he had nothing better to do than eat. If, however, he tells me he had a one-sandwich or, best of all, a no-sandwich day, that means he was too happily occupied to feed his face.

Since nothing stands in the way of my lunch, I calculate the success of my outings by the number of pictures I take. Although I pack a camera wherever I go, there are three circumstances in which I don't make any exposures: (1) lousy weather, (2) such awesome surroundings that film, which can never do more than freeze one brief moment of a lesser reality, can't begin to capture what my memory can, and (3) I'm so involved in physical activity a camera is only in the way.

Since I have a waterproof Nikonos, the weather must really be miserable to keep me from taking pictures. When I'm able to document an outing on many rolls of film, beginning with the plane trip in and ending with birds posed at the dock, I've not had as significant an experience as if, after the week's trip, I've taken only a few shots.

That was the case of the Alaska sea-duck hunt. In order to capture on film the panorama of snow-capped peaks framing China Poot Bay, the strings of ducks trading below them would have been reduced to tiny dots. Yet to take close-ups of the waterfowl would have been to lose the epic proportions of their habitat. Rather than esthetically rob Peter to pay Paul, I put my camera aside to let my soul absorb as much as possible of that epic time and place.

Biologists and statisticians say that sea-duck hunting has become the most rapidly growing form of wildfowling in North America, because most sea-duck populations represent virtually untapped resources, and because in an era of diminished dabblers and divers, sea ducks offer the last, best shooting. This may all be true, but I believe a larger reason for the growth of sea-duck hunting is what Sir Ralph Payne-Gallwey observed more than a century ago: a wildfowler is someone "who loves to use a gun on wild birds in wild places. . . . This is especially the case if the gunner is even slightly an observer of nature, and takes an interest in noting the habits and plumage of the numerous tribe of wildfowl he will have a chance of seeing and shooting during a fairly hard winter."

There is no harsher winter environment than coastal Alaska in November, the beaches of New York in December, or seaside Virginia in January—states and months where and when I've sampled sea-duck shooting. Yet the rigors of the weather only serve to enhance the earned aspects of the hunt.

Upland bird hunters have their share of special moments, but the attention of grouse, quail, and woodcock shooters is focused on their dogs and less on the birds being sought. Wildfowlers sometimes see superb dog work, but the greatest part of our satisfaction comes from the wild settings in which we find our quarry and the wonderful mystery of the birds themselves. These ingredients form what Sir Ralph called, "the backbone of wildfowl shooting."

Maine

The sea-duck hunting season is now keenly anticipated from British Columbia to the Chesapeake Bay, and from the Maritime Provinces to northern California. Even on the Great Lakes, where the quantity of old squaw purposely shot each fall once numbered only a few dozen birds, many hundreds are now taken by wildfowlers from the breakwaters at Duluth to rocky points near Kingston.

Yet no area of the continent has seen such a surge in sea-duck hunting over the past decade as Maine. Two reasons account for the phenomenon: the first has to do with local shooters switching from the beleaguered and now tightly regulated black duck to the more generously regulated sea ducks. By 1983, the black-duck kill in Maine was down 42 percent over the three-year mean kill for 1979–81. During the same period, the Maine eider kill rose 217 percent—22,436 eiders killed in 1983 in comparison with an earlier three-year mean of 7,071.

Once upon a time, eiders were shot exclusively by New England watermen for recreation and then salted for food, which coastal families ate as one of their few sources of red-blooded protein. In the spring, island-nesting eiders yielded many clutches of fresh eggs to foraging families from the mainland. By 1907, such unregulated harvests had reduced summer eider numbers in Maine to roughly fifty pairs nesting on Old Man Island in Machias Bay.

What brought the birds back was a combination of luck, the birds' own resilience, and a state wildlife department that cares about sea ducks. Unlike their European counterparts, most American waterfowl biologists disdain the study of sea ducks. That we know anything at all about surf scoters—a uniquely North American species—is due entirely to European studies of white-winged (velvet) and black (common) scoters.

The behavior of eiders and scoters differ in several respects that have helped the less migratory eider to cope with increasing human settlement and use of its coast. Scoters are non-colonial nesters of the Arctic flood plains. By contrast, when eider hens find a congenial island site, they're happy to share the area with other hens; and more than two hundred nests have been found concentrated on a single acre. Since they are large birds, eiders can cope with the ever-swelling herring and greater black-backed gull colonies found along the coast of Maine. In some cases, eiders nest close alongside incubating gulls, possibly even deriving some protection from immature gulls that prey on the eggs and chicks of any poorly protected sea bird. Since breeding gulls are always fiercely hostile to non-breeding gulls, the nesters help keep vagrant gulls away from nesting eiders as well.

On the debit side, the most common, yet most easily prevented, form of eider mortality is caused by picnickers, yachtsmen, and other recreational users of Maine islands in early summer who come ashore, scare both eiders and gulls into the sea, take their strolls and pictures, and leave. When the gulls return to shore first, they raid the eider colony, taking as many eggs and nestlings as their own nestlings can eat.

Fortunately, eiders don't stay at their nests more than twenty-four hours after the last duckling has hatched. Once the young are in the sea, they form *crèches* guarded by several hens, including some that didn't nest or may have lost their own young. Predatory fishes are more of a threat to baby eiders than predatory birds, just as later in their lives, the only enemies mature eiders seem to have, besides hunters, are sharks and seals. (On my first eider-hunting trip to Maine, I lost a crippled drake to a harbor seal.)

In 1965, seven years after he documented the expansion of the ring-necked ducks' breeding range into New England and eastern Canada,

Howard L. Mendall initiated a project with the Maine Cooperative Wildlife Research Unit to protect and expand the breeding range of eiders. Nearly forty breeding islands were acquired by various state, federal, and non-government conservation agencies. Although forty-three so-called priority islands remain outside direct control, some of these are managed by cooperative agreements with island owners who provide predator control and other forms of protection to nesting eiders.

As a result, nesting eiders have doubled their numbers at least four times over the past thirty years and extended their range southwestward as well. Today, between 20,000 and 30,000 pairs are found nesting along the Maine coast. According to winter waterfowl inventories conducted by the state in cooperation with the U.S. Fish and Wildlife Service, eiders are now more abundant in Maine than all other waterfowl species—including geese, black ducks, mallards, scaup, teal, mergansers, goldeneyes, and other sea ducks—combined!

Thus, the major reason for the phenomenal growth of sea-duck hunting in Maine is that the state is about the only place in North America where a wildfowler has an excellent chance of acquiring one of the grandest of wildfowl trophies. Maine is selling as many out-of-state small-game licenses these days to eider hunters as it once sold to woodcock hunters heading for Washington County or to teal shooters off to Merrymeeting Bay.

Having missed even seeing an eider in Alaska, I scheduled my first wildfowling trip to Maine the following January. That expedition was memorable in providing me with enough mature drake and hen eiders from which to select an ideal pair for mounting. It was also memorable in addicting me to Maine sea-duck hunting.

"You can sit in the open so long as you don't move until you're ready to shoot," my host, Charlie Kelley, advised.

Nonetheless, I felt exposed and conspicuous on the rocky islet as five eiders labored toward us into a 20-knot wind. Against Charlie's advice and my own reason, I scrunched down a little more.

"The ducks fly better on calm days than rough ones," Charlie had said earlier, and I could see why the bulky, four to six-pound birds would be reluctant to squander much energy on fighting the wind.

"Hold your fire until they lift their heads just before landing," counseled Charlie.

The three black-and-white drakes and two brown hens were so large

205

that I was sure they were in range until I glanced down at the decoys and calculated the flying birds were still more than seventy yards away. Charlie's decoys—foam Herter's geese repainted to resemble eiders—were only a dozen yards from the islet because Charlie and his regular gunning partner, Dave Farrell, like to take their shots under thirty yards.

As the birds got closer, I heard them grunting above the sound of the breeze and slapping waves. The birds banked slightly, and the greenish highlights of the males' white heads and the reddish glow of the females' feathers briefly shone in the early light before the birds swung back into the sun and became silhouettes again.

The eiders raised up, but instead of dropping their feet for a landing, they sheared off on the wind. One second they were only twenty-five yards out and still coming; the next, they were already thirty-five yards away.

"Shoot!" yelled Charlie.

Since I was on the extreme right of our group, I picked the drake that was farthest right. At my shot, he folded, rolled, hit the water—and disappeared. I stood up to improve my shooting angle, popped a new shell into my over-and-under, and kept the gun to my shoulder for when the bird resurfaced. He bobbed up ten seconds later, dead.

Charlie was already in one of the two boats he and Dave always take eider hunting. (Nothing like having a backup engine in January, as we were to be reminded later that morning.) The three drakes had been knocked down, but one was a swimming cripple.

A pair of eiders came unexpectedly around the corner of the islet. They saw Charlie in the boat, veered between him and the rock, saw us, and began to climb. I was the only one reloaded, and as the two birds approached twenty yards up, I hit the drake with my first shot and cold-cocked him with my second. He fell into the sea with a mighty splash and lay just a few yards offshore.

Jim Phillips was our fourth companion that frigid dawn. He believes the reason so few doubles are scored in sea-duck shooting is that you must wear so many layers of clothing to survive the sub-Arctic conditions that you can't swing your gun in wide arcs or react quickly enough to take advantage of doubling possibilities.

I believe there's another reason: no birds are harder dying than eiders, scoters, and old squaws. Even birds that fall in such a way that all your previous experience tells you the birds are dead before they hit the water will sometimes dive and stay down a worrisome time before floating up.

A sea duck is like a feathered Antaeus. But, whereas the strength of that mythical giant came from his contact with Mother Earth, the sea duck's strength lies in its contact with Mother Ocean. I've sometimes thought of Hercules' sad victory over Antaeus when lifting a still-striving scoter, old squaw, or eider from the sea and had the bird shudder and die in my hands.

Sea-duck shooting is like hunting dabblers in a cattail marsh without a dog: you can knock down doubles so long as you don't care about retrieving every bird. If you value the birds and want to recover each one you knock down, you must keep your eyes on the quarry until it's safely in hand. Frequent doubles in sea-duck hunting are incompatible with responsible sportsmanship.

Eiders are magnificent fowl whose chunky bodies and swift flight make them seem like miniature World War II torpedo-bombers attacking low across the sea and from out of a rising sun. Because the birds are often only fifteen yards away when you fire, you kill better with number-6 and even 7½ shot than with the 4s and 2s you thought you might need to bring down the goose-sized birds.

Eiders are so trusting that you could probably use bleach bottles to attract them, but most veteran shooters, like Maine resident John Marsh, say they have "too much respect for the ducks" to do that. As a result, the carving and painting of sea-duck decoys is becoming a popular sideline of the growing sport.

The last time I returned to Maine to hunt sea ducks, the ledge selected by my hosts included a panorama of Cadillac Mountain on Mount Desert Island, the highest point along the western Atlantic Coast north of Rio de Janeiro. Scoters, old squaw, and eiders churned toward our decoys in virtually endless lines. We hardly had time to reposition ourselves after killing the cripples and collecting the dead before another string of ducks hove into range. Most memorable of all, I shot a hen eider that had been banded by state biologist Alan Hutchinson sixteen months earlier on Browney Island, not far north of where we were hunting. It was strictly a no-sandwich, no-picture-taking outing—trophy wildfowling at its very best.

Postscript

Since most hunters have not yet hunted sea ducks, there are relatively few places you can find a guide. For information about Mike

McBride's camp, write Kachemak Bay Wilderness Lodge, Homer, Alaska 99603. Charlie Kelley and Dave Farrell are not for-hire guides, but Bob Oberlander and Tom O'Hearn on Cape Cod are. Oberlander lives at 427 Gilbert Street, Mansfield, Massachusetts 02048; and O'Hearn can be reached care of P.O. Box 581, West Dennis, Massachusetts 02670. Although I've not hunted with either man, they get high marks from hunters who have. Oberlander charges $120 for a morning party of two, and O'Hearn as much as $300 for an all-day hunt for two. This is comparable to the $1,500 Mike McBride charges for five days of hunting with four-star room and board included. You won't see many eiders in Kachemak Bay, but then you won't find too many harlequins on Cape Cod.

A final thought—sea-duck limits are generous—possibly too generous. It makes me uncomfortable to realize how fast this sport is growing and that we know so little about the life histories of such complicated birds. Considering, too, that most sea-duck shooters don't eat the birds they kill, despite their delicious flavor if properly prepared, I would prefer the federal government to err on the side of caution and reduce the present average daily limit of seven birds a day to four. Indeed, it's been my experience that the smaller the limit, the greater the trophy experience. Each bird is more highly prized, and the shooting is all the sooner done so the gunner can concentrate on all the other ingredients of the total hunting experience.

─── 15 ───

Woodcock

I have included a short chapter on woodcock (originally written in 1980), because I have a special affection for these upland shorebirds. One of my lapel pins has a design of four silver feathers on blue surrounded by a silver circle attesting to my membership in the British *Shooting Times'* Woodcock Club. This pin is earned by those who have taken a right and a left at woodcock, a feat I've somehow managed to pull off twice in my shooting career.

Although British writer J. C. M. Nichols complained that the woodcock "never by any chance gives a really high sporting shot" and sometimes comes out of cover "as low and straight as an owl," every woodcock I've encountered, including those I've approached from behind a pointing dog, flushed wonderfully unexpectedly, so that even when they flew "as low and straight as an owl," I all too often missed.

Like that other legal-quarry shorebird, the snipe, woodcock are here-today-gone-tomorrow game throughout most of eastern North America. Their unpredictable appearance represents a bonus opportunity for grouse hunters in the North and for quail shooters in the South. The woodcock is as truly a *wild* fowl (and, incidentally, occupies much of the same range) as the black duck.

Some years ago, I testified before a House Subcommittee on the decline of this sporty bird. That testimony represents one of the few times I may have influenced federal management policy. Ironically, my suggestion that we reduce the length of the woodcock season from 107 days to the present thirty-five means that in my home territory I rarely bag a woodcock nowadays. This is because the Commonwealth of Virginia does not zone itself for purposes of migratory bird management. Consequently, a woodcock season set in October to benefit hunters in the mountains all but eliminates woodcock hunting on the Eastern Shore where major flights don't appear until December—after the state-wide season is closed. Still, such personal sacrifice is preferable to what existed a relatively few years ago when woodcock in the South were hunted into the third week of February—after many had begun courting and a few even nesting.

Besides, if I feel an irresistible urge to hunt woodcock, I can always visit Canada where some provincial game departments are beginning to manage land for the birds much as the British and Irish began doing long ago.

Are There Enough?

The jingling bell drifted from left to right in the damp, dense thicket, but I could see nothing of its source. Like Peter Pan's fairy friend Tinker Bell, the ghostly pointer moved swiftly, yet unperceived.

Periodically I thought I glimpsed something white through the vertical screen of dowel-sized tree trunks. But when I'd look again, the white something was gone, and the tinkling ranged away among the luminous shadows of the alder bottom.

A dog's collar bell can have a hypnotic effect on hunters as well as upland gamebirds. Staying up late the evening before to reminisce with old friends reinforces with fatigue the soporific sensation of the invisible sound.

Stooping, side-stepping, slipping on mossy rocks or deadfalls, Eddie Provost and I had already visited two coverts by the time the sun cleared the eastern hills. Flash had made game in both areas, but the cover was so dense that by the time Eddie and I had gotten into position, the birds were gone.

Gone? Woodcock—renowned for such tight-sitting that New England dog handlers used to rate them as the *ne plus ultra* gamebird on which to train pointing pups—gone?

Yes, we were only into the second week of Maine's woodcock season but the birds were already as nervous as black ducks on Thanksgiving dawn. As duck hunters have discovered about their quarry in recent decades, shooting pressure can and will alter a gamebird's behavior. In the case of ducks and geese, the birds begin feeding at night to avoid gunning gauntlets at dawn and dusk. In the case of woodcock, the tight-sitters are flushed and shot, while the runners live to run away another day.

In past decades, relatively few Canadians hunted timberdoodle, and the birds were wonderfully innocent when they crossed the border into New England and the Upper Midwest. Now with the Canadian retrieved kill approximately 150,000 birds—and with an additional crippling loss of approximately 30,000—a significant percentage of woodcock have already been exposed to dogs and gunfire by the time they fly across the St. Lawrence or the Great Lakes.

When you add to that the pressures of opening week in, say, Michigan and Maine—when the bulk of the nearly 400,000 birds killed in those two states are shot in the first few days of the season—well, no wonder the surviving woodcock are jittery!

Some woodcock hunters—mostly those who shoot them incidentally to other game—don't believe that woodcock can and do run away from a pointing dog. Although woodcock won't run as fast or as far as that three-minute-miler, the pheasant, or even as compulsively as late-season quail and grouse, in ideal woodcock habitat a bird doesn't have to go many yards before it is able to flush out of sight of the hunter.

This odd little bird with upward-looking eyes and downward-looking bill seems as though it couldn't toddle more than a few steps without bumping into a tree or falling over its own beak. Some hunters refuse to believe the evidence of their own eyes and their dogs' noses, insisting that a huge flight of woodcock is in, when the hunters are actually only chasing the same few birds around in circles.

Woodcock are an upland shorebird, and all shorebirds are excellent runners. Some species, like the sanderling, which trots back and forth at the edge of the surf to snatch mole crabs and other delicacies from the sucking sands, appear to spend most of their lives on the run. Why wouldn't woodcock—the only bird in North America that was, until recently, hunted during both legs of its migration—revert to the running habits of its ancestors.

I had just decided to go left, instead of right, around a clump of birch when the ghostly music of the bell stopped. The sudden silence was so complete, I could hear a dog barking far away down the valley and the celestial murmur of a jetliner on its way to Europe.

"Up here, George!" called Eddie. "Come right and find an opening. Hurry!"

I crashed through the middle of the bypassed birch clump and veered to the right of Eddie's voice. The alders fought back, whipping my cold cheeks and colder ears and occasionally sneaking in a jab below the belt. I was still not in sight of the dog when I flushed a woodcock directly under my feet.

The bird twittered up so close and unexpectedly, it looked like Eurasian woodcock, one nearly twice as large as its American cousin. The bird had as much trouble finding a hole in the alders as I had. When it crossed what only a woodcock hunter would call an "opening," I caught the bird with a charge of 8s.

"Steady!" Eddie commanded his dog thirty invisible yards away.

"I've got a bird down," I called. "I'll stay here to mark it. Move ahead with Flash and see if there's another."

There wasn't. I had shot the woodcock that Flash had tried to pin, but the bird had probably upped and run as soon as the dog had locked onto point.

And so it went during most of the week. Only three of the birds I eventually shot were taken under circumstances that an upland purist would call "classic." Probably my most memorable kill came at the conclusion of a desperate hundred-yard dash up a logging road to cut off a woodcock zig-zagging ahead of the frustrated Flash.

Sure, there have always been running woodcock. And sure, I've been blessed with days when the birds flushed from under a dog's nose. Yet I seem to be finding more edgy woodcock with each passing season, and not just in Maine. The woodcock I've hunted in Maryland, Virginia, and Georgia are as inclined to run—maybe more so—than those I've found at the upper end of the flyway.

Was this my imagination, or are woodcock sustaining the kind of pressure that might alter behavior? I did some homework, and what I learned was both a revelation and a shock:

There were more than twice as many woodcock hunters in the 1970s as there were in the 1960s. (Reduced limits and seasons and reduced habitat, especially in the Atlantic Flyways, have trimmed this rise in the 1980s.) Still, the current retrieved continental harvest is estimated to be 1.6 million birds. That figure is comparable to all the geese—Canadas, snows, blues, white-fronts, brant, even emperors—killed across the continent in an average season. While the attention of wildlife biologists was diverted elsewhere, the woodcock became one of the most important gamebirds in North America—and one of wildlife management's biggest headaches.

The species was once mostly hunted in the northern tier of the United States from Minnesota to Maine. It was practically an unknown quantity to hunters below the Mason-Dixon Line. Despite generous daily limits and lengthy seasons, after the birds slipped into those parts of the country where the Adirondacks and Alleghenies are called the Blue Ridge and Smokies, they were all-ye-all-ye-in-free.

However, with more affluent Southerners looking for more ways to enjoy the great outdoors, and with agribusinessmen mopping up the last little corners of quail cover from the Carolinas to the Mississippi, most any old boy with a bird dog began to look to woodcock to keep his pooch and himself finely tuned throughout the fall.

Hunting pressure on the timberdoodle has grown so dramatically in the South that harvests in Alabama and Mississippi have gone from an "unknown-minor" category in 1960s' hunter surveys to more than 60,000 retrieved kill today. Virginians, who once also fit the "unknown-minor" category, presently collect more than 40,000 birds each fall, and in Georgia, former game director Jack Crockford is concerned that hunting pressure may already have eliminated the woodcock wintering population along those portions of the Chattahoochee River that lie within a few hours' drive of suburban Atlanta.

Californians are so eager to cash in on the nation's enthusiasm for woodcock that they stocked several hundred individuals of the American species during the 1972–1973 season. The stocking apparently didn't take. However, since any woodcock is exotic in the West, why Californians don't experiment with the Eurasian species, which frequently weighs more than a pound, is puzzling. After all, if the introduction backfires and the birds become too much of a good thing, Californians may as well be blamed for an elephant as an aardvark!

A handful of concerned biologists have watched the spiraling interest in woodcock hunting with spiraling dismay. They're not opposed to hunting; indeed, many of them enjoy it. But they are well aware that *quality* sport depends on an abundance of birds and a scarcity of hunters, and the American woodcock is still a surprisingly unknown quantity.

Wildlife biologists are not even sure whether there are two separate flyways for the species divided by the eastern mountain ranges or whether the birds migrate in a more or less random pattern. Biologists don't even know whether the spring surveys of "singing males" and the fall surveys of wing samples can provide them with anything approaching statistical reliability for proper management. Finally, and most worrisome of all, biologists don't know—not even to the nearest half million—how many woodcock there are in North America.

On the other hand, wildlife biologists do know that guess-timate management is prone to failure. They also know that the woodcock's fascinating courtship ritual holds a special appeal for nonhunting birders who will not sit idly by and allow the U.S. Fish and Wildlife Service and the Canadian Wildlife Service to discover maximum tolerances for the species by accident—particularly if the accident involves a dramatic decline of birds on their breeding grounds. Of course, natural causes beyond the control of man might bring this about, too, but wildlife biologists understandably get the blame.

More research is urgently needed, but the costs are high and apparently exceed the public's willingness to pay. Woodcock do not come to baited traps as waterfowl will, nor do they congregate in huge flocks the way blackbirds will. As a result, the average cost of capturing and banding a single woodcock is about $40.

Yet research is just one of the expenses associated with preserving wild fowl. As more woodcock singing grounds in the northern states grow up into mature forests or are converted to Christmas-tree farms and shopping centers, and as more of its wintering habitat is drained for flood control and soybean production, more areas will have to be set aside and specifically managed to maintain the species. Marginal habitat will have to be improved to insure adequate breeding and feeding grounds. Yet Southern wildlife managers can't even agree on what constitutes prime wintering habitat.

Appeals to sportsmen have been generally disappointing. Mention a Webless Migratory Bird Hunting Stamp to finance research and habitat preservation, and most hunters will hold their heads in pain at the thought of still another tax burdening their recreation. Some hunters wouldn't mind if they knew their fees would be earmarked for woodcock research and rehabitation, but they correctly suspect that each new federal administration tries to sidetrack such funds into paying for something else. The only authority presently requiring a special ($2.25) woodcock stamp is New Jersey's Division of Fish, Game, and Wildlife, and this agency does nothing more specific with the funds than plow them into general revenues where they are more likely to beef up retirement benefits for state bureaucrats than help woodcock. What is particularly irksome about the example is that New Jersey's Cape May County represents one of the most important migratory concentration areas for woodcock in North America. (In 1988, the U.S. Fish and Wildlife Service began acquiring some of this critical habitat just as it started doing the year before at Cape Charles, Virginia.)

Elsewhere, no other state —including Maine, Michigan, New York, Pennsylvania, and Wisconsin, where hunters kill more than 100,000 woodcock annually—has a woodcock stamp. There is even less interest south of the Mason-Dixon Line. Only Canada requires all woodcock hunters to purchase a migratory bird stamp. Unfortunately, this money is used only to obtain harvest and productivity data from a sampling of people who buy the stamps.

Most frustrating to conscientious wildlife biologists is the fact that even after they discover critical information about the life history of woodcock, the information is rarely applied in any meaningful way to hunting regulations. Long after it was learned, for example, that there is a population of woodcock indigenous to the South, and that these birds frequently begin nesting as early as late January, hunting seasons in most southern states continued to run well into February.

Not many years ago, while hunting quail on the Eastern Shore of Virginia, I heard a familiar, but unexpected, sound coming from behind a mound of earth pushed up by a bulldozer. The sound was so incongruous, I thought it must be a spring peeper or cricket frog out of tune with the season and out of tune, period. When I crept over the rise, I found a woodcock in the sweetgum-rimmed clearing strutting and peenting for all the world as though I was a hen coming to mate. (Fortunately, February woodcock seasons are now history.)

The ticket to successful game management is a concerned and informed constituency of sportsmen. Yet many hunters don't know how to differentiate woodcock from snipe, and some don't even know that both birds are game. If you think this an exaggeration, consider the annual woodcock wing survey. It differs from the waterfowl wing survey in that the latter's participants are randomly selected, thanks to the federal duck stamp program, which makes such random selection possible. By contrast, woodcock wing contributors are volunteers, eager to play their small roles in the work of conservation. They represent a biased data base, but one you would think was better informed than the average hunter.

Yet every year, surprising numbers of non-woodcock wings turn up in woodcock survey envelopes. The most common mistakes involve rail, quail, and snipe. But woodpecker wings also show up, especially from those parts of the country where pileated woodpeckers are locally called "cocks of the woods," "peckerwoods," and "woodcocks." One hopes at least that the mountain men of West Virginia, Tennessee, and North Carolina eat what they shoot.

Superficially amusing, the implications of such ignorance are not at all funny. If the current crop of woodcock wing contributors represents the best and brightest of the bird-hunting fraternity, then we better start developing mandatory hunter education courses that will stress bird identification along with the more typical emphasis on hunter-safety. A fraction of the funds raised by a woodcock stamp could be used for such training. As for the mugwumps unwilling to buy any more hunting stamps, good, they should stop hunting. There are already too many of us plowing through the coverts now. If another $10 or $20 stamp is enough to keep them at home, they're not the sort of guys who get gooseflesh when a dog's bell falls silent in northern alders or southern cane. They don't deserve that wonderful little wild fowl, the woodcock.

Postscript

All attempts to date to enlarge the U.S. Migratory Bird Hunting and Conservation Stamp to include dove, rail, snipe, and woodcock (as well as ducks and geese) have failed. Since woodcock continue to decline, daily limits have been reduced from five to three. Unfortunately, three was selected on the basis of no more scientific data than five, or the earlier number, eight. If woodcock continue to decline, the daily limit may be reduced to two, or even one, until the opportunity to hunt becomes so thin, woodcock aficionados will stop trying to find the birds. At that point, the species will be declared threatened and federal funds may at last be made available to restore something which—if we started *now*—could readily be perpetuated at far less cost.

— 16 —

Canvasbacks

The Last Canvasback

Waterfowl gunning for the market ended officially on July 3, 1918, when President Woodrow Wilson signed an act of Congress implementing the Migratory Bird Treaty between the United States and Canada. Yet for more than half a century afterward, market hunting was a way of life in little enclaves all along the Atlantic Coast. Before World War II, it was a vigorous tradition frustrating state and federal law enforcement agents. Today, diminishing waterfowl numbers and the simple fact of men growing old are bringing the last of the commercial hunters out of the marsh.

I wrote the first version of this story in 1957 for my college literary magazine. Fifteen years later, Audubon bought a revised draft. Since Audubon doesn't ordinarily publish fiction, the editors were concerned that my characters and the incidents weren't true. I persuaded them that the story was based on real people and real events, and it was subsequently published in May 1974.

Toward eight in the evening the bright moon appeared from behind a piled bank of black cloud, permitting the two poachers to start down Folly Creek. Their boat drove crisply through a glaze of ice until they left the sheltered landing area and turned into the open channel. There, gusts of wind rushed across the low marsh and threw sheets of spray into the little scow.

"Keep it balanced, Sam! Get to your right!" yelled Foxer from the stern.

"Why don't you stay in the lee?" asked Sam. "We're not even to the main channel, and Lord knows how sloppy that'll be."

"We're going to get wet no matter what we do! At least we've got the tide under us out here. I'll run the boat unless you think you can do better!"

Sam started to look back at Foxer, but salt spray burned his eyes and made them water. He turned forward and rubbed his wet face with the back of a woolen glove. When he opened his eyes, he found he'd rubbed some grit or lint into one of them. He took his right hand out of its glove to remove the particle.

"Every time," he muttered to himself, working his index finger at the edge of the eye. "Stubborn—just like his father."

Sam was Foxer's uncle and the oldest member of a three-man team that was once characterized by state warden Carroll Belote as "the single greatest threat to wildfowl on the Eastern Shore of Virginia." Like most watermen, Sam, his brother, Billy King, and Foxer took on a variety of jobs to make ends meet. The only difference was that, in their case, much of their income was illegal.

They tonged oysters and trapped muskrats in the winter, and crabbed and netted sea trout and spot the rest of the year. But none of these activities came close to the money they made shooting and trapping wild ducks for private clubs and restaurants in Philadelphia, Baltimore, and Washington. At an average price of two dollars a bird, there'd been seasons when the three men made more money in a month of hunting than in six months of fishing. Even though they knew their middleman was making 100 percent profit on what they sold him, they begrudged him nothing. In many ways, his risks were greater than theirs.

Billy King had been the most productive member of the team. He ran a string of duck traps. He admired the black duck's sagacity, but he smiled at its fatal fondness for shelled corn. In town, when men got to talking about the wisdom of wildlife as country men do, Billy always stuck up for the black duck even though he admitted "you can bait one from here to Hell."

Billy set his traps in the bottoms of guts where it was difficult for airborne wardens to spot them and where ducks came naturally to feed on a falling tide. The birds entered the traps with their heads down gobbling grain. Then they couldn't figure how to get out after the tide came in. When the water was high and the ducks drowned, Billy came by, pretending to be oystering or checking eel pots.

Billy King sometimes worked both tides a day and made more money than his son and brother did trapping muskrats. Furthermore, the buyer took the ducks just as they came from the traps, while Sam and Foxer had to skin out their 'rats and market the carcasses to a different buyer.

Then Billy King was caught.

It was a put-up job. Federal agents had been watching him closely for two seasons, but they could never catch him with any evidence. Determined to get him, the agents live-trapped several black ducks at the Chincoteague National Wildlife Refuge, brushed them with phosphorescent dust, and then planted the birds in one of Billy King's traps.

When Billy King sneaked into the landing that night, the agents were waiting. With the dust smeared over his hands and the boat's gunwales and engine, he and his rig lit up like a Christmas tree when the spotlights went on.

Billy King asked for a trial by jury, and the verdict was "not guilty." Not because the jury believed his story about finding the ducks tangled in a derelict crab pot. But because they disliked the way the Feds had framed the arrest.

But Billy King never hunted or trapped again. He was badly scared by the trial and went to work in the oyster boats for the last few years of his life. He was ashamed—not of what he'd done—but that he'd been caught. For that reason, maybe, he fished harder than other watermen. Billy King was twice penalized for exceeding his shellfish quota, and on three occasions he got into scrapes with Maryland fishermen when he was found working their side of the Chesapeake line. The last run-in cost him a week in the hospital at Nassawadox.

Then one January, Billy King went out in a storm to tong oysters. His boat was discovered two days later lying on her side in a marsh across the bay. Billy King's body was never found.

Ever since his father's death, Foxer talked of giving up waterwork and his partnership with Sam. For two summers he'd taken a job pumping gas and working as a clerk in a Chincoteague motel. Although he continued hunting with Sam during the winter when the motel was closed, Foxer talked more and more of giving it up and going to work in Salisbury.

"That's a coming town," he said. "I can get a job selling things and make twice the money we do shooting ducks."

But Sam was sure Foxer was only talking. He felt that if he ignored Foxer's crazy talk, it'd eventually stop. Sam just couldn't imagine any of his people working for somebody else.

The more silent Sam became, the more aggravated Foxer became. He needed someone to argue it out with, so Foxer told Sam it wasn't like the old days. Their old middleman had retired, and the new contact sold only to a couple of embassies in Washington. Although prices were up and their buyer had found markets for all the diamondback terrapin they could catch, the demand for wild geese and black ducks was tapering off.

Sam listened but said nothing.

The motor was throttled back. Foxer was looking for the cut, a winding trench of water gouged by the tides through the marsh north of Cedar Island.

"Load up, Sam. This is it."

There were often ducks hidden in bends of the cut.

Sam loaded each of his two barrels with 5s and laid the old double across a pile of burlap on the floor of the boat. The moon was bright in a haze that suffused the whole sky with blue light. Except for the black marsh, it didn't seem like night.

Suddenly the horizon rose on either side. They were in the cut. With the wind blocked off, the cold became less intense. Sam shoved his right hand back into its glove and put his head down between his arms to warm his ears.

He closed his eyes. A year ago Foxer had given him a woolen pullover for his head, but the old man refused to wear it. "I taught him all he knows, and there's more he won't ever begin to know." Then he went to sleep.

Sam awoke briefly in a daze. The motor had been turned off and tilted from the water. Up ahead he could see Foxer's back straining with the painter, dragging the scow along one side of the cut. Then he went back to sleep.

The double roar of Foxer's gun startled Sam into consciousness. He took his gun and scrambled from the seat over the side into the shallow water. He stepped up on a mussel-covered bank and saw Foxer run ahead, crouch, and fire once again—the flame of his gun bright against the dark horizon.

Foxer slowly got to his feet and waded into the cut. Sam followed the bank until he stood above Foxer picking up a pair of ducks.

"Was that all?" Sam asked.

"No. Maybe seven. The last shot was for this cripple."

"Why didn't you wake me?"

"You were asleep."

Foxer climbed the bank and, holding his broken gun and the two birds, looked down into Sam's face.

"That's what I asked," said Sam. "Why didn't you wake me? If I'd been up here, we could have gotten more."

"That's right, Sam." Foxer put an empty casing in his coat and stuffed another shell into the right chamber of his shotgun. "I told you when we came in here to watch for ducks. There wasn't time to tell you again. If you're getting too old to stay awake, that's one thing. But don't try to blame me for us not getting more birds."

Foxer passed Sam, walked to the boat, and threw the black ducks into the bow. The scow was lodged at an angle in the narrow channel.

"If you don't mind, stay out of the boat 'til we get her through the cut. She's hit bottom a couple, three times now, and the tide's still running out."

For several minutes, Sam stared across the dark island as Foxer and the boat slowly moved along the bank and disappeared into the night. When Sam finally reached the mouth of the cut, Foxer was waiting with the engine running.

The trip to Burton's Wedge was across open water. Foxer guided the boat along the exposed edge of the tidal flat to avoid the high following waves the wind drove up from the channel. Finally he saw the light at Sandy Point that marked the entrance to the narrow bay.

Sam opened his gun and rested the stock in the crook of his arm. Above the roar of the motor he heard the frantic *quack-quack* of a startled black-duck hen. Then he saw the climbing wings, lifting up, driving down, with fast silent strokes—sixty yards ahead, and now above the bank of rolled cloud. The bird drove up at a sharp angle and finally turned and headed for the barrier island and the sea beyond.

Fifty years ago, tens of thousands of wildfowl had wintered on the great seaside marshes of Virginia. It was not uncommon for Sam to kill thirty ducks in a morning's flight. Now the sky was mostly barren and the marsh empty, except for scattered groups of hiding birds.

Although the enormous flocks of diving ducks had dwindled, the black ducks had survived, even prevailed. With the first touch of dawn, the blackies rose high above shotgun range and flew on hard-driving wings beyond the Atlantic breakers, there to settle down and sleep away the day. At dusk, they returned to the marsh and fed through the night.

Sam wondered at ducks being able to change, when it was so hard for people.

Foxer cut the engine and the boat glided into a small cove. While Sam slowly climbed over the side, Foxer jumped out and dragged the scow into a gut and secured it with a line tied to a cement block thrown into the grass. Then, tying a burlap sack over his shoulder and stuffing his coat pockets full of shells, Foxer started off. Sam got his sack and shells and followed.

The first pond they came to had four blacks on it. They approached the pothole within a hundred yards then split and came in from opposite sides. Sam approached the edge first, and as the birds began their leap into the air, he gunned down two with one shot when their silhouettes cleared the horizon. He crippled another that was no more than a shadowy blur. The remaining duck passed directly over Foxer's head offering him an easy target against the moonlit sky. Sam reloaded and killed the cripple; the tight pattern seemed to lift the bird from the water with its spray of shot.

The secret of night shooting was in accepting silhouettes as three-dimensional birds. Experience taught you to compensate for the lost senses of distance and color. As long as you killed or crippled your birds over water, you could find them. A dead bird in the marsh was difficult to locate without a light; a cripple was impossible to find without a dog—and a dog was a luxury. Foxer's and Sam's incomes combined were less than $10,000 a year. Although the money was tax-free, the two men knew a dog would cost them more than he'd be worth.

Using the same hard measure, Sam and Foxer never shot a bird in the air if they could kill it on the water. Even by loading their own shells, the price of fuel meant the cost of killing a duck was 10 percent of its value—even if you killed one with each shot. That both men were also crack wing-shots was beside the point. Economics demanded the first shot be on the water, the second in the air. That is, if they could catch the birds unaware.

Two more ponds, and they had six more ducks. Finally, they made their way to the outlet of Finney Bay. They crouched low in the grass stubble as they cautiously crept near, their shadows blending with the shadows of the shore. There, not more than twenty-five yards from the bank, rested two pods of six birds each.

The two men hardly breathed, listening to the ducks gabble and watching them put their heads under for food. The birds were perfectly framed within the gleam of the moon's wake. Foxer lifted his double.

Suddenly Sam saw a canvasback drake bob to the surface just beyond the two groups of black duck. It held a strand of grass in its bill as it swam closer to shore. With a quick twist of its head, the canvasback swallowed nearly the whole strand. It dipped and shook its head once more, and the rest of the plant disappeared.

With the crash of Foxer's gun, Sam swung his double under the rising black ducks to the single canvasback running across the surface of the water. His first shot broke around the bird; his second caught the drake as it began to veer out of range. The canvasback fell to the water, a cripple.

"What're you shooting at?" yelled Foxer, as he reloaded and fired at a black duck flopping on the water not far from shore.

Sam didn't reply, but ran along the bank, then stumbled into the knee-deep bay and began to wade after his canvasback.

Another shot crashed, and then one more, as Foxer went about the task of killing cripples. The bird ahead of Sam was swimming rapidly for the mouth of the bay and the deeper waters of the channel. Sam stopped, put the gun to his shoulder and pulled the trigger.

Nothing—he'd not reloaded.

"Damn! Oh, damn!"

Sam waded at an angle to the wounded drake in an attempt to turn it back into the bay. The bulge of water about his knees washed and splashed over the barrels of his gun as he broke it and reloaded. He paused and fired at the swimming bird. The shot patterned the drake, but with a flip of its tail, the canvasback disappeared beneath the surface.

Sam continued to push in the direction of the channel. When the water reached his thighs, he began to wander back and forth, smashing the surface with a gloved fist.

"I've got to keep him in," he thought. "He can't get away."

"What'er ya shooting at?" asked Foxer from the shore behind Sam. "What're ya doing now?"

Sam turned and waded toward Foxer's shadow. He continued to strike the water with his fist.

"There's a canvasback here!" he said.

"One can?! Sam, we could have killed all twelve of those black ducks if you'd been shooting where you're supposed to!"

Sam could see Foxer clearly now, holding several black ducks by their necks.

"I killed a canvasback," he said, and then stopped and stared out over the bay, hoping the drake would come up again—even for an instant.

"Where is it?" asked Foxer.

"It dove."

"Cripes sake, Sam, you took a long shot on a single when we had a dozen bunched in front!"

"I told you it was a canvasback. He'll bring more than twice as much as one of your black ducks."

A cat's paw of wind scurried across the water between the men and vanished into the darkness of the bay.

"Sam, when you and daddy first took me into the marsh to shoot ducks, you told me it was a business, not a sport, and to keep quiet when the other boys in school started talking big about hunting. With them, shooting was a way to prove themselves. But with us, it was our livings, and there was no boasting and no sharing with the world anything we'd seen or done. That was good advice, Sam. But you seem to've forgotten it. The last few trips have been full of little grandstands, like you making me do all the work and you shooting at a single when you could have killed four or five! You know I want to give this business up, and you're fast pushing me to it!"

"It was a canvasback."

Foxer was silent a moment. Then he dropped off the bank and waded out to the older man.

"Come on, Sam. The wind's dropping, and we can still try the ponds on Parramore. It's a good night for it."

Sam felt the gentle weight of Foxer's hand on his shoulder.

"Come on," Foxer said.

As Sam started to wade in, the canvasback broke the surface not thirty yards away. It had turned and was now well inside the bay, not far from where it had first fallen. The rush of Sam's shot swept the bird about and twisted its head down on the water. One wing jutted out and feebly sculled at the surface.

"Shoot!" yelled Sam, as he hurriedly broke his gun to reload.

"Don't worry, he's finished."

"No, he's not! Shoot! Please shoot!"

Sam dropped a good shell in the water as he fumbled with wet gloves to jam new cartridges into the chambers. He snapped the barrels closed and brought the gun to his shoulder as the bird dived.

"Foxer! He's gone!"

"You hit him good. He'll be up again."

"No, he'll grab hold and stay down!"

Sam waded to the spot where the drake had disappeared. He shuffled around the mud on the bottom, trying to find the hiding bird. Finally, he stopped and waited. Beads of water clung to his brown woolen coat and streamed off the barrels of his gun.

"Let's go, Sam! We're wasting time."

"No. You go if you want."

"That one bird isn't worth it! We cripple and lose half a dozen a night. If he's on bottom, he'll stay there and we'll pick him up on the way back."

"No, he's liable to come up if we leave and get away."

"That bird was dead when it went under, Sam! He can't get away. Let's go!"

"You go ahead."

"You're not coming?"

"That was the first canvasback I've seen on the seaside in six seasons. I mean to get that bird."

"Don't be stubborn, Sam!"

"Leave me alone, Foxer. Get out of here and go on!"

A moment of silence passed before Foxer said quietly, "I'm going to give you just one minute to make up your mind to come on, or we'll own up now and call it quits. You've got no one else to do this damnable business with, and you're getting too old to manage the boat and motor by yourself. It'll be over, Sam. I'm serious. You understand?"

Sam waded to the mouth of the bay. He found the bar where the water was only ankle deep, and he kneeled down and leaned on the stock of his old double.

"I'm staying here, Foxer."

"Then we're through."

Foxer turned from the bay and vanished into the marsh.

Sam sat back on his heels and looked up at the sky. The moon was smaller now that it was overhead, and the light it reflected and the shadows it cast seemed more intense.

"I walked these marshes before that boy was born."

Sam could feel the tide dropping beneath him. Soon the bay would be little more than a mud flat.

The first bird Sam ever hit had been a canvasback. Out of a flock of over a hundred, he'd dropped a single drake. It had fluttered along the surface a short distance before diving. Sam spent the entire day trying to find that bird. He never did.

A pair of black ducks crossed high over Sam's head, their wings beating furiously, silently. Sam thought he heard the muffled roar of a gun.

"This is the first canvasback in six seasons," he said to himself. "They're all gone now."

An hour later the tide was full out, revealing the back of the drowned bird not more than thirty feet from where Sam kneeled. He got up and slogged over to retrieve the drake and a cluster of oyster shells it had gripped in death with its bill.

Sam lifted the water-soaked canvasback for inspection, and even in the moonlight, the brick-red color of the head was distinguishable from the black-and-white body. The feet hung limp. Sam noticed a tiny snail—only a particle—in the bird's eye, and he brushed it out with a gloved hand.

Sam was very tired when he reached the canal where the boat was hidden. Foxer was waiting. He'd killed only one more bird.

How Much Is A Canvasback Worth?

Old-timers will tell you that the Golden Age of the canvasback was their grandaddys' era—the 1880s and 1890s—when tens of thousands of decoys were carved around the shores of the upper Chesapeake, anchored on the Susquehanna Flats in the autumn, and shot over all winter until spring ice grinding down the river cleared out both the birds and the decoys.

Old market records provide clues as to why cans' were once called "feathered gold." At a time when the father of retired decoy carver Madison Mitchell was averaging $14 a month farming near the mouth of the Susquehanna, he also earned $5 for each pair of canvasback he shot and only a dollar for each pair of "blackheads" (scaup).

Yet those same records suggest that the Golden Age of the canvasback actually occurred a century earlier, after British and German troops had been sent back to Europe and Americans explored and cleared, worked and played, like never before and rarely since.

About 1810, ornithologist Alexander Wilson recalled a clever deal he struck with a New Jersey waterman after "a vessel loaded with wheat was wrecked near the entrance of Great Egg Harbor in the autumn and went to pieces. The wheat floated out in vast quantities, and the whole surface of the bay was in a few days covered with Ducks of a kind altogether unknown to the people of that quarter.

"The gunners of the neighborhood collected in boats, in every direction, shooting them, and so successful were they that, as Mr. Beasley informs me, two hundred and forty were killed in one day and sold among the neighbors at twelve and a half cents apiece, without the feathers. . . .

"They continued for about three weeks, and during the quarter part of that time a continual cannonading was heard from every quarter. The gunners called them Sea Ducks [but] they were all Canvass-Backs, at that time on their way from the north, when this floating feast attracted their attention, and for a while arrested them in their course.

"A pair of these very Ducks I myself bought in Philadelphia market at the time, from an Egg Harbor gunner, and never met with their superior, either in weight or excellence of flesh. When it was known among those people the loss they had sustained in selling for twenty-five cents what would have brought them from a dollar to a dollar and a half per pair, universal surprise and regret were naturally enough excited."

Elsewhere, Wilson remarks that "it has not been uncommon to pay from one to three dollars a pair for these Ducks; and, indeed, at such times, if they can, they must be had, whatever may be the price."

To provide some idea of the contemporary value of those canvasbacks, land in the western portions of many of the former colonies sold for as little as a penny an acre in 1800. Thus, a pair of canvasbacks were worth between a quarter and a half section of land—land which, even as cutover woodland today, is worth hundreds of dollars an acre, and better than a thousand when cleared for farming.

Granted, our eastern states were land-rich and labor-poor in 1800. And in the century that followed, both land and canvasbacks fluctuated enormously in price the way any commodity does. However, even after market shooting was outlawed—thereby taking canvasbacks off the commodity list—sportsmen and epicureans remembered the bird for its exquisite taste and lavish price. As Alexander Wilson noted, "The Canvass-Back, in the rich, juicy tenderness of its flesh, and its delicacy of flavor, stands unrivalled by the whole of its tribe in this or perhaps any other quarter of the world. Those killed in the waters of the Chesapeake are generally esteemed superior to all others, doubtless from the great abundance of their favorite food which these rivers produce."

First Can'

When I moved to the Chesapeake country in the mid-1960s, I was looking forward to sampling many specialties of the region ranging from raw oysters and rockfish stuffed with crabmeat to sea squabs and canvasback. In those days, the oysters, rockfish (striped bass), and sea squab (puffers) were still abundant. The canvasbacks, however, were already declining.

I had seen wild canvasbacks before: a dozen or so spliced into rafts of broadbill bobbing on the Hudson River where the rail lines run down from Dobbs Ferry to Manhattan; or a hen can' as out of place in a flock of bluebill bobbing on Palm Beach's Lake Worth as the Queen Mother would be in a crowd of cheerleaders.

During my first fall on the Chesapeake, I saw many hundreds of canvasback rafted on both sides of the Bay Bridge between Annapolis and Kent Island, but I never saw those birds over my decoys. Still I knew that such a meeting was inevitable, for this was the Chesapeake, and the Chesapeake is canvasback country.

In December the following year, I was hunting from a blind on one of the tributaries of the Chesapeake when I noticed a distant smudge of "smoke" curling up the river. "Are those blackbirds?" I innocently asked one of my more experienced companions.

"Blackbirds, hell! They're canvasbacks! And coming this way!"

A rabbit could not have been more mesmerized by a snake than I was by that genie-like cloud of birds writhing and undulating their swift way over the varnished surface of the river.

"There must be thousands of them," I whispered.

"At least," said one of my companions, as we began to hear the winnowing of their wings like wind preceding a storm.

One puny lot of possibly a hundred birds sheered off the main mass and swung our way. Shameful to admit, I fired my first round into the bunch and naturally never cut a feather. Then I picked a drake, pointed well ahead of it, and squeezed the trigger. My shot train passed behind. A small voice soothed, like a Marine sergeant I once knew, "Steady, lad, steady." I picked another drake, swung past him, and kept swinging as I squeezed the trigger.

"I got one! Holy Cow! I killed a canvasback! Quick! Get the boat somebody! I've got a canvasback out there! Hurry! The tide'll carry him away!"

I was oblivious to the fact that my companions had several canvasbacks of their own on the water, and that the tide, just about at its lowest ebb, wasn't going anywhere. Still, even after my companions calmed me down, I never took my eyes off *my* drake from the time it was lifted into the boat to when it was flung, a little irreverently I thought, into my arms by friends who'd killed their share of cans' before.

The bird was no less magnificent in hand than it had been in flight. A little smaller or thinner, perhaps, than what I'd imagined, but the early-morning sunlight warmed the brick-red tones of the head and fired the ruby eyes. At that time, I didn't know a taxidermist who could duplicate such beauty, so I decided to pluck the bird and share it with a special lady friend—with side dishes of wild rice, spinach salad, and a bottle of red wine.

One of my companions said the cans' we killed had been roosting for the past week on the lower reaches of the Choptank, and that they had been flighting upriver each morning to feed. Since the specific scientific name for the species is *vallisneria,* meaning wild celery, I assumed this succulent aquatic plant was what the birds had been eating. Unfortunately, clams and minnows must have been that flock's fare, for I've eaten mergansers with less pungency than my first regal canvasback! My girlfriend bravely ate her share, insisting that it had an "interesting" flavor, but then she was in love, and so was I, and eventually I married her because anyone who could find positive ingredients in that particular meal was worth marrying!

The Birds' Dilemma

And so the once and future glory of the canvasback is riddled by the reality of increasingly degraded wintering habitat where birds are hard-pressed to eke out a living on shellfish laced with viruses and PCBs because the rooted vegetation for which the Chesapeake was once renowned is almost gone. Rooted vegetation needs sunlight that is increasingly absorbed by algae. It also needs the proper blend of fresh and salt water, and the Chesapeake and lower portions of its tributaries are losing their freshwater supplies to human consumption, irrigation, and evaporation at an ever-accelerating rate. Such consumptive losses of fresh water are expected to increase fivefold by the year 2020. A U.S. Army Corps of Engineers' study predicts that within thirty years, fresh water will be disappearing from the Chesapeake system at a yearly average rate of more than 2.5 billion gallons *every day.* To comprehend this amount, the entire volume of the bay including the sea water flushing its lower reaches, is only about 13,000 billion gallons.

The Corps has predicted that between 20 and 40 percent fewer waterfowl will use the Chesapeake by the first decade of the twenty-first century. Especially hard hit will be canvasbacks. Not only will there be fewer underwater plants for the birds to eat, the small clams that make up the bulk of the cans' present diet are expected to suffer declines of at least 30 to 60 percent.

The only bright spot in the Chesapeake story is a stretch of the Potomac below Washington, D.C., where the exotic water plant, hydrilla, flourishes upstream of the river's brackish water zone. The Corps of Engineers had planned to spend millions of dollars in an undoubtedly futile effort to eradicate the formerly unwanted weed. Then biologists pointed out that hydrilla provides summer cover for the beleaguered striped bass and winter fare for the even more beleaguered canvasback. Some biologists even proposed introducing the foreign plant to all Chesapeake tributaries.

Until that proposal is acted upon, however, a consequence of generally degraded wintering habitat is that surviving canvasbacks are forced to concentrate on a shrinking number of suitable feeding grounds, where not only is the risk of epizootics greater, but competition for scarce food seems to favor drakes over hens. In a study conducted in South Carolina in the early 1980s, biologist William C. Alexander found that canvasback drakes characteristically defend feeding territories where a favored food, like banana water lily, is available, or when food in general is scarce.

"When a female entered one of these predominately male feeding areas," writes Alexander, "she was confronted at almost every turn by territory-holding males and forced to swim elsewhere on the pond. For an equivalent amount of foraging effort, the larger, more aggressive males can maintain a substantially higher caloric intake than females. Thus, it is possible that the average female canvasback in this area is forced by hunger to venture into more dangerous parts of the ponds; during the day, the canvasbacks that swam from open water into the dense surrounding cattails were approximately 75 percent female. These areas are inhabited by river otters and alligators. Birds feeding in these areas were more vulnerable to predators than those feeding in a group."

The poor condition of canvasbacks returning to the breeding

grounds coupled with persistent summer droughts have resulted in a steady decline in continental numbers over the past half century. Although 1961 and 1962 represent the species' two lowest breeding populations ever—396,000 and 385,000 birds, respectively—the canvasback never really recovered from intense diving-duck shooting in the 1950s.

Although North American wildlife agencies reduced the canvasback daily limits, they were reluctant to close the season. With hunter numbers increasing through the 1960s, 1970s, and into the 1980s, sportsmen continued making profound inroads into canvasback populations, especially following a drought. Although the average breeding population supposedly rose to 575,000 birds from 1976 to 1985, the canvasback population fell to its third lowest recorded level in the spring of 1985 with only 411,000 birds.

Shooting pressure is the only aspect of a migratory bird's life over which wildlife agencies have any real control. In 1936, when the old U.S. Biological Survey determined that canvasback populations had fallen well below a million, it closed the hunting season nationwide with no exceptions and despite the protests of many hunters who observed that in some wintering areas there appeared to be "lots of birds."

Ironically, there were probably more canvasbacks in North America on the eve of that 1936 national closure than there were during the 1970s and 1980s when tens of thousands of canvasbacks were legally shot all across the continent. During the more recent decades, canvasbacks had a champion in H. Albert Hochbaum, author and illustrator of *Canvasback on a Prairie Marsh* (1944) and guiding spirit of Canada's Delta Waterfowl Research Station. Al was determined not to let politicians and statisticians smother his favorite bird with mumbo-jumbo. In 1984, he wrote me to say that during the spring, "fewer canvasbacks than ever returned to their prairie breeding grounds. Even in the continuing drought, the worst since the 1930s, there was good canvasback nesting habitat without birds to use it. Nevertheless, the gutless politicians and shackled biologists proclaimed another open season. They are willing to sacrifice future production for immediate pleasure. Duck hunters go along with this out of the mistaken belief that ducks can be made out of dollar bills—that by sending money to another country, Canada, they can maintain a resource that is being lost at home.

"Canvasbacks have a potential life span of twenty to twenty-five years. There is evidence that the older a hen gets, the better, more successful mother she becomes. Under present hunting practices, few hens live to their third year. As the numbers of young birds get smaller, the older birds, particularly experienced mothers, come under increasingly heavy gunning pressure. A rancher couldn't handle his stock this way; nor are we managing canvasbacks for the future."

Year after year, Al fought the business-as-usual perspectives of administrators in the Canadian and American wildlife services. Year after year he won a few more of them over to his—and the canvasback's—side. Finally, in the summer of 1988, the canvasback season everywhere in the United States was closed. Unfortunately, Al never learned that the most significant part of his crusade—he also wanted Canada and Mexico to close their canvasback seasons—was won. He died in 1989, on March second, at his home in Portage la Prairie, Manitoba.

Clubs, Conservation, and Whyfors

— 17 —

Clubs

I think I would have enjoyed the oc-
casional company of a nineteenth-century Virginia gentleman named Alexander Hunter. Although a dandy and a snob, he was also a devoted
wildfowler with little patience for pretense.

How can one be both a snob and unpretentious?

Easy, if you believe you embody a class and a way of life intrinsically superior to other forms of human existence, yet are modest and grateful for your fortunate birth and upbringing.

A major part of Hunter's outdoor life was spent with men of similar attitudes on Atlantic coastal marshes. Hunter was contemptuous of pretenders to his social order, and he scorned sycophants and thieves seeking to exploit his good fortune and refinement. Although his gentleman's code prevented him from making a scene with cheats and liars in the marsh, he didn't hesitate to call spades by their proper name in print. There is nothing reserved about Hunter's warning in *The Huntsman of the South* (1908) regarding the greed of North Carolina's Goose Creek Islanders:

"Every sportsman who ever shot over the blinds at Currituck or vicinity will endorse every word I write about the grasping rapacity of these islanders, and I know that those who are yet to go there will be glad that they have read these lines, for they show prospective hunters what to expect. To those contemplating a trip to these famous ducking grounds, one word of advice. Estimate the expense of your jaunt, multiply the total by three, and you will then have enough left, *if you are economical,* to get home."

Even more than the grand larceny and blackmail (a guide named Tim refused to sail Hunter's party half a mile across the shallows to a tender waiting to take them home until he was paid $15—scalper's wages by today's standards), Hunter was appalled by the short-sightedness with which the watermen treated local resources:

"Nearly all the able-bodied Goose Creek Islanders own boats, and nearly all of them have, hidden away under the bow, a box some two feet square, one side of which is closed with a sliding lid. Inspection of its contents will reveal a kerosene lamp and a tin reflector.

"A dark, calm night is chosen, and the boat is noiselessly propelled by a pole along the estuaries and creeks of the North Carolina sounds where the ducks congregate to sleep. The gunner sits in the bow, with his ears open, and so keen is a trained pot-hunter's hearing that he can detect the swimming of the ducks as they move away. The pusher sends his craft along with hardly a ripple. The gunner now opens the slide and a dazzling glare flashes over the water. The ducks, bewildered by the light, mass together and swim slowly in a circle, blinking at the blinding gleam. The gunner fires at point-blank range, and dozens are killed at one discharge, and as many more are crippled, and flutter away and die on the marshes. The rest fly aimlessly away and the next morning migrate to distant points.

"Hunting waterfowl by fire-light is a grave offense against the State laws, and heavy penalties are exacted if the offender is caught. But, ah! there's the rub. It is almost impossible to capture these pirates, for as soon as the shot is fired and the dead ducks gathered, the lid of the firebox is closed, the craft glides away in the darkness, and the reflector is not used again until some remote point is reached. It is needless to add, this kind of shooting drives all the ducks from the neighborhood."

Modern glorification of poachers, as in Harry Walsh's *The Outlaw Gunner*, is proof of decay in the sporting tradition. Anglo-Saxons have always sentimentalized outlaws, from Robin Hood to the rebel alliance in *Star Wars*. But there is nothing imaginary about the harm done to wildfowl and wildfowling by poachers in Hunter's day or our own.

Fortunately, the outlaw gunner is finally fading from the wildfowling scene, but only because there are less risky ways to make a living. Trapping or fire-lighting ducks and selling them to hardnosed middlemen entails more effort and risk of imprisonment than living on the dole, and poaching is certainly less lucrative than ordinary crime. Sadly, the more uncommon the outlaws become, the more their mythology appeals to adolescents of all ages looking for local color or role models after which to pattern their own outdoor activities.

In my first winters as a wildfowler, I romanticized renegade watermen and wrote my first version of "The Last Canvasback" as a college sophomore, which means, appropriately enough, "wise fool" in Greek. Later, when I began connecting some of these individuals with the duck traps and bait I found contaminating my favorite hunting spots and with the methodical neck-wringing slaughter of ducks for sale, I developed a less sentimental view of the "subsistence hunter."

Virginian Richard L. Parks in his contribution to *Duck Shooting Along the Atlantic Tidewater* (1947) peeled away sentiment from reality in describing the folly of creating still more hunting regulations to deal with the poaching cancer:

"When the powers that be realized the waterfowl were heading toward that limbo where went the Passenger Pigeon, they feverishly began passing laws—laws that were well meant but difficult to enforce—laws that played into the hands of the unscrupulous. To a shorter hunting season! To less shooting! To fewer hunters on the marshes! These are the toasts of the duck trappers as they pluck our ducks and guzzle their rot-gut beside the roaring woodstove by night! For one duck trapper can bag more Blackducks in a season than a thousand license-paying sportsmen."

In Richard Parks's day, the sporting-club system, which once held poachers at bay, was already moribund. Alexander Hunter and Dwight W. Huntington, however, lived during the heyday of the wildfowling fraternity—when chains of club marshes in the major flyways offered wildfowl their best hope of protection. Writing in *Our Wild Fowl and Waders* in 1910, Huntington noted that "nearly all the best marshes and the desirable lands about the ponds and lakes in the United States which are frequented by wildfowl during their migrations now are owned or leased by individuals and clubs.

"The best shooting points about the Chesapeake Bay and on the outlying beaches also are controlled in the same way, and the number of duck clubs is increasing rapidly. . . . The marshes about the great lakes in the United States and Canada are owned and controlled by many clubs. The center of abundance of these clubs is from Sandusky Westward and around the Western end of Lake Erie to the St. Clair Flats, where there are excellent duck clubs, both in the United States and in Can-ada. . . . There are many duck clubs in the vicinity of Chicago and Northward at Fox Lake and other desirable places. The whole vast region along the Illinois River in the vicinity of Peoria and Havana is occupied, and there are hundreds of clubs about the marshy lakes of the Western and North Western States. On the Pacific coast the duck clubs already are numerous in Oregon and Washington and abundant in California from the vicinity of Sacramento South to Los Angeles, where there are literally miles of clubs.

"There are a few clubs about the great reservoirs in Ohio; and there are many clubs in New England, especially in Massachusetts. Along the Atlantic coast there are many insular clubs, which own for the most part the islands where their club houses are erected. The Princess Anne, the Ragged Island and the Back Bay Clubs, a short distance from Norfolk, Virginia, mark the beginning of a long line of clubs (most of which have fine club houses), which extends Southward through Currituck Sound to the waters of the Albemarle and Pamlico. . . . To the Southward there are many more clubs, notably those about the mouth of the Santee, in South Carolina, and the number is increasing."

In the decade prior to the outbreak of World War I, there were more than forty clubs for gentlemen-wildfowlers along just that portion of the Atlantic Coast between Capes Henry and Hatteras. Membership was not cheap. "To belong to a crack club on Currituck Sound," Hunter wrote, "is almost as expensive as keeping a yacht, for the keepers and attendants are regularly employed all the year around, and the extras amount to a large sum." Yet such large sums were well spent on behalf of the clubs' marshes and the wildfowl using the marshes. A major portion of those sums was spent on gamekeeping the grounds so that the selective killing of a relatively few birds by club members was more than offset by patrolled protection of the flocks.

Prime wintering habitat, even those marshes under close club control, invariably attracted trespassers. At North Carolina's Swan Island Club, whose eighteen—mostly Bostonian—members visited only a few weeks each year, "the keeper there," wrote Hunter, "showed me a novel contrivance to keep poachers off the grounds. On top of the house was a tripod on which was mounted a large rifle that revolved on a pivot. When the keeper discovered, by aid of a powerful fieldglass, any marauder, he promptly sent a bullet in his near proximity, and the detected party always took the hint and moved on. There are several thousand acres in this tract, and there is always good shooting, for the ducks have learned to gather there when gunned out of the sound."

Clubs became, in effect, waterfowl refuges for most of the wintering season, except for those few weeks when members visited. Even during that period, club rules generally prohibited the killing of hens and afternoon shooting. In addition, all larger clubs had sanctuary zones where no shooting at all was allowed. Overall, club marshes represented a kind of waterfowl Shangri-la compared to the free-for-all killing taking place on the unkeepered marshes and bays.

Hunter described the amenities of a number of these sporting fraternities, including the Currituck Club, the exclusive Narrow Island Club (each share cost $25,000), the Palmer Island Club (although each share cost "only" $5,000, this club offered some of the best canvasback shooting in North Carolina), the democratic Widow Mitchell Club, the "most companionable" Light-house Club Company, and the crude, rude, and socially unattractive Poor Man's Club, whose members divided their time "between sitting in their blinds and snoring in their bunks." Yet all private clubs shared the positive feature of a lower ratio of hunters to habitat than on any of the non-club marshes in the area.

Hunter's favorite sporting resort was his own Ragged Island Club not far from Cape Henry. Insularity is an important club virtue, for remoteness from routine is essential to the therapeutic process we call *re-creation*. Although the old site of the Ragged Island Club is no longer insular, remote, or even therapeutic, it was in 1890; and its isolation meant that Hunter and his clubmates could relax and be candid in ways unimaginable in their ordinary Victorian lives. The best proof of this was the visit to the club by President Benjamin Harrison. "To see the President roughing it with the boys," wrote Hunter, "was to witness the acme of the freedom of a republican government. When the Prince of Wales accepts an invitation to hunt, he always has some of his boon-companions along. If the Emperor of Germany, or even the President of the French Republic, was to honor one of his subjects with a hunting visit, a numerous staff would surround him; the best detectives of the country would be engaged for the occasion. Here in free America the ruler leaves his office and goes to an isolated island, away from all mail and telegraphic facilities, accompanied only by one colored servant, and surrounded by his political enemies. It was a picture that would have caused European royalty to open its eyes."

Times change. I was briefly part of Jimmy Carter's press retinue in 1976. I saw how frustrated the President-elect was in his desire to walk his back fields to hunt quail without at the same time being hounded by a battalion of Secret Service agents and hand-wringing aides-de-camp. A similar panoply and entourage would have quickly persuaded the members of the Ragged Island Club that President Harrison should hunt elsewhere!

The Clubs Decline

Enormous changes in sporting habits were precipitated by equally large changes in political philosophy during and after World War I. Through increases in federal income taxes, death duties, and other obligations to the government, the American people transferred power previously held by the rich to elected officials. The theory was that no single person in a political office would ever have as much control over so many peoples' lives as had financial potentates like Andrew W. Mellon and John D. Rockefeller.

Oh, how naive this theory was! The perquisites and trappings of the rich ended up being concentrated in governmental departments. The rich no longer build mansions and mausoleums to house their glories; the federal government does!

244

Beginning in the 1920s, accelerating in the 1930s, and culminating in the 1950s, the U.S. government acquired many of the best private duck clubs in the country and converted them into national wildlife refuges. The change-over did not make wildfowl any more secure than they had been in the network of privately maintained marshes. Indeed, in some areas, poaching actually increased on the now poorly guarded wetlands.

The theory behind the transfer of power was that whereas the old duck clubs had been exclusive and open only to the well-to-do, the new refuges would be open to everyone. The reality was that in order to please the greatest number of people who do not hunt, wildfowling on some national wildlife refuges was stopped entirely. On refuges where shooting was allowed, first-come, first-serve pass-shooting (better known as sky-busting) became the accepted way for every man to have his "fair chance" at a duck or goose. As soon as a ticket-holder got his bird, the next gunner waiting in line stepped forward to get his.

Organizing a national wildlife refuge system was a benefit to waterfowl but, as with the breakup of the Bell telephone system, something that worked was sacrificed for an ideal that, perhaps, works less well. The old duck clubs protected birds and, in many instances, better than federal refuges do today. Furthermore, the loose-leaf manuals of monthly directives found in each refuge manager's office never address the sportsman's code. And that is the part of the wildfowling tradition that has suffered most in the marshes where it all began.

In some refuge acquisitions, the federal government didn't use its power of eminent domain, because the life span of most outdoor fraternities is only as long as that of its oldest founding member. Many clubs begun before the Civil War were already suffering from tired blood and declining memberships when the ducks began to disappear in the late 1890s. In cases where the early clubs survived a changing of the guard, their new members were generally not as well-heeled as their lightly taxed predecessors had been. Sons and grandsons bred to a conspicuous consumption they could no longer afford willingly parted with reunion marshes for modest sums or tax advantages arranged for by family attorneys. By the 1930s, with duck populations and the nation's economy at new historic lows, duck clubs were folding monthly.

Some states, and even some non-government conservation groups, got shares of the wetland spoils. A few clubs survived, however, and new ones were founded following World War II when both the ducks and the men overseas came back. Just as in the late 1860s and 1870s, the late 1940s and 1950s were postwar boom years in which society expanded and energetic men made lots of money. The newly rich looked around for suitably luxurious ways in which to consume their wealth. And just as sporting journals founded after the Civil War had encouraged that era's industrial monopolists to devote some of their riches to establishing duck clubs—many in the recently defeated South—national sporting magazines after World War II encouraged a new class of monied professionals to devote a portion of their incomes to re-establish duck clubs—especially in the still ailing South and undeveloped West.

Dozens of new or refurbished clubs were hatched from the eastern shores of the Chesapeake to California's Imperial Valley. The new club rosters were less often made up of mining and manufacturing magnates than of less fabulously wealthy but better educated doctors and lawyers. Such service-oriented professionals were also better conservationists than their predecessors had been. Whereas the old club members had thought of waterfowl management mostly in terms of what their clubs could do, the post-World War II generation of members championed waterfowl conservation on a continental basis.

With increasing pressure from booming agricultural interests in the upper midwestern United States and Canada, the late 1940s and 1950s were Ducks Unlimited's finest years. Whereas in 1900, the world of wildfowling was divided into market-men and sportsmen, bad guys and good guys, by 1950, almost every person hunting ducks described himself as a sportsman. Unfortunately, most outdoor-oriented youngsters growing up today lack the influence of a sportsman's club and, hence, have no more suitable model for the word *sportsman* than a poorly educated and overpaid jock "going for the gold." In a society where fascism is confused with patriotism, and bullies are called heroes, youngsters are encouraged to believe that "getting everything you desire" is better than living a life of moderation. Under intense pressure "to win," the unaffiliated hunter succumbs to cheating and belatedly learns, if he learns at all, that the only person he's beaten has been himself.

An Old-Fashioned Club

In a cynical and overcrowded world, the need for each of us to cultivate a spiritual oasis shared with a few like-minded friends is not readily perceived by the majority of people numb with the mediocrity of modern life. I occasionally come across such a sanctuary for the soul, and sorrow for the many who'll never know the completeness it offers. But I sorrow for its members, too, for their oases are doomed by death, taxes, and the popular, but thoughtless, faith that standards set by the many are fairer—hence, better—than standards set by the few.

I enjoy spending time with Bill Nickel, a neighbor and occasional legal advisor, because he's a dedicated wildfowler and an outdoor aristocrat. He shoots the same battered Browning his father gave him as a boy, and the well-worn condition of his truck, boat, trailer, and clothing are further proof he values a full life over a full wallet. Like me, Bill is an expatriate Long Islander conditioned to a way of life that was dying in the Great South and Peconic bays even as we were growing up with a need to live that life. On Long Island, you either accepted the conversion of farm fields and marshes to shopping centers and suburban housing, or you devised some plan of escape. You either took a job in the Big Apple and climbed a corporate ladder, or you sought somewhere to live like the Long Island of long ago.

Like me, Bill has two brothers and is the son of a physician. His father belonged to a small eastern Long Island hunting club made up mostly of other physicians. Bill and his brothers hunted with their father until increasing competition for declining numbers of ducks drove the family south to search for a more promising land. They found it on a barrier island in coastal Virginia.

Bill had told me wonderful stories about the Parramore Island Club, and one rainstormy July day, we left my open fishing boat to take shelter at the clubhouse. We were unable to get in, but no matter to Bill: he peered through the windows, gazed across the beach, and was recharged by boyhood memories. We stood under the dripping eaves and were devoured by clouds of mosquitoes while Bill told tales of past Parramore hunts. The mosquitoes didn't seem to bother Bill, and he didn't suffer later from the deer tick larvae that had burrowed into my calves and ankles. It was an interesting visit, but I regarded it as a bad omen for any future contact I might have with that particular club.

Happily, the omen was wrong. In December 1985, shortly before the start of the third segment of that year's duck season, Bill asked me to join him, his brothers, his father, and several of his father's friends—including the club patriarch, Dr. Carl J. Schmidlapp—for a hunt. We'd go out to the island opening day, have dinner, and hunt the next dawn. Since club rules disallowed afternoon duck shooting, I could spend my afternoons poking around the dunes or forests for a deer. We'd stay the second night and return to the mainland Sunday morning. I agreed to go, but a small part of me hoped that some emergency would crop up to give me an excuse to bow out. I was so backlogged with work, I wasn't feeling right about taking off two whole days for just a few hours of duck shooting. Perhaps, also, I was prepared to be disappointed. I have visited more than one sportsmen's club where the casuistry of the membership impressed me rather more than its avowed concern for wildlife.

Bill and I arrived early enough Friday afternoon for me to take a solitary walk up toward the north end of the island. I put Jed, my yellow Labrador puppy, in one of the spare kennels and set off down a mist-shrouded road running back from the ocean to a weed-choked slough and a high dune line known as Italian Ridge. Here I left the cross-island road and wandered north on a pine-needle-padded path through an ancient loblolly forest in whose clearings a few less venerable black cherry and American holly grew. Hurricane Gloria had thrown over several of the giant pines, and the sight of their smashed branches and broken trunks in the fog was both sad and sustaining. The fall of those once-dominant trees would give other, younger pines their places in the sun, and the great woody corpses would subside into humus enriching the ambitious youngsters.

After strolling through the dark forest for nearly a mile, I made my way down the steep western slope of the ridge to a slough to continue my walk through the marsh. The going was rough, though I was pleased to find that Bill's promise that none of the island's wetlands had soft bottoms was true. I flushed two great blue herons and a solitary black duck before hearing the muttering of a great concentration of birds behind a large bayberry thicket. One of my carefully taken steps must have splashed louder in the fog than the others, for a sudden hush fell over the birds, and I marveled at their capacity to distinguish my step from that of a deer's.

As I rounded the edge of the bayberry bush, the first black ducks leaped up. A muddy gutter meandered from the cattail-thickened slough out to a saltgrass meadow, and a vast flock was feeding in the drain or resting on flashes of water on the marsh. The ducks roared into the air. Many had to wait for others overhead to clear before the waiting birds could jump and join the exodus. I jogged across the meadow, flushing still more ducks that had been feeding with their heads underwater. In all, I counted nearly 2,000 black ducks with nary a mallard in the crowd. With the birds gone, the misty landscape was suddenly bleak and foreboding, and I hiked back to the clubhouse.

At dinner I met members and friends of what is known as "the New York contingent" of the club. Since the core membership of Long Island physicians can't maintain the club by itself, the doctors share expenses with a "Richmond crowd," which generally arrives in January. Although January struck me as a better month for duck hunting, the New Yorkers have so long used December for their pre-Christmas reunions, Bill doubts they would consider trading dates, even if the Richmond crowd wanted to.

"You gamble any time you mark your duck-hunting calendar months in advance," Bill reminded me. "But with the wind switching to the northwest and gusting to thirty, the temperature expected to drop forty degrees tonight, and with all the many 'white ducks' [light-bellied puddlers like pintail, wigeon, and gadwall] passing through, we'll probably have the best shooting of the season tomorrow!"

At dinner, I told Bill and the others about the concentration of black ducks I'd seen that afternoon. There was some skepticism, less for the actual numbers I'd seen—Bill had explained I was a compiler for one of the National Audubon Society's Christmas Bird Counts—than for the location where I'd seen the ducks. Bill Steiger rallied to my defense by reminding the other old-timers that, although there was little open water left in the freshwater portion of the northern slough, an extremely high tide had flooded all the marsh that afternoon, and that the gut draining the upper portion of the island might well have been an ideal place for black ducks to gather on the ebb.

The club regulars were not being rude by picking at my testimony. Since club members were reluctant to shoot black ducks, even though they were legal quarry, the members didn't want details for the sake of ambushing that particular flock. Rather, they wanted to know where birds had been seen that afternoon to make decisions about where they'd hunt at dawn. Although the club has a caretaker, who also serves as a chauffeur for the truck that carries the gunners up and down the beach, every member and guest is strictly on his own so far as actual hunting is concerned. Each man makes up a kit of shells, inflatable decoys, and snacks the evening before. After he's dropped at one or another marked location along the beach, he marches west until he finds a pond from which he flushes a satisfactory number of ducks. He then puts out his decoys and waits for the birds to return. If none do, the hunter moves again, Indian-style, depending on where he expects to find more birds. He may pass four or five ponds and put up dozens, even hundreds, of black ducks before putting his decoys out. He may not get what he's after, and he may decide to kill a consolation black duck, but few members or guests do. It's wildfowling at its best. With only nine hunters on the entire island, each of us would have nearly 1,000 acres of dunes and marsh and wooded ponds to explore, and from their happy chatter, I guessed that most of the crowd was as much looking forward to the wandering as to the shooting.

Since I was new to the island and unfamiliar with its subtleties, I asked Bill if I could hunt with him. I sensed he would have been happier hunting by himself, but he agreed, provided we shoot only "white ducks." He organized our kit while I joined Doctors Ayers, Nickel, and Schmidlapp for a rubber of bridge. Unlike the younger generation of gunners who worried all evening about where they'd go the next day, the older members had made up their minds rather quickly because, for them, the hunting of memories was at least as important as the hunting of ducks. So long as they avoided killing a black duck and got a few shots at teal, pintail, or gadwall, they'd have a happy outing.

After the card game, I climbed the stairs to the old coast-guardsmen's dormitory where other guests were already asleep, their snoring synchronized to the pulse of the surf on the beach a short distance away. Undressing in the dark, I suddenly realized how relaxed I'd become in the past half-dozen hours, and I pitied all those who'd never know the peace of such a magic realm.

The Hunt

A century earlier when the dawn arrived, we would have traveled in a horse-drawn wagon down the beach. Not only would it have taken an hour longer, the wagon-driver would have waited for the tide flooding through the toppled cedars to turn. By contrast, Dave Tyler's four-wheel-drive truck slalomed through the fallen trees, dropped the last of us off on a slow turn, and was on its way back before a horse-drawn wagon would have gotten a mile from the clubhouse—which a century ago was nearly half a mile from the surf, while today it stands only a few hundred feet from the eternally rising sea.

Bill had decided to hunt the southernmost ponds on the island, figuring the birds would be most active that morning over the marshes and meadows tapering toward Little Machipongo Inlet. His brothers had been down that way during the early season, and we found a plank for a seat in the middle of a jerrybuilt blind on an island in the middle of a pothole. A few black ducks left the pond as we approached, but I couldn't see how this one spot, more than any of dozens of duplicates on the island, would provide the kind of shooting I knew Bill anticipated. Still, this was his territory and his excitement was contagious.

We'd not finished putting out the last decoy when black ducks began working to us. As soon as we got in the blind, they started landing. The first shootable birds didn't appear for another ten minutes. I'd been watching a pair of black ducks swimming twenty yards away, when Bill whispered, "Four teal—on the upper end of the pond."

The birds had zipped in and landed while we were looking elsewhere. We sat still and hoped they'd swim nearer, but with the cold wind blowing toward us, the teal elected to stay at the upper end of the pond where the water was calmest. More black ducks arrived, and a few landed in the middle of the decoys bouncing and straining at their anchor lines.

"It's now or never," declared Bill as he unexpectedly stood up.

It was difficult concentrating on the little ducks with so many larger targets jumping closer to us. Fortunately, however, when the teal leaped up, they did because the other ducks were jumping and not because they had seen us. They drifted back on the wind just enough for us to collect all four.

That many ducks down at one time was the most Jed had seen so far in his youthful career, and I had to leave the blind to show him where the last bird had fallen far out on the meadow to convince him that there really was another duck there. We were soon back and settled in for another ten minutes of black-duck landings.

During the course of the morning, some two hundred blackies came to the decoys by ones, twos, threes, and small flocks up to seven. These were the ducks that actually pitched to the decoys; my estimate does not include the many *hundreds* more that worked over us but flared without landing. In all, we saw several thousand black ducks in a little more than a hundred minutes for an average of three coming or going every sixty seconds. That's spectacular wildfowling, even when you're not firing a shot.

The next two shootable birds were easily killed. Bill recognized them as gadwall flighting in with half-a-dozen black ducks several long seconds before the flock was within range. We stood and took the pair directly overhead: Bill's hen fell to his right, my drake, behind the blind. The blackies rocketed away on the wind. By the time they were distant specks, Jed had retrieved both gadwall.

Although we had to wait nearly fifteen minutes for the next shootable pair, we were almost fearful they'd arrive too soon and curtail the black-duck-watching. So engrossed were Jed and I in peering through the blind's branches at a black-duck drake swimming just a few feet away that Bill's sudden call to arms had the dog out of the blind after the black duck and me slow on my feet and slow to locate the towering gadwall hen that Bill's quick killing of the drake had left me. Although I blew feathers from the duck's body with both shots, she limped out to the beach before going down behind a clump of wind-twisted cedars north of an overwash.

"I'll pick up here," said Bill. "Hurry over to the beach and get that bird before it blows out to sea."

As soon as I crossed the dunes, I got out binoculars to scan the ocean. There were no whitecaps for half a mile offshore. I glassed north and south where the duck might be, but saw only a distant flock of gulls working over something that didn't look much like a duck. By the time Bill joined me, Jed and I had searched the beach and the thickets for seventy-five yards on either side of where we thought the duck went down. Bill joined in the search, but after I told him about the distant flock of gulls, he became pessimistic. He thought the bird had limped out to sea, even though my quick arrival and search of the sea convinced me she hadn't.

"Go back and shoot another duck," Bill suggested.

"I don't think so," I replied. "I count downed birds as bagged birds on my own marsh, and I don't see why I should break the rule out here."

"That's a good rule," Bill acknowledged, "and I know we agreed to kill only four ducks each when we came out this morning. But even if you'd found your gadwall, the law still allows two bonus teal. I'm not going back to the clubhouse with you having only three ducks! I want you to shoot another bird."

We returned to the blind, and I soon shot a green-winged teal drake. We went back to the beach, hung the ducks on an upturned root of a fallen cedar and stacked our guns and other equipment around them. Dave Tyler would come by with the truck later in the morning to pick everything up. In the meanwhile, we could enjoy an unencumbered three-mile hike back along the surf.

We'd not walked a hundred yards when I spotted the missing gadwall hen lying dead above the tide line. She had been shot in her left eye and later, when plucked, I found four other pellets in her neck and body. Yet after dropping out of sight behind the cedars, she'd beat on against the wind before collapsing some fifty yards above the spot where Jed and I had turned back from our search.

With the lost-and-found gadwall swinging from my hand and old and new memories to share with Bill, I strode happily along the beach and watched Jed chase shorebirds over the surf.

When we got back, a dozen mallard, gadwall, and wigeon were hanging on nails driven into the north side of the shed—and a black duck. When Bill discovered that the "mistake bird" had been shot by his father, he rubbed his hands in anticipation of the hearty ribbing he'd give Dr. Nickel at lunch.

Surprisingly, Dr. Nickel freely admitted he'd shot the black duck. His confession, however, was only a preamble to his description of how, while sitting disconsolately with the black duck that had looked like a mallard at dawn and thinking of some defense for the abuse he knew he'd get from his sons, he'd looked up and seen three gadwall hovering over the decoys. Three quick shots, and the ducks were his.

"The first two splashed into the pond," said the seventy-eight-year-old physician. "I knew I'd have no trouble finding them. But I was worried about the last bird which fell into some reeds behind me. I went to look for him first. Once I had him in hand, I didn't care whether the whole world knew I'd started the day with a black duck—so long as they also knew I'd gotten a triple on gadwall!"

The son who'd teased his father walked over and shook the doctor's hand. If the red gods grant me seventy-eight years of life, I pray they also grant me the will to hunt ducks, the skill to kill them cleanly, and a son who will always share my passion for such things.

My visit to the club impressed me with the fact that I was hunting not only in a very special place, but with some very special people. When at lunch we debated the pros and cons of closing the black-duck season entirely to let the species rebuild its population, the discussion did not sound as hollow as such talk does among people whose good intentions too often exceed their deeds.

When another guest, Bruce Buckley, said he'd be content to come to the island just to watch black ducks work to his decoys, no one doubted the sentiment, for that was exactly what Bruce had done for the past two mornings. Although countless black ducks had come and gone within range, he never fired his gun. You could see, however, by the sparkle in his eyes that he'd had a great time merely anticipating the pintail and wigeon the red gods decided not to send him.

After lunch, I offered to help the senior members repair a shed roof. "Oh, no," they laughed, "you're much too heavy! Get your rifle and go find a deer. Roof repairs are our specialty!"

As I started up the trail running north through the dunes, I looked back on four young/old men climbing ladders and unrolling tar paper. I saw that such sharing is what keeps them coming back, year after year, to this wildfowler's retreat.

At dinner the night before, Dr. Schmidlapp had spoken with melancholy about his generation being the last to experience such refined recreation. When a hurricane or the sea finally destroys the clubhouse, he said, all that the club stands for will perish with it.

Yet as I watched those grand old men in ragged clothes reinforcing the roof of an ancient shed, the metaphor of death and time that occurred to me was of the fallen patriarch pines along Italian Ridge whose fiber and substance are already being passed on to another generation.

A melancholy postscript: In the early-morning hours of July 12, 1989, a violent thunder-and-lightning storm swept down the Eastern Shore of Virginia. At dawn, Bagley Walker and I were running offshore to go fishing when we noticed smoke several miles south at the site of the Parramore Island duck club. We hoped the fire wasn't so far along we wouldn't be able to anchor offshore, swim through the surf, and rescue some artifacts and the shooting logs. But we were too late. All four walls were ablaze and the roof and lookout cupola had already fallen into the inferno below. Above the roar, we could hear the erratic popping of paper shotgun shells like Chinese firecrackers in a funeral pyre. The blaze marked the end of an era. Older club members say they're too old to start over; younger members say they don't have the money. A club's values may be passed on by people who hunted there, but a club's traditions can't be. You need a clubhouse and time—lots of time—to do that.

— 18 —

The Native Question

The heyday of Canada's James and Hudson bays' hunting camps is history. Although a few old-timers still hunt there, after the camps were turned over to native corporations, their quality went quickly downhill. The Cree seem to care little about pleasing visitors. The natives know, for example, that local geese don't fly until mid-morning, so they don't leave camp until 9:00 A.M. Most

255

Americans don't understand or even care about the goose flight schedule. They know only that they've taken off a week from work and paid good money to come to Canada to hunt geese, and they want to be on the shooting grounds at dawn. They don't care whether they get birds; they just want to be there.

But the guides don't even get up until 8:00 A.M. For centuries their survival was based on an economy of motion, and they see absolutely no point in going early, even to please clients who would probably return next year if they have a satisfying time this year—and satisfaction may consist of nothing more than knowing that the guides have done their utmost to please their clients. But the natives live each day as it comes. Prospects twelve months hence are so remote as to be meaningless.

This here-and-now philosophy of life has resulted in some serious abuses of subsistence hunting. Rumors of overkill of every kind of Arctic wildlife filter down from the Far North. Thus, I made an expedition to Baffin Island less in the context of recreation than to report on how much remains of the subsistence tradition.

In *Arctic Dreams,* Barry Lopez writes that "hunting in my experience among Eskimos—and by hunting I simply mean being out on the land—is a state of mind." Well, that's true of all hunting. "The release of the arrow or bullet is like a word spoken out loud," Lopez continues. "It occurs at the periphery of your concentration." Again, that sensation is not unique to the Inuit.

The question is not whether some Inuit feel the hunting experience more keenly than white or black hunters—nor even whether Inuit are superior hunters to whites and blacks. Hunting capabilities, after all, are based on experience and environment. The Inuit would make awkward woodland hunters just as, initially at least, Iturbi Forest pygmies would fail on the tundra.

The real issue is whether there are any mechanisms in Inuit culture to prevent food-resource overkill. Does an Inuit's undeniable intimacy with the unforgiving Arctic environment provide him with an intuitive grasp of conservation and its long-term value to the survival of his hunting culture? Or is the Inuit treatment of nature no better than that of other primitive peoples suddenly granted the magic of outboard engines, aluminum boats, and waterproof ammunition?

My inquiry was more than a matter of curiosity. Throughout the northern polar regions of the world, nesting geese and swans are coming under increasing hunting pressure. In one of the most productive goose-breeding grounds on earth, the Yukon-Kuskokwim Delta of Alaska, the human birth rate is also one of the highest on earth. The human population has swollen more than 50 percent in the past fifteen years to over 20,000 today, while during that same period the goose population has plummeted. Emperor geese fell from an estimated 139,000 in 1964 to 71,000 in 1984; white-fronted geese fell from an estimated 500,000 in the late 1960s to fewer than 100,000 by 1984; and most precipitous of all, cackling geese, a "geographic variant" or subspecies of the Canada goose, fell from an estimated 380,000 in 1965 to only about 21,000 birds twenty years later.

Is there a cause and effect between Inuit population growth and goose declines?

During the past twenty years, the human population in California, winter home of both cacklers and white-fronts, has also risen dramatically—from approximately fourteen million to twenty-four million. Furthermore, Alaskan Inuits take only eggs or kill replaceable birds, while Californians have destroyed irreplaceable habitat. Between 1950 and 1985, Californians drained and developed four million acres of wetlands and other wildfowl wintering grounds. Within the state, there are only 300,000 wetland acres left, most of them controlled by hunting clubs.

Meanwhile in the Atlantic basin, a swelling Inuit population on Greenland is applying increasing pressure to the only white-fronted goose population wintering in the western British Isles. The white-fronts that winter on England's Severn Estuary and that inspired Sir Peter Scott to establish his Wildfowl Trust headquarters at Slimbridge mostly come from breeding grounds in northern Siberia. On their way west, however, they cross and join the migratory path of lesser white-fronted geese migrating from Greenland and Scandinavia.

Greenland may be a huge island, but most of it is mountainous and inhospitable to nesting geese as well as people. Most all the island's larger life forms are drawn to its relatively few river valleys and estuaries for food and reproduction. The Danish government does not conduct aerial surveys or make waterfowl estimates the way the U.S. and Canadian governments do. All we know for sure is that a rapidly rising population of more than 40,000 Greenland Inuit continue to tap a shrinking population of white-fronted geese for eggs and meat. Each year the nesting colonies of white-fronts on Greenland grow smaller. Once-prime nesting grounds haven't seen many or any birds in over a decade.

Hans-Pavia Rosing is a Greenland Eskimo and president of the Inuit Circumpolar Conference, a civil rights organization made up of native peoples from Greenland, Alaska, and northern Canada. In March, 1982, he told a *New York Times* reporter that "for too long, we have let the outsiders push us around in our own land. We are now determined to protect our lands and our waters, and to share in their destiny."

These are noble sentiments, but they're apparently inspired more by politics and economics than by an understanding of how nature works. The territories of all Arctic peoples, including the heretofore ignored and forgotten natives of Siberia, are being surveyed for their mineral wealth by various government and industrial agencies. So far, only the natives of Alaska have made a settlement with their federal government, and the natives of Canada and Greenland want to get comparably generous slices of their region's economic pies.

In the meanwhile, neither the Canadian nor Danish government has pressed the Inuit to abide by management restrictions on the slaughter of wildfowl and other game. Some observers feel that federal governments want the Inuit thoroughly besotted with carefree killing so that conservation itself can be used as a lever during further negotiations with native peoples over the "more valuable" mineral rights. Thus, the government might allow the Inuit to maintain traditional hunting rights in exchange for a petroleum company's right to drill for oil in a likely looking river valley or estuary, or to cross a wildfowl nesting ground with a pipeline once a corporation had discovered oil nearby.

Such economic tradeoffs are already being made on the Greenland white-fronted goose's wintering grounds: the Wexford Slobs in the southeastern corner of Ireland and the island of Islay in the Inner Hebrides off the west coast of Scotland. Eastern Atlantic white-fronts feed on peat bogs, and, as ornithologist Dr. Richard G. B. Brown has noted, "as far as anyone knows, they have nowhere else to go."

The problem is that peat is also a valuable resource for people, especially in Ireland and northern Scotland where it has been dug, dried, and burned for fuel for centuries. When the human population of Ireland was controlled by periodic plagues, famines, and emigrations, there was more than enough peat for both birds and people. Today, however, a power plant is planned for the Wexford Slobs that will exploit vast fields of peat that once attracted large flocks of white-fronts.

And on Islay, the government is bulldozing a road to Duich Moss so that the peat on this formerly remote white-fronted goose wintering ground can be reached for cutting and burning to smoke the malt for the whiskey for which the island of Islay is world renowned.

The ordinary citizen can take a stand only on issues in which he sees clear moral choices between right and wrong. Yet in Greenland, Ireland, or on Islay, there are no bad guys wearing black hats. The Inuit, the Irish, and the Scots merely want to continue doing what they have always done, only on a larger scale, because there are now too many of them—and all of us.

As Dr. Brown commented on the situation on Islay, "Geese or whiskey? Put like that, it's a comic dilemma—though in sober fact it's a very sad one. It's not the kind of problem you can solve by changing your brand or by picketing your local liquor store. I doubt if it can be solved at all. The real point is that we have finally outgrown this planet, and the future will be a series of increasingly painful choices between our own species and all the others. The others will inevitably go to the wall when it comes to the crunch, and our grandchildren will find the world a poorer place in which to live."

Summer Snows

One snow-flurry day in August I helped a party of Inuit hunters haul their boats and gear over the falls on the Robertson River near the northern end of Baffin Island less than one hundred miles from the magnetic North Pole. My Inuit hosts had been mildly contemptuous when I expressed interest in their Arctic char fishery near the mouth of the river. Fishing is women's, or children's, work in Inuit society, and the American men who come north each summer just to catch char puzzle Inuit men. Americans are also regarded as a sinister force. The money they bring buys new boats, motors, and ammunition, but that means able-bodied men must take time off from the real work of hunting to help the women cook and care for the hermaphrodite-like visitors who believe that playing a fish on delicate tackle is as masculine an activity as hunting caribou or seals.

As soon as I made clear that I wanted to share the hardship of an upcountry hunt, my Inuit hosts appeared to forgive my feminine interest in fishing. Furthermore, since I was more than a head taller than the tallest of them and heavier by seventy-five pounds, I made myself valuable as a pack animal. Soon I was just one of the boys—albeit a somewhat retarded one, since I couldn't speak their language or share in their plans and jokes.

We ran upriver mile after mile against the clear, swift, melting current of the icy river with the swirling snow thinning periodically so I could see a vast and brooding landscape through water-spotted bifocals. We were searching for caribou, but since any game would do, we were foraging as well. Periodically, Sheatie Tagak would run the lead boat ashore. Jacob Peterloosie would follow with the two teenaged boys and myself gripping the gunwales to keep from falling backward when we hit the shingle beach. We'd scramble up to some high point to lie down and scrutinize the surrounding hills. The Inuit held their binoculars vertically and looked through them with one eye. The Inuit's first magnifying lenses were telescopes obtained from European ship captains in the eighteenth and nineteenth centuries. Using a single eye to spot distant objects is now too ingrained a habit to be changed by the advent of binoculars.

At one stop, the two Inuit men discussed something that seemed to involve a choice regarding a snow-mottled valley ahead. They led the rest of us back to the boats in a purposeful way suggesting the hunt had begun in earnest. For some reason, however, everyone seemed less keyed up than I'd imagined we'd be; and as soon as we rounded the next headland and entered the lower basin of a large lake, I saw why. We were on our way to a nesting colony of greater snow geese, and the kids were already laughing and arming themselves with tent poles.

As soon as we arrived, men and boys jumped onto the stony beach, and I was left to secure the boats while the others dashed ahead to run down wobbling, rocking geese fleeing over the broken ground. It surprised me that so few of the adult birds flew, for when I examined them later, they were sufficiently fledged after the summer molt. Yet most of the adults stayed with their broods and tried to lead them in a circle back toward the water. Few made it. The adults were shot with .22s, while the young grays were clubbed by the frolicking boys. It took several trips to bring all the birds down to the boats, and by the time the geese were packed in the bows, between the seats, and around the gear, it looked as though we were seated on two outboard-powered icebergs. I don't know how many dozen birds were killed, but I do know that when we slowly motored away from the shore, I looked back at an eerily empty valley that had been teeming with wildfowl only an hour before.

The Caribou Slaughter

I thought the hunt was over—that we'd run downstream to put the women to work picking birds—that we'd continue looking for caribou the next day. But we ran upstream and in the second valley beyond the one where the snow geese had been, Sheatie spotted a small group of caribou. Eventually, I, too, saw their tiny forms on the mountainside. When one moved, I could make out others among the lichen- and snow-spotted rocks. We left the goose-laden boats pulled up among some boulders and started a circuitous stalk that would bring us behind the ridge toward which the caribou were feeding.

"Tuwawi!" ("Hurry up!") commanded Jacob as he trotted forward in that graceless but competent manner with which an Inuit can consume miles of tundra without tiring. Sheatie had guided the hunt all day until the caribou were spotted. Then Jacob, the older man, took over. The five animals spooked once, apparently from our odor, and we had to duck and run and crawl behind the ridge for another mile. We finally climbed into a saddle on the ridge and took cover behind some boulders. The nearest *tuktu* was feeding just one hundred fifty feet away. Sheatie took aim with his .22-250 but waited respectfully while Jacob looked down his ancient .303 Enfield whose sighting plane was striped by dirty adhesive tape binding the rusty barrel to the stock. With Jacob's shot, the nearest caribou collapsed as though the tundra had been jerked from beneath its feet.

The four other animals, including a *nurak* (young caribou) and a lactating female *(armaluk),* looked up and shifted nervously. One of them began walking toward its dead comrade. At Sheatie's shot, it sat down and then toppled over when it tried to regain its feet. It began crawling down the slope on its paralyzed hindquarters while the Inuit shooters concentrated on downing the remaining animals.

The boys were called forward to take shots, and the killing became more erratic. A third caribou was hit twice during a volley of half-a-dozen rounds from Sheatie's rifle. The animal fell, got back up, and ran after the limping mother and calf. Suddenly the wounded bull went down for good as though only belatedly realizing he was dead.

The two remaining caribou disappeared into the swirling snow, and Sheatie and one of the boys ran after them. I followed more slowly and found the calf dead half a mile farther along. I returned to watch Jacob skin the first animal he'd killed. Periodically, we heard shots reverberate from the mountain walls close to the opposite shore of the lake into which the mother caribou was finally driven and slain.

Five up; five down. The next day, the Inuit would find only two caribou in the vast Robertson River drainage, but that was because, they said, the hunters that day were not as good as Sheatie and Jacob. There would be more caribou in time, they said—as always before.

In the sense that hunters today kill about as many caribou as their fathers did, replacements for these animals do seem to spring mysteriously from the earth as the Inuit elders have long believed. But what modern Inuits do not know, and natural historians do, is that the scattered groups of caribou on Baffin Island are mere remnants of great herds that once supported a far larger local Inuit population. A mere handful of hunters presently roam this region, in pursuit of a mere handful of game. The killing they did with me was only scavenging in the ruins of a once-great hunting tradition diminished by the very technology that makes their meager success possible.

Conservation

Although the Inuit once used every scrap of game they killed, increasingly meat is left on the tundra by hunters who bring out only the saleable hides and antlers. Sheatie indicated we'd have cached less except for the thickening August snow that was bringing on an early Arctic dusk. We were more than thirty miles from camp, and the downstream run would mean going through several rapids and over one waterfall in the dark. Thus, the hearts, livers, and entrails of all the animals were left for the foxes and ravens, while most of the meat was hidden under rocks. Scavengers would settle for the organs, Sheatie said, and leave the caches be.

"That's fantasy," said the wildlife officer for the Northwest Territories at Pond Inlet. "Feeding foxes and ravens attract polar bears, which dig out the caches. Many of those the bears don't find are never relocated by the Inuit. The waste of game is unbelievable. The Inuit aren't subsistence hunting anymore; they're shooting to hear their guns go off!"

Jacob, Sheatie, the boys, and I salvaged the caribou heads with their edible eyes, tongues, brains, cheeks, noses, and antlers for carving into cash artifacts for the tourists who visit Pond Inlet—along with the hides, tenderloins, and precious stomach fat. Down on the lakeshore, we opened the kerosene stove that had already provided tea earlier in the day. We supplemented a package of dehydrated onion soup with hunks of caribou meat boiled in a pot that saw double duty as a boat bailer. For those of us too hungry to wait, we ate slices of raw tenderloin.

The lactating female caribou was towed from the middle of the lake where she'd drifted, and as soon as the animal's fur was scraped free of its soggy burden of icy water, Jacob knelt and drank from one of her udders. This was a familiar act to the old hunter, but Sheatie had apparently not done it before. He was curious, and after a few words with Jacob, he, too, knelt and stroked the nutrient-rich milk into his mouth. The boys laughed and, through shy glances at me, showed their embarrassment at what their elders were doing. When the animal had been butchered, the boys threw the empty milk gland into the water and stepped on it, demonstrating their contempt for old ways, and then watched it slowly wobble back to the surface.

A hunting culture is markedly different from other societies. Its language is rich in animal imagery, but generally poor in philosophy. This is because hunters depend on their knowledge of the real world of wildlife for survival; there is little leisure for pondering abstract thought. The Inuit have dozens of words, not only to describe every part of a goose or caribou, but to describe every stage of such creatures' life cycles. Even though snow geese are on Baffin Island only three months of the year, the Inuit look on them as *their* birds. All talk of a need to allot portions of the goose population among other exploiters in southern Canada and the United States falls on uncomprehending ears. The United States is more remote to the Inuit than the moon, which is where some older Inuit believe snow geese fly when they leave the Arctic.

In the Inuit religion, there may or may not be a life after death, but if there is, the Inuit believe it is only a spiritual continuation of the life they've known on earth. Only enslaved peoples—meaning highly civilized ones—believe (because they must believe) in a life after death superior to this life. The Inuit are not afraid of death, but this does not mean they are unafraid of other things. They are superstitious and accept ancient myths about wildlife as fact. While it may be true that such myths inspire a rapport with wild creatures transcending the sentimental affection for animals common to Western civilized peoples, such myths interfere with Inuit education in wildlife management.

I asked a young English-speaking Inuit fisherman why he killed small Arctic char that he didn't intend to eat when, by releasing them, he could catch them again many summers hence when they would be of a size worth keeping. He was puzzled and said, "The char are mine; I caught them." That was explanation enough.

Likewise, when we got back to the boats with those portions of the caribou the Inuit had decided to take downstream, the Inuit threw out all the snow geese to make room for the caribou hides and heads. With careful repacking, the Inuit might have saved some of the birds and still had sufficient freeboard for a safe passage downstream. But they threw out every goose as though the birds were inferior game that would diminish the value of the more highly prized caribou. The entire colony of greater snow geese went drifting into the dusk. On the run downriver, we passed their ghostly bodies wedged between rocks and stranded on gravel bars.

Although the conscious overkill of geese by some American sportsmen is morally more reprehensible than what the Inuit had done, the result is the same: dead geese that will never perpetuate their kind. Some wildfowl can sustain much persecution, but no species can sustain it indefinitely. The Inuit are a practical and intelligent race. Although conservation is obviously not an inherent part of their culture, it could be made a part of their lives if their leaders could be persuaded of its value and if these men would in turn try to teach the younger generation just now searching for values beyond materialism.

Like most peoples, the Inuit are increasingly dependent on a technology they do not fully comprehend. The problem is not in the Inuit's full-scale adoption of modern tools, electronics, and machinery, for, in most respects, technology has resulted in more interesting and more secure lives than those their fathers knew. Only armchair travelers would argue that the Inuit were better off before they made their first contact with the Europeans and Americans. The problem is not in the technology, but in the fact that sophisticated cultures find it so much easier to export goods than values. Americans and southern Canadians continue to introduce new tools and toys to the Inuit without showing them how to maintain or recycle the old ones. We not only fail to introduce self-restraint with our innovations, we fail to show the Inuit how to perpetuate the wildlife species on which Inuit pleasure and profit—if no longer their survival— are based.

Only a handful of Inuit in the entire Arctic basin are being trained in the fundamentals of wildlife management, and rarely are the best and brightest minds selected for this vital work. The tide of contemporary prosperity in Alaska, Canada, and Greenland is already ebbing. The promise of unlimited mineral wealth may turn out to be an illusion. What will the Inuit do if their cash economy reverts to barter even as their outboard engines revert to rust?

The choices are limited, but they will be even more so if hunters of the North do not soon develop some appreciation for the philosophy of common sense we call conservation.

19

Fair or Fowl Lobbying

Although he had stayed up late the night before with whisky sours and wonderfully lucky poker hands, the Senator looked chipper the next morning at dawn when he came down for breakfast.

"Waterfowling has sure changed from when I was a boy," he said. "We'd have been out and killed a duck or two by now."

"Geese don't get up quite as early as ducks, Senator," I explained. "We have plenty of time."

We almost had too much. After sitting for nearly two hours in a field pit with only distant flocks of geese, old war stories, and progressively stale jokes to share, the Senator was restive, and the rest of us were anxious.

Suddenly the guide began calling with great urgency. By looking where he was looking, I saw seven birds heading our way. Please, I silently prayed, for the sake of your kith and kin, give us a shot.

The birds worked closer.

"Oh, my," the Senator breathed. I glanced over at this gray eminence of American politics, his eyes bright with excitement and longing; he was a boy again.

"They're going by!" yelled the guide. "Take the one on the end!"

We shoved our camouflaged lids forward, and the four of us stood to shoot. Four shots sounded together, and the nearest Canada seemed to stumble, tried to regain its balance, and then collapsed to the ground with a resounding thump.

"You got him, Senator!"

"I did, didn't I?"

"Good shooting, sir!"

Of course, there was no way to say for certain who'd killed the bird, but all of us were playing pre-assigned roles: the modest guide who called the birds; the Senator who excelled in shooting as he did in politics; and his two companions who were there to do everything short of buying one to make certain the Senator got a goose for Thanksgiving dinner!

As we started back across the field, I underscored the point of the outing: "If those drainage projects get funded, sir, I'm afraid they'll mean even fewer birds than we saw this morning."

"We can't have that!" the Senator declared. "The farmers will holler bloody murder, but I've survived that before. I want you to talk with my legislative assistant when we get back, okay?"

"Okay!"

Although political lobbying is a twelve-month, round-the-clock industry, the activity peaks when certain kinds of legislative proposals are made, and only diminishes during summer and holiday recesses. The goal of every good lobbyist is to use time in the valleys to influence the peaks, and the very best lobbyists know that this is largely a matter of separating congressmen from their Washington offices and getting them onto terrain where the lobbyists are in control.

The autumn that President Reagan toured the nation, charming the electorate with his version of tax-reform, a number of representatives and senators were in goose pits on the Eastern Shore of Maryland hearing about the "critical need" for exceptions from lobbyists for the oil and mining industries, hotels and restaurants, and other businessmen with little desire for change in the status quo.

With so many hunters among America's corporate executives and legislators, more than a little of the nation's business gets done in duck blinds. The long, idle hours of waiting and companionable talk seem conducive to financial dealing: decisions are made to take over Company X or to select A over B as chairman of the board.

Nowhere is lobby-fowling more intense than along the eastern shores of the Chesapeake. Lobby-fowling may affect the choice of a man for political office or help determine which company gets a military contract. It influences which bills get through Congress and helps determine how much you'll pay in taxes next year.

Legislators rule on their home turf, and their Washington offices are their home away from home in the nation's capital. Tempting a senator or representative to compromise his constituents' interests is well nigh impossible so long as the congressman is surrounded by staff members and memorabilia from home. You can host all the Kennedy Center theater parties you like, but as soon as your targeted congressman returns to his house or apartment in or near the District of Columbia, you have lost most of the little influence provided by a free meal or a catered evening at the theater. By contrast, promise a congressman some fun and anonymity, and he's yours for the weekend!

Ever since the first days of the Republic, lobbyists of one stripe or another have used our fields and streams to seduce lawmakers into going along to get along. George Washington was a hard nut to crack, because his favorite sport was riding to hounds, and it's very difficult to discuss special interests while chasing foxes over the Virginia countryside—even if you can also find an able lobbyist who is an able horseman.

But Washington himself served as a kind of lobbyist during the formation of our Constitution. He was presiding over a deadlocked gathering of states' representatives during the hot summer of 1787 and wisely requested an adjournment to let weather and tempers cool. Washington then invited Gouverneur Morris and Robert Morris (no relation) to go fishing with him on the Schuylkill and Delaware rivers. The convention would not reconvene until September 17th, and Washington's wanderings with the Morrises became a kind of working vacation from the heat and congestion of Philadelphia.

The men fished for perch in the Delaware at Trenton and for trout in the Schuylkill not far from Valley Forge. In the shade under streamside trees and in the evenings at local inns and homes, the three men resolved several sticky issues regarding the proposed Constitution, the most important of which was the role of slavery.

In turn, Gouverneur Morris knew that no matter how the Constitution was worded, not every state would willingly be submerged into a federal framework. Thus, he and Washington persuaded Robert Morris to accept a "majority clause" making the Constitution binding on all the states once a majority had ratified it.

A good thing they did. Only Delaware wholeheartedly endorsed the finished document. Rhode Island and North Carolina flatly rejected it. These two states, however, were pulled into the Union, kicking and screaming all the while about their martyred rights, thanks to the cooperation of three angling friends who also happened to be among the most influential politicians of their generation.

Although angling has continued to be an important lobbying activity, it was increasingly overshadowed by duck hunting after the Civil War. One trouble with angling—particularly fly fishing—is that it has to be done alone to be done well. It's difficult to catch a senator's attention when he's intent on catching a trout. Then, too, fly fishing requires skills that many legislators lack. Shooting, by contrast, is something every American presumes he knows something about, and even when a legislator is a lousy shot, his companions can contrive to make it appear otherwise. When political campaigner Hubert Humphrey posed for pictures in 1970 for the now defunct *Rod & Gun* magazine, he proudly cradled an old double-barreled shotgun in one picture, but fished off his dock with spincasting tackle in another. He wasn't about to be caught by the camera with a fly rod in his hands! Furthermore, while it was okay for President Jimmy Carter to hunt quail, since he had done that from boyhood days in Georgia, even staff members began grumbling about his deceitfulness when he told the press he was going to Camp David but sneaked off to Pennsylvania instead to fly fish.

Just as Humphrey and Carter were the last Democratic heirs to political momentum initiated by Franklin Roosevelt, President Benjamin Harrison was the last heir to a political dynasty established by his great-grandfather, who signed the Declaration of Independence, and by his grandfather, who was our ninth President. If there was any one President who established wildfowling as the *ne plus ultra* activity for Washington politicians and lobbyists, it was Benjamin Harrison. In his reminiscence about Harrison's visit to the Ragged Island Club in *The Huntsman in the South,* Alexander Hunter recalled that:

"The President was introduced to all the members present, and they were soon discussing plans for the next morning. He expressed a wish to be put into a blind as early as possible in the morning, and to be left there with a retriever, saying that he would hunt as the others hunted. He wanted no extra attention, and declared that he did not mind exposure, and could stand anything the rest could.

"Our distinguished guest was called at 3 o'clock the next morning, and he soon came in, looking bright and cheerful. His costume consisted of rubber hip boots, dog-skin vest, and waterproof blouse, over which he wore a thick 'dreadnaught' coat. His gun was the handsomest one I ever saw, and I do not think there is another like it in America. It was made for him by a prominent American manufacturer, and the inscription, 'Protection to American Industries,' was cut on the barrels. It was a 12-gauge with exquisite barrels, and the triggers and guard were of pure gold, while rich chasing adorned the piece all over."

Although protocol generally forbids direct political or business negotiations while hunting, it does not prohibit an admiring constituent from making a utilitarian gift to an illustrious sportsman. If the gift is also valuable, well, that merely reflects the intensity of the constituent's admiration. Benjamin Harrison's shotgun supporting "Protection to American Industries" was accepted on that basis.

Grover Cleveland, whose two terms as President bracketed Benjamin Harrison's, was also an avid wildfowler; like Harrison, he was not averse to accepting tokens of esteem, particularly if they helped him hunt ducks. In an era when aluminum was still something of a semiprecious metal, W. H. Mullins of Salem, Oregon, presented President Cleveland with a fourteen-foot "unsinkable" duck punt weighing just thirty pounds. According to the manufacturer, "the softest stroke of the paddle will set it in motion. Its draught is so small that it can run among the thick reeds where the ducks love to hide in the daytime."

Maybe. Unfortunately, President Cleveland was an enormous man;

the Secret Service was required to extract him from the marsh whenever he got stuck. A delicately balanced boat may have been too tippy for a man of Cleveland's girth.

Theodore Roosevelt was more of a bird-watcher than a bird-shooter. His hunting passion was for big game, and he sacrificed a potential second elected term in the White House to go on safari in Africa, where not even the most intrepid lobbyist could find him.

Franklin Roosevelt was less passionate and more calculating about the effect of outdoor recreation. Constantly looking for ways to impress the electorate with the idea that he was healthy and vigorous despite his confinement to a wheelchair, FDR avidly fished or hunted waterfowl because he could do both these activities sitting down in a boat or blind.

One tale touching on FDR's hunting prowess was reported from a meeting in the Oval Office on August 12, 1937, between the President, Secretary of Agriculture Henry A. Wallace, Senator Harry B. Hawes of Missouri, and Carl Shoemaker, conservation director of the National Wildlife Federation. This is how Shoemaker remembered the discussion, which was about the creation of a Presidentially-sponsored Wildlife Week:

"The President was in a jovial mood as he sat behind his big desk cluttered with ships, anchors, and other naval miniatures. We lined up in a semicircle facing him. The group had selected Senator Hawes to state the purpose of the meeting, but first the Senator had to tell a story about a retriever dog he once owned. It was a good yarn and reminded the President of one time he was out goose hunting.

"It was a clear day and shooting was poor. Finally, Roosevelt said, he saw two geese overhead coming into the decoys. They were pretty high, but he stood up and fired at the lead goose and hit it. He then swung around and fired at the second one, but he didn't know whether or not he hit it because the first goose landed on his head and knocked him down in the blind. He thought it might have killed him!

"Everyone laughed, and Senator Hawes, with a smile, remarked, 'I'll bet that John L. Lewis wished it had.' That was at the time Lewis [president of the United Mine Workers of America] was having a row with the President over the coal mines."

Either that goose hunt took place before 1921, when Roosevelt contracted polio, or Shoemaker was contributing to the image of an un-handicapped chief executive. There would have been no way for *President* Franklin Roosevelt to stand unaided to shoot a goose.

At about the same time FDR began wildfowling with financier Bernard Baruch at his Hobcaw Barony in South Carolina, two Germans were shooting ducks in the marshes of the Spree River and initiating a technological revolution that has led to a trillion-dollar industry.

Fritz Pfleumer, a devotee of the Dresden Opera, was annoyed by the then hoarse and scratchy phonographic copies of his favorite singers' voices. He conceived the idea of using magnetized particles embedded in plastic tape to record audio signals. He fenced off his notion with a ring of patents and turned the concept over to AEG, a large electrical company in Berlin, for further development.

Unfortunately, AEG was an engineering firm, not an innovative facility. It tried to apply given technology to solve the problems associated with converting Pfleumer's ideas into reality. The AEG project resulted in a recording tape with a narrow frequency range and obtrusive background noises.

Fortunately, the president of AEG belonged to the same hunting club as Dr. Frederick Gauss, a leading chemist of the Badische Anilin-und-Soda-Fabrik (BASF). One morning the two executives shared the same blind, and when the AEG president confided his problem to the BASF scientist, Gauss immediately and correctly surmised that the problem was with the magnetized tape and not with the recording equipment.

Between shots at passing ducks, he suggested that the iron filings used as magnetic particles were too large to accommodate the small waveforms of the higher audio frequencies and too irregular in shape to assure a quiet background. Before they left the marsh that morning, the two men struck a deal: BASF would develop a superior tape to be marketed with recorders built by AEG.

By early 1934, BASF had refined the process of chemically precipitating tiny uniform particles of ferric oxide onto plastic tape—a process that is still used in the manufacture of recording tapes today. After Reich-Marshal Hermann Göring learned of the superiority of magnetic tape over wax cylinders for recording his speeches, he asked the director of the Reich-Rundfunk (German radio) to make sure all his stations used tape recorders. By the late 1930s, industrial spies and attorneys from France, Great Britain, and the United States were trying to steal or break through Herr Pfleumer's protective ring of patents.

Today magnetic tape is not only the foundation of the music and video-recording industries, it is used in everything from computerized banking to the exploration of space. About the only place it is not likely to turn up is in a North American duck blind or goose pit. It is illegal on this side of the Atlantic to use recorded duck or goose sounds to attract birds—and unwise anywhere to tape conversations concerning business or politics.

20

Why We Do What We Do

The glory of wildfowling is in pursuing game that has not yet been belittled by the manipulations of man. Sea ducks, greater snow geese, and brant nest in areas where man has little leverage. And they winter in the wildest zones left along our increasingly settled coasts. Although oil spills kill tens of thousands of sea ducks annually, the fact that we rarely think of oil and, what some wildlife managers still call, "trash ducks" in the same context may be in the birds' best long-term interest. Most every time research embraces a species—be it the condor or mallard—the bird seems to be soon pressed down under the weight of its own data. Species we tend to ignore—vultures and scoters, for example—fare better.

Wildfowling is like going on safari. You must see lots of game to have memorable days. *See* lots of game, not shoot lots. Wildfowlers are naturalists at heart, and while we must kill a bird or two to participate in those great days in the morning, we don't need to kill many birds to frame our outings with exquisite memory. We need only confirm that there are places on our overcrowded planet where something truly wild still exists, offering sustenance to souls turned anorexic with too much civilization.

Some wildfowlers assume that the only great hunting is now abroad—that after more than a century of land and water abuse, the USA is too well-drained, channelized, manicured, and managed to provide genuine sanctuaries for *wild*fowl and *wild*fowlers. But my favorite forms of wildfowling have more to do with states of mind than particular locations. If you bring to even well-trodden paths the perspectives of the naturalist/sportsman, you can have better hunting today than our nineteenth-century ancestors had. My four favorite wildfowling states of mind involve the coast, reunions, messing-about, and solitude.

Coastal gunning is an austere and occasionally hazardous sport. That's part of its appeal. Despite public launch ramps and lighted channel markers, it's hunting in wilderness no less fearful than our great-grandfathers knew. Sea-duck shooting is the most austere and risk-riddled variety of such gunning. I always hunt sea ducks from boats with well-conditioned engines. Doubtful second-hands are used for summer angling when it's not necessarily fatal to get wet or spend a night adrift. In addition, I file an outing plan with people ashore and never hunt past 11:00 A.M. to give them plenty of time to organize a search party before dark if I don't return by noon. I try to hunt with partners who bring their own boats and motors so that if their engine (or mine) fails, we still have a fifty-fifty chance of getting home alive.

This is not hyperbole. You could pay a potentially fatal price for the sight of harlequin ducks swirling out of the snow toward an islet that isn't there at the peak of the tide, or of eiders racing over a sea that's not frozen only because it's in turmoil. In circumstances where survival is triumph enough, a steady flight of birds, a good ratio of kills to fired shots, and a safe return are ecstasy!

There are milder forms of sea-duck shooting—days on which you strip to a T-shirt to soak up the Indian Summer sun. I've hunted sea ducks in almost luxurious comfort in the Chesapeake. My companions and I shot from spacious skiffs tended by larger bay boats. There's much charm in those classic hulls and the watermen who serve them, but I prefer my gunning where birds flight low over a white-crested ocean backed by snow-peaked mountains. Sea ducks are orphans of the wildfowler's world and, as such, they're adopted by only the most hardy among us.

A reunion hunt involves special friends or family. It takes place on particular holidays or in particularly memory-laden locations. I know three generations of one family who've been hunting opening day in their home state since there was only a single generation of hunters. The quality of shooting has declined over the past thirty years, but not the quality of the reunion. So long as the grandfathers and grandsons get some shooting, the fathers—who organize the hunt—are satisfied. They could move the whole show to another state, or even another date, and get more birds. But if you don't understand why they don't, you don't understand the appeal of a reunion hunt.

Reunions for me involve old friends or colleagues who, due to our different schedules, rarely see one another during the year. My friends and I try to pick a different reunion site each winter. If only three or four of us can make the outing, those who go make hundred-dollar phone calls to those who didn't so that all can share, vicariously at least, in the highlights.

Had Kenneth Grahame's Water Rat in *The Wind in the Willows* been exposed to the sport, he would have made a splendid wildfowler. When the Mole allows as how he's never before been on a river in a boat the Water Rat solemnly states that "there is *nothing*—absolutely nothing—half so much worth doing as simply messing about in boats."

Had the English character of the Water Rat been an American Muskrat, he would surely have substituted the word *canoes* for *boats*. Messing-about on North American rivers calls for nothing less than that distinctly North American craft.

The size of the river is important. It must be crooked and alluvial.

Too broad and deep, and you might as well be on a raft with Huck and Jim. Too shallow, and you'll spend more time walking your canoe through the riffles than paddling around sharp bends where ducks startle into flight less than twenty yards away. And, of course, if the river is too swift and tumbling, you're into another kind of messing-about entirely, known as white-water canoeing.

When I was in college, crisp autumnal Saturdays were too rare to spend in a stadium—even though by parking cars before a football game, selling my student-discount ticket, and working the press box during the game, I could earn $60—back when $60 would buy a case of shotgun shells with change to spare.

Usually, however, I'd cajole one or another of my equally nonconformist friends to help me lug a collapsible kayak/canoe down to the river that flowed near the college where we'd assemble the curious craft and set off downstream. It was the same river every outing. Yet in all other respects, it was new and different. Bags of wood duck and mallard with an occasional black duck or ringneck pheasant hung from our shoulders by the time a driver, who'd just put his lights on in the gathering dusk, would pull over to let us pile our bagged-up boat, birds, and shotguns into the trunk of his car for the ride back to school.

Messing-about, like reunion hunting, is layered with memories from an accumulation of seasons. You may not mess-about with the same companions every year, but for new partners to share your enthusiasm, they must have their own storehouse of messing-about memories.

A couple of seasons back, several friends in the U.S. Fish and Wildlife Service and I got together on Virginia's Shenandoah River for a first-class October mess-about. One of the boys—although we're all in our forties and fifties, it's difficult to think of us in the messing-about context as anything other than "boys"—owns a cabin and a couple of canoes on the river to which each of the rest of us brought food, drink, a fly rod for the smallmouth bass, and a shotgun for the wood ducks. It was as serene a time as serendipity can be. Others preferred sleeping late and messing-about in the afternoon. My pattern was to make the dawn flight, catch a midmorning nap, then play Squanto for one of my companions who fired off an occasional shot at ducks from the bow while I fired off an occasional cast for bass from the stern. Messing-about doesn't get much better than that!

Yet several times a season I must hunt alone. I do this when the weather urges me to, or when I need to put a problem or project into perspective. You can only hunt safely alone in places where you don't need a boat. I usually hunt alone in the marsh across the road from my home. In solitary hunting, I rediscover the reasons I abandoned conventional pathways twenty years ago to make my way *my* way. Even the most frustrating winter week is set aright by a nor'easter flooding the marsh and concentrating wildfowl where I can sit and watch them come.

Solitary hunting suits anyone who needs religion in his life but not congregations. The vaulting sky over a marsh is higher than the tallest cathedral. The marsh is grander than the greatest temple. The day dawns just for you and the ducks. It is a soul-wrenching experience—a lesson of mortality amid an infinitude of life. Solitary visits to a marsh transfigure mere duck hunters into that most profound embodiment of the sporting fraternity, *the wildfowler*.

A
WILDFOWLER'S
ALBUM

With pintail populations at historic lows, how much better to treat each drake pintail as the trophy bird he is, even on days when the ducks won't quit coming. Mattamuskeet guide John Mullet sends out his Chesapeake pup for a downed pintail in a flooded field of Japanese millet.

Shooting out of a Core Sound blind is a unique wildfowling experience. Your guide drops you off at dawn, checks on you at noon, and picks you up at sunset. Each hunter is expected to wear chest waders and do his own retrieving.

Most of the birds Art Carter and I saw at Core Sound were divers, like the hen broadbill running along the water and the banded redhead drake that even Art is a little dazed to be holding after wishing so hard to get one.

Is a tundra swan the ultimate wildfowling trophy or only a parody of optimum sport? I seem uncertain of the answer as I examine my prize in a North Carolina field.

Although modern agricultural combines leave less corn for ducks and geese to scavenge than they did 30 years ago, the real problem is rising wheat prices which have turned millions of acres of once grain-scattered stubble into vast winter lawns. The "grass" feeds the geese, but offers scant food for wintering ducks.

Opening morning in Ohio was so slow that my host, Oakley Andrews, and guide, Cyrus Nielsen, had ample time to reminisce about seasons in the not distant past when mallards poured by "Lucky 16" in such numbers, shooters killed only drakes, yet were still out of the blind by eight or nine AM.

North American wildfowlers are increasingly traveling abroad for the kind of shooting that once existed nearer home. Bob Ziemke's face reflects satisfaction as well as the early morning sun as he emerges from an Argentine pothole with a double of Chiloe wigeon.

Part of the pleasure of gunning abroad is in sampling new species. The white-winged duck above is *pato overo*, the Chiloe wigeon; the bird below is *pato capuchino*, the silver teal.

Because I'd left my hunting clothes at home, I may be the only person in South African history to kill a double on Swainson's francolin while wearing a button-down shirt. Alfred, the Zulu dog handler, crouches at left with an extra box of shells. Fortunately, I didn't need it. I killed six francolin and six guineafowl with just the shells stuffed in my pants. (Photo by Kenneth Garrett)

John Richards holds a breech from a cannon once used by Sir Peter Scott for puntgunning.

One of the pleasures of hunting in the UK is in meeting men cut from the same wildfowling cloth. By using "B.B." as his nom de plume and "D.J. Watkins-Pitchford" as his nom de paintbrush, Denys Watkins-Pitchford has convinced countless admirers that he is two different people. Although eighty when I snapped this picture, he was impatient to be off to Scotland to hunt geese.

A member of a finite and rather secretive society of British punt-gunners, John Richards shows off specialized equipment which has changed little in 150 years. (The boat's trailer is the only innovation.) The staffs used for shoving the boat through the shallows have weighted, forked ends so they can be withdrawn from the muck with a minimum of resistance and not float to the surface once they're free.

Dr. M. Bagley Walker, Jr. hefts a 4-gauge shotgun in John Richards' driveway overlooking the Dee Estuary. John enjoys letting Americans shoot the 4-bore, but encourages them to take overhead shots so they'll be driven deep into the mud by the gun's recoil.

An émigré reader objected to my calling Cossack guides, "Southern Russians." He insisted that Cossacks are "Ukrainians". That may be, but Sasha (on the left) and Vladimir (on the right) called themselves Russians, and I'll take their word for it. Note that push-poled gunning skiffs used east of the Sea of Azov don't differ much from wildfowling craft in other parts of the world. The wildfowling fraternity is based on such practicality and common sense.

Atlantic brant populations rise and fall mostly on the basis of breeding success or failure. The year this picture was taken was obviously a good one on their Arctic nesting grounds.

Professional rail-hunting guides are increasingly rare, but that won't stop two people willing to take turns poling and shooting from a steady platform in a flooded marsh. Shirley Belote turns his flat-bottomed scow so that his nephew will be in a better position to take several rail crossing a channel in coastal Virginia.

That's not mud on the belly of the brant in Norman Seymour's left hand. It's a dark-bellied specimen from the eastern Atlantic race of brant which occasionally wanders to North America from more traditional wintering grounds in Ireland.

Wildfowlers want to *see* lots of birds, not kill them all. After discovering a spectacular flock of snow geese, gunning partners, Tom Lomas and Jim Malone, were more inclined to shoot film than shotgun shells—but then they already had a brace of birds apiece.

Wildfowlers spend more time in winter marshes than any naturalists. As a result, we see things seen by few others and speculate about their implications. For example, in these sequential photographs, a pair of orphaned immature snow geese (left) attempts to join a family of two adults and three young. One of the adults drives off the orphaned birds. Will such rejection affect the orphans' odds of survival? How successful as parents will such orphaned birds eventually be? Wildlife management concerns itself with the fate of species. Wildfowlers concern themselves with the fate of individual birds as well.

Biologists hope to learn more about Canada goose short-stopping by neck-collaring birds so flocks can be readily traced in their movement up and down North America's flyways. A high percentage of neck-collared birds are shot by hunters who say they didn't notice the collar until the bird was down. Possibly embarrassed by this, and certainly stirred by stories about neck-collared geese dying each winter when ice-balls freeze over the plastic bands, many hunters feel that neck-collaring should stop. "Biologists can't do a thing to prevent short-stopping," one hunter insisted. "The only reason they push the collaring program is to provide jobs for themselves or graduate students."

A quarter-century ago, wildfowlers seeking rugged sport and exceptional trophies hunted goldeneye and shot only the larger and more wary drakes. Goldeneye populations are now declining, so the same rugged sportsmen find their recreation in sea duck shooting, especially drake eiders. John Gottschalk holds a pair of goldeneye in Virginia.

For over a century, an oak and heart-pine structure stood on the beach of Parramore Island, Virginia, housing first a Life Saving Station (later called Coast Guard) and then a duck club where Bill Nickel, shown with our morning's kill, was first exposed to the honorable standards that once made such clubs indispensable to the training of America's business and political leaders. When the club was struck by lightning and burned in July 1989, another link in the continuity of the sporting tradition burned with it. In the surf are the ribs of an old slave ship that have shifted with the sands even as the clubhouse itself was once pulled from the reach of the ever-rising sea.

An ice-coated Jim Phillips contemplates his good fortune in surviving another sub-zero morning in Maine.

I've had many grand companions in 40 years of wildfowling, but my very favorite was a golden retriever named Golden Shores' Rye on the Rocks, alias Rocky. He didn't know the meaning of the word *quit*. Ice might cling to his coat and his teeth might chatter, but he'd plead to stay if I suggested we go home. His nose was exceptional, and toward the end of his life when arthritis made it painful for him to charge about, I only used Rocky to retrieve downed birds in my home marsh when guests' dogs failed to do the job. When I put him down, Rocky died with all the dignity of a gentleman. But then he always was one.